THE
FOOTNOTE HISTORIAN'S TRILOGY

GEORGE WASHINGTON'S BOY,
THE JOURNALS OF OSBORNE P. ANDERSON,
LADY PATRIOT

TED LANGE

Order this book online at www.trafford.com
or email orders@trafford.com

Most Trafford titles are also available at major online book retailers.

© Copyright 2016 Theodore Lange.
All rights reserved. No part of this publication may be reproduced, stored in a retrieval system, or transmitted, in any form or by any means, electronic, mechanical, photocopying, recording, or otherwise, without the written prior permission of the author.

Print information available on the last page.

ISBN: 978-1-4907-6705-5 (sc)
ISBN: 978-1-4907-6706-2 (hc)
ISBN: 978-1-4907-6707-9 (e)

Library of Congress Control Number: 2015918802

Because of the dynamic nature of the Internet, any web addresses or links contained in this book may have changed since publication and may no longer be valid. The views expressed in this work are solely those of the author and do not necessarily reflect the views of the publisher, and the publisher hereby disclaims any responsibility for them.

Any people depicted in stock imagery provided by Thinkstock are models, and such images are being used for illustrative purposes only.
Certain stock imagery © Thinkstock.

Trafford rev. 06/06/2016

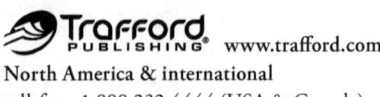 www.trafford.com

North America & international
toll-free: 1 888 232 4444 (USA & Canada)
fax: 812 355 4082

Dedicated to

My Lovely Wife

Mary Lange

Thanks to

Tracy Sprague

For Being a Wonderful Editor

Introduction

A history teacher once told me that history is written by the victors. African American participation in American history is often recorded as a footnote. I wanted to put the footnote on the page.

My quest for the facts behind the footnote started with my journey as an actor. I love to research the characters that I embody and find layers that I can add to my portrayal. Discovering little known facts about a time or era and looking for anecdotes that might provide a character with idiosyncratic options can lead an actor away from obvious choices. This provides the actor with an abundance of rich levels based on the character's history. The characterization avoids the cliché and becomes a real human being. When I decided to become a playwright, this passion for historical research became an integral part of my writing process. I feel compelled to avoid the headline and to reveal the story of the footnote.

This trilogy of plays explores footnotes from the American Revolution, Harper's Ferry, and the Civil War. All of these plays are based on historical events and facts but the emphasis is on the African American point of view. My bibliographies document my fact-finding journey and validate my creative choices. Thus, from history student to actor to playwright, I have adopted another moniker…*The Footnote Historian.*

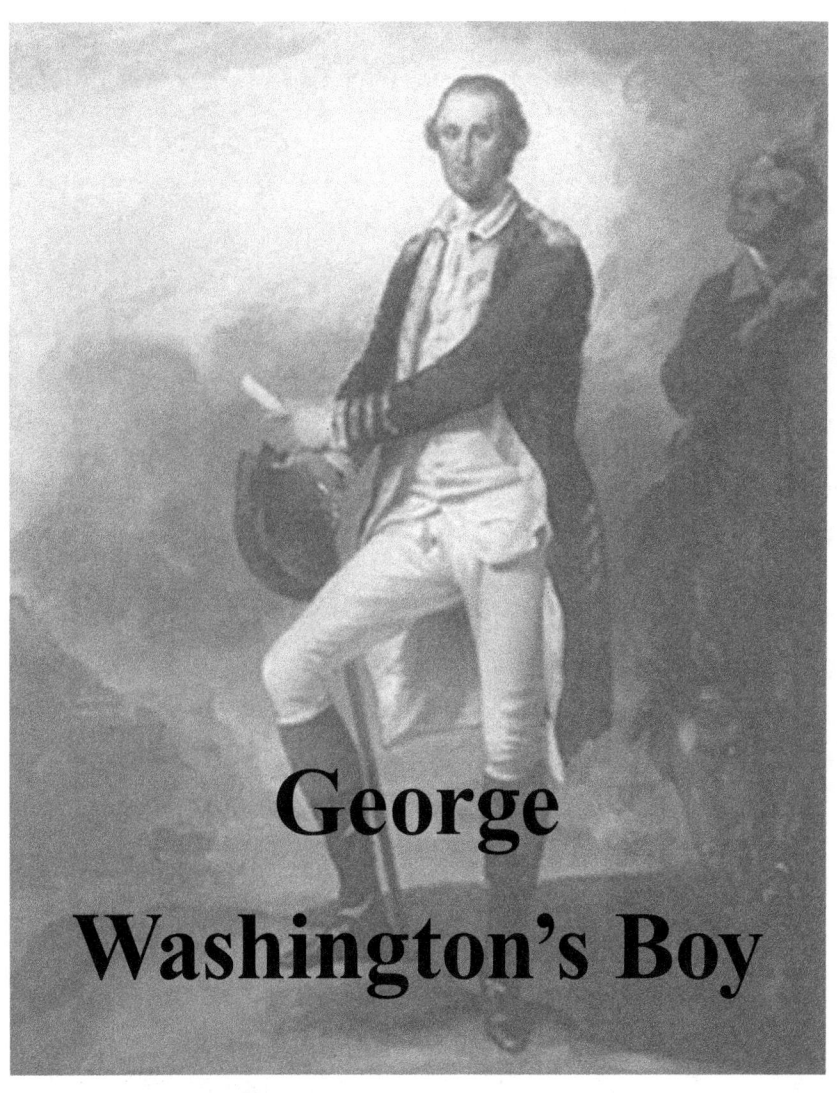

George Washington's Boy

George Washington (1780) by John Trumbull

Dedicated to

John Bishop

and

to my sons

Ted IV and Turner

and

to my wife

Mary

Thanks

To Tom Whayne, my high school drama teacher

and

To Tay McArthur, my high school history teacher

and

To Kay Ley, my favorite editor

George Washington's Boy opened February 3, 2007, at the Horse Shoe Theatre at Los Angeles Valley College, Los Angeles, California with the following cast:

BILLY LEE	Adam Clark
GEORGE WASHINGTON	Gordon Goodman
ALEXANDER HAMILTON	Bryan West
ONA JUDGE	Chrystee Pharris
MARTHA WASHINGTON	Connie Ventress
NATHANIAL GREENE	Morgan P. BROWN
HERCULES	Ken Sagoes
DOCTOR CRAIK	Morgan P. BROWN
VENUS	Tiffany Adams
MARGARET THOMAS	Trisha Mann
JOSEPH WHIPPLE	Robert Pine

Director:	Ted Lange
Set Designer:	Victoria Profitt
Costume Designer:	Mylette Nora
Lighting Designer:	Aaron Bronsal
Stage Manager:	Melissa Alva
Producer:	Mary Lange

George Washington's Boy opened August 2, 2007, at the Sawtooth Center, in Winston/Salem, North Carolina, at the National Black Theatre Festival with the following cast:

BILLY LEE	Adam Clark
GEORGE WASHINGTON	Gordon Goodman
ALEXANDER HAMILTON	Bryan West
ONA JUDGE	Chrystee Pharris
MARTHA WASHINGTON	Connie Ventress
NATHANIAL GREENE	Andrew Jones
HERCULES	Ken Sagoes
DOCTOR CRAIK	Andrew Jones
VENUS	Tiffany Adams
MARGARET THOMAS	Trisha Mann
JOSEPH WHIPPLE	Bernie Kopell

Director:	Ted Lange
Set Designer:	Victoria Profitt
Costume Designer:	Mylette Nora
Lighting Designer:	Aaron Bronsal
Prop Master:	Chubie Egbuho
Costumer:	Amber Dykes
Producer:	Mary Lange

The Setting

Act I

It is the night before Christmas, 1776. George Washington prepares to fight for freedom from the British as his slave, Billy Lee, struggles to read about freedom. Washington decides to cross the Delaware and attack Trenton. Under the backdrop of the Revolutionary War, Washington sets up winter camp at Morristown, Pennsylvania. Washington continues to teach Billy Lee to read, as he manages his army, and tries to boost the morale of his troops. Billy Lee strives to read so that he might learn more about the philosophy of war and the Americans' fight for freedom even as they subject his people to slavery. Washington falls ill and almost dies in Morristown. He is saved by the speedy intervention of Martha Washington and her favorite cook, Hercules. Billy shares with some of the other slaves what he has learned about freedom from Washington and reading books about chivalry. Billy realizes that freedom is a right for all Americans and begins to plot his escape. Washington recovers from his near-death experience and Billy Lee faces death to escape to freedom.

Act II

Fourteen years later, the war is over. The Americans have won their fight for freedom but all Americans are not free-slavery is still legal. Washington, the First President of the United States, maintains a residency in New York. Billy Lee, crippled from his attempt for freedom, continues to serve Washington. Washington struggles with his own philosophies as an advocate for freedom while continuing to own slaves. The spirit of freedom has grown and even though Billy Lee feels he can no longer physically run, other slaves from the Washington household begin to claim their freedom. Billy Lee falls in love with a free black woman, Margaret Thomas. They marry, but as Billy Lee is still a slave, they must live in the slave quarters at Mount Vernon. The hope for freedom is ever present as Billy Lee attends Washington on his death bed and Washington gives his last will and testament to Billy Lee.

Author's Notes

I was on a flight from Los Angeles to New York to spend Thanksgiving with my sons and cook them Thanksgiving dinner. They were both going to college in the Big Apple and while on the flight, I read *His Excellency, George Washington*, by Joseph J. Ellis. The author mentioned Washington's slave, William Lee. I never knew that Washington had a personal slave, also known, at that time, as a valet or body servant. While in New York, I also happened to visit The Metropolitan Museum because I wanted to see the painting of *Washington Crossing the Delaware*. By happenstance, I saw Joseph Trumbull's 1780 painting of *George Washington*. In the right hand corner behind the horse, there is a slave. I realized that this must be William Lee. When I saw this portrait, I was intrigued. Here he was again. Who was William Lee? He must have been someone of importance to have his portrait painted with Washington; yet, I'd never heard about him until this trip to New York. Also, as an actor, I'm always looking for a character that I could play. Maybe William Lee could be the one? And so my quest began to learn about this slave who was the personal valet to Washington. Who was this slave who witnessed the architects of a new American nation fighting for their freedom while imprisoning their own slaves? What was his untold story?

Even though American historical research from 1176-1799 is voluminous and even though the facts confirm the existence of slaves, their personal stories are rare. Many were dehumanized under the guise of labels such as personal valets or body servants, but they were in fact, slaves. The house slaves lived behind the scenes, combed their masters' hair, packed their mistresses' clothes, and cooked food for the household. All the while, they were privy to the innermost secrets and thoughts of their masters. In my research of slave life during the American Revolution, I conducted internet searches, talked to experts, visited Morristown, Philadelphia, and Mount Vernon. I discovered that while I would never play William Lee, his story and others of this era should be told. I've included a bibliography of the books I used to uncover their sagas.

When staging the play, it is vital that the actors honor the unwritten rules governing the relationships between the master and slaves that existed at that time. Slaves never looked directly into the eyes of their masters. It was forbidden. There are times when William Lee and Washington are alone, yet William never abuses this unwritten law. This will contrast with the moments when the slaves are alone and are free to share their true humanity with each other.

At the end of the play, William's final speech to Washington is a moment of solace and reflection for both characters. It reflects the essence of their relationship and should portray the gravity of the scene with an inner spirit and strength.

The mood of this play is created with the excerpts of classical music indigenous to the time period. The classical strains of Beethoven and Mozart perfectly counterpoint the scenes and the dialogue of the play.

This play paints a picture of slavery during the early days of our country--their lives, loves, and struggles for freedom. Is it accurate? We were not there--we only have the side of the victors. With *George Washington's Boy* we envision a history written by those in the shadows.

One more thought: a play is meant to be heard. After I finish writing a play, I like to hear it read. So, I gather some good friends and actors and we read the play aloud. I serve them a big bowl of spaghetti, salad, and red wine. We read the play, drink some wine, and discuss what works. The red wine definitely creates a mood where everyone feels comfortable voicing their opinions. So, please feel free to gather a few friends, drink some red wine, and say these words out loud--the power of the spoken word will connect you to these characters and you will hear their stories told!

George Washington's Boy

Synopsis

The fight for freedom from the British, the Declaration of Independence, and the first presidency of the United States are presented from the viewpoint of George Washington's closest confident, ironically, his slave, Billy Lee. Based on historical fact, Billy Lee served his master throughout these monumental times and was privy to the innermost thoughts and actions of George Washington and the beginning of a new nation.

Cast of Characters

George Washington is a Virginia planter who became a General and the first President of the United States of America.

Billy Lee is George Washington's mulatto slave.

Alexander Hamilton is a twenty-year old patriot.

Nathaniel Greene is a general, who walks with a limp in his right leg.

Martha Washington is George Washington's wealthy wife.

Ona Judge is a beautiful, young, brown-skinned slave girl, owned my Martha Washington.

Hercules is a dark-skinned slave, who is George Washington's cook.

Doctor James Craik is George Washington's personal doctor.

Venus is a beautiful, young, mulatto slave girl.

Margaret Thomas is a free black woman, resident of Philadelphia.

Joseph Whipple is a New Hampshire employer looking for a maid.

ACT I

Scene 1

Music cue: Beethoven Symphony No. 9, the Overture, Coriolan. Lights fade up slowly on: Washington's Headquarters, Bristol, Pennsylvania just outside of Trenton. Christmas Eve, 1776. Washington is pacing and listening as Billy reads slowly. He is not a good reader but he is getting the words right.

BILLY

"These are the times that try men's souls. The summer soldier and the sunshine patriot will in this **chris-is** shrink from the service of his country."

WASHINGTON

Good. Now William, this word is *crisis*. The summer soldier and the sunshine patriot will in this *crisis* shrink from the service of his country. So…what is the name of the book?

Music fades out.

BILLY

The… AH- mer – ree- kan…. Crisis.

WASHINGTON

That is very good. Very good. I'm proud of you.

BILLY

Massa George, I'm reading better than the last time, huh?

WASHINGTON

Yes, William. Your progress is admirable. I am fascinated by your sudden interest and diligence in reading.

BILLY

Well, everybody's talking about this here war and I think it would help me better to know what we fighting for.

There is a knock at the door.

WASHINGTON

Come in. It will…and I think you should pay particular attention to the writings of the Bible.

Alexander Hamilton enters.

BILLY

Yes Sir.

WASHINGTON

But for now I want you to read the rest of that page.

ALEXANDER

Merry Christmas, Your Excellency. I think my time could have been better served, but I finished passing out the pamphlets of *The American Crisis* as you ordered.

WASHINGTON

Alexander, I've been watching the weather.

ALEXANDER

Yes Sir. The men are freezing and the food is low.

WASHINGTON

I think this may work to our advantage.

ALEXANDER

General, I don't see how low morale, inadequate clothing, and empty bellies can help our cause.

WASHINGTON

Perfect time for a battle. I want to attack Trenton.

ALEXANDER

But, General, it's Christmas and it's snowing.

WASHINGTON

The best time to fight those Hessians.

ALEXANDER

I don't understand, General? Won't Colonel Rall have his men posted?

WASHINGTON
I hope to catch that "Old Lion" sleeping. Traditionally the Hessians like to celebrate Christmas. They will not be expecting a battle. I have it on good authority from one of my spies...

ALEXANDER
Has he been accurate in the past?

WASHINGTON
John Honeyman, a local farmer, an immigrant, Scotch-Irish--no love for the British there. Colonel Rall has been underpaying him for meat and produce supplies. Honeyman has given me precise information on how many soldiers are in Trenton, which houses they are staying in, and how many sentries are sent out each evening--also where they patrol.

George hands the papers to Alexander.

ALEXANDER
Sounds promising. But what about Cornwallis' troops in New Brunswick?

WASHINGTON
They are fifteen miles away. I don't think they will be prepared to march on Trenton. By the time they arrive, we will be gone.

ALEXANDER
Those Hessians are well-trained...

WASHINGTON

The Hessians like a good Christmas feast. Lots of drink, lots of food. A full belly and a noggin full of Madeira take the edge off of a soldier's wits. I'm hoping they will not be in any physical condition to do battle. I want to cross the Delaware tonight.

ALEXANDER

Your Excellency, may I speak unencumbered?

WASHINGTON

That is why you are one of my aides.

ALEXANDER

General, we've been fighting for two years. We haven't won a battle since Bunker Hill. New York was a disaster. There are desertions every day. The army is ragged. Men are marching with no shoes, thin clothing, and are poorly armed. Everyone is hungry. It may be presumptuous of me, but I think the men need to rest. This is the perfect time to do it. The Hessians are not going to attack us. We need this time to lick our wounds and recuperate.

WASHINGTON

Necessity, dire necessity will--nay, must justify this attack.

ALEXANDER

You want to cross the Delaware in the dead of winter and at night? I think attacking Trenton is a bad idea.

WASHINGTON
Alexander, we must inspire the men. We win this battle--they will be wearing Hessian boots on their feet instead of rags.

ALEXANDER
And beef in their bellies?

George crosses back to the maps on his desk.

WASHINGTON
Exactly. I've got Henry Knox and you with the artillery. I will cross at Mc Konkey's Ferry with Nathaniel Greene. I want Sullivan to lead his soldiers down River Road, closer to the Delaware. General Greene and I will take Pennington Road and we'll wait for the sound of gunfire from Sullivan's men as a sign that his army is ready to assault Trenton.

ALEXANDER
Aren't you worried about General Howe?

WASHINGTON
I have it on good authority that he is on his way back to New York to have a dalliance with a married woman named Elizabeth Loring.

ALEXANDER
Ahh, the spoils of war. Where will you want me to gather the men so that you can speak to them?

WASHINGTON

I'm not going to speak to the men.

ALEXANDER

Your Excellency, the men are going to need words of encouragement. The thought of attacking Hessians may unnerve some of the men, especially after the failures in New York.

WASHINGTON

I am not an orator. I am a general. They won't know who we're attacking 'till we get there.

ALEXANDER

Please forgive me General for speaking so boldly, but these men need a morale booster--and that can only come from you.

WASHINGTON

What do you think of Tom Paine?

ALEXANDER

Common Sense is the Bible for most of the patriots. It's clear, well written, and precise.

WASHINGTON

Inspirational?

Washington hands the pamphlet to Alexander.

ALEXANDER

Well, yes… inspirational.

WASHINGTON

Did you read his new pamphlet, *The American Crisis*?

ALEXANDER

Yes Sir, as I was passing them out. "These are the times that try men's souls."

WASHINGTON

Words cannot be more eloquent than these. The men will pass these pages among themselves. That will be our morale booster. I want you to bring the other officers here within the hour. I will lay out my plans in detail and we will discuss our options. Tarry not.

ALEXANDER

Yes, General.

Alexander starts to leave.

WASHINGTON

Alexander, we must learn not to look back. The future holds victory.

Alexander leaves.

BILLY

Massa George, you gone let everyone talk?

WASHINGTON

What?

BILLY

When you have meetings with your soldiers…you let everybody talk. Colonels, Captains, Lieutenants. Everybody has a say. Why? You the leader. You the General. Why you let Mr. Hamilton question your orders?

WASHINGTON

I am just having a conference with the Generals.

Washington pulls a book out of his desk that he has been reading.

WASHINGTON

Can you pronounce the title of this book?

BILLY

Lee- Mort- Tee. Dee –Art- Her.

WASHINGTON

Le Morte D'Arthur. French. Translated it means, "The Death of Arthur."

BILLY

Good book?

WASHINGTON

A very good book.

BILLY

Who is Arthur?

WASHINGTON

A leader. A general. He had soldiers fighting for him. He called his soldiers, knights.

BILLY

Knights.

WASHINGTON

Yes, William, knights. Come here. I want you to see how the word is spelled. It starts with the letter K. Do you see that? His knights helped Arthur to become the King of England. He united the land. They called it Camelot. It became a country.

BILLY

Just like the way you trying to do, uniting the colonies. Trying to make a whole new country.

WASHINGTON

Yes. When we win this war, the colonies will become like Camelot…and Camelot became a utopian society.

BILLY

What's that…utopian?

WASHINGTON

Get me the *Doctor Johnson Dictionary, Second Volume*.

Billy goes to the book shelf and gets the dictionary. It is a huge book, ten and one-half inches wide, seventeen inches tall and three and one-half inches thick.

WASHINGTON

Utopian comes from the word utopia. Let's find the word and see its definition. It is spelled U.T.O.P.I.A. Here it is…now what does it say?

BILLY

Utopia: an imaginary…is…land, eye…land. Dee…scribed in Sir Thomas Moore's book *Utopia*, 1516. An eye deal place or state.

WASHINGTON

Good William, very good. It is the ideal place or world for a person to live in. Where there is equality for every man.

BILLY

That's what you trying to do?

WASHINGTON

Yes. Arthur made new laws and gave his knights a chance to speak. Everyone sat in a circle. They sat at a special table. Arthur tried to be a wise leader. He listened to his knights, then made a decision.

BILLY

Just like you…everyone always sits in a circle.

WASHINGTON

I try to get the best out of my men.

BILLY

You want the colonies to be like Camelot when the war is over.

WASHINGTON

Yes, William. I want to make a new country…free from the tyranny of our enemy. I want a union of states. I want our citizens to have liberty. I want to strive for the higher ideals of men.

BILLY

This Camelot…did it have slaves?

WASHINGTON

What?

BILLY

In the utopian society, were there slaves? Who worked the fields in Camelot?

WASHINGTON

Peasants.

BILLY

Is that another word for slave?

WASHINGTON

No. They were free.

BILLY

So Camelot ain't had no slaves?

WASHINGTON

There were no slaves in Camelot.

BILLY

Is that what you trying to do, Massa George?

There is a pause, the General thinks for a moment, then...

WASHINGTON

William is Nelson ready?

BILLY

He's fed, but he ain't saddled.

WASHINGTON

Go saddle him. I want him ready. Brush him first. That will warm his blood.

BILLY

Yes Sir.

Billy leaves with the King Arthur book. Washington crosses to his desk and starts to draw up his plans. Music cue: Mozart Piano Concerto No. 2, Adante.

Music fades as there is a Black Out.

SCENE 2

In the darkness, the sound of a cold wind blows, a gun fires, and a cannon fires. Finally, there is silence. Softly, birds sing like on a peaceful plantation. Lights up on the Mount Vernon Plantation, Virginia, January 1777, Martha's bedroom. Ona Judge is a fourteen-year-old slave. She is packing clothes into a trunk. Martha enters.

ONA

Ma'am, you want me to pack these papers?

MARTHA

Oh--those are letters Ona. Very important letters. They stay here. Be sure you pack my hats.

ONA

Yes Ma'am. These letters about the war?

MARTHA

Goodness no. More important than that. These are love letters from my husband.

ONA

Yes Ma'am, love letters. How long we gonna stay in Morristown?

MARTHA

For the winter, I miss him so. I ever tell you how I met Mr. Washington?

ONA

No Ma'am.

MARTHA

I thought he was the most striking young man I had ever seen and quite a good dancer. He was polite, gallant, and charming. We met at a ball.

ONA

Love at first sight.

MARTHA

For me, yes. For him... not really. He liked someone else. A pretty lady... Sally Fairfax. Thank goodness she was already married. I just had to arrange a way to meet him in a private setting instead of a public forum.

ONA

How did you do that?

MARTHA

This is a secret Ona. So you must promise to keep my confidences.

ONA

Miss Martha, I promise.

MARTHA

First I tried to get as much information regarding him as possible. I found out we had a mutual friend, William Chamberlayne. And William told me, George was in the habit of riding on Thursdays with his boy, Billy Lee. At the end of his ride on the way back to Mount Vernon, George usually stopped by William's for a strong drink and good conversation.

ONA

Was he riding Nelson?

MARTHA

On no, my dear, this was long before he found Nelson. Sooooo, on one particular Thursday afternoon, I managed to be visiting my friend Mister William Chamberlayne. George stopped by as was his custom and while William supplied the strong drink, I supplied the good conversation.

ONA

You didn't get bored?

MARTHA

Certainly not. I am a lady. I know how to keep a conversation going.

ONA

Yes, you do.

MARTHA

He had wonderful stories how he fought battles in the French Indian war. He talked of his lineage and how he inherited Mount Vernon from his brother Lawrence's widow. I talked about my first marriage to Daniel Custis, my children Patsy, and little Jacky. Oh, we did not get bored.

ONA

A lady must know how to keep the conversation going.

MARTHA

He told me of an adventure he had in the Ohio country. I shouldn't tell it, but it was so exciting to hear him describe it to me. Daniel Boone was with him. It happened on the Monongahela. George was under the command of a general named Braddock.

ONA

A Virginian?

MARTHA

No, a British Officer. They were to take a French Fort called Duquense.

The French had sent out nine hundred men, mostly Indians.

ONA

How many troops did the General have?

MARTHA

They had some British regulars and George was heading the Virginia Militia. In total there were about thirteen hundred men. They were surprised by the enemy at the edge of a clearing in a forest. Within the first ten minutes their ranks were being demolished. The British were used to fighting in concentrated rows. The Indians were hiding behind trees and rocks. They were using the forest as a shield from the British musket balls.

ONA

Don't seem fair.

As she talks, Martha crosses to a desk, opens a drawer, and pulls out a pair of leather military riding gloves. She holds the gloves as she continues her story.

MARTHA

George and the Virginia troops were caught in the middle. So they were being fired on not only by the enemy but also by the British regulars. George said, "They behaved like men and died like soldiers." As the Indians got the upper hand, most of the British soldiers broke and ran. General Braddock rode into the heart of the fighting trying to rally his men. He was cut down by enemy fire, shot in the shoulder and the chest, and mortally wounded. It fell to George to lead the men. Riding back and forth, he stopped the men from their panic. He had two horses shot out from under him and four musket balls passed through his coat--but he was unharmed. They had nine hundred casualties that day, while the Indians only lost twenty-three.

ONA

He's a brave man.

MARTHA

How could I not fall in love with a man like that? I asked for a token. He gave me these.

ONA

Gloves.

MARTHA

Not just gloves. These are his military gloves. The ones that he carried with him on that trip. I must make sure I bring these gloves for good luck.

ONA

Someday I want to be courted.

MARTHA

What? What did you say?

ONA

Nothing. Should I put these love letters away?

MARTHA

No give them to me.

ONA

Yes, Miss Martha.

MARTHA

Now, I must go ask Hercules to pack us a scrumptious lunch for the trip.

Martha exits the room. Ona admires one of her hats.

Black Out.

In the darkness, there is the sound of soldiers marching.

SCENE 3

Music cue: Mozart Piano Concerto No. 21 in C major, Adante. Lights up on: Jacob's Three-Story Tavern, Morristown, New Jersey, January 1777. George Washington is sitting at his desk as he finishes writing a letter. His hair is shoulder length and unkempt. Billy walks into the room carrying an ornate wooden box. He sets the box on Washington's desk and pulls out combs of varying sizes, two brushes and a hand mirror. Washington seals the letter he has written, while Billy combs and brushes Washington's hair and ties it in a queue. Washington's uniform is laid out, with his coat, boots, sash, and sword. During the scene, Billy dresses him.

BILLY
Massa George, I am almost finished with the King Arthur story.

As the music fades, there is a knock at the door.

WASHINGTON
Come in. Not now William.

Nathaniel Greene enters. He walks with a limp. Billy ties Washington's hair with a black ribbon.

WASHINGTON
Nathaniel, did you read this?

Washington crosses to his desk and gets another newspaper.

WASHINGTON

Freeman's Press from Philadelphia?

GREENE

No Sir.

WASHINGTON

Supporting our victories in Trenton and Princeton?

GREENE

Those victories have certainly boosted the morale of the men. Permission to report Sir.

WASHINGTON

Please General Greene, give your report.

GREENE

(*reads from his notebook*) Yes Sir, we've got the men in the southeast part of town on flat open fields. They have pitched their tents there.

WASHINGTON

What is our food supply?

GREENE

There are some small farms in the area. Food looks good-- corn, wheat, rye, oats, plenty of vegetables, and stored fruits. Morristown has about seventy homes. Population is close to 350, give or take a child. The churches—mostly Presbyterian. This town has two silver smiths and a saddle maker, Dan Smith.

WASHINGTON

Very good work, General Greene. I want you to go the churches and convert them into hospitals. Talk to the pastors. They should be sympathetic. Send this Dan Smith to me. I want him to make a saddle for Nelson.

GREENE

Yes Sir.

WASHINGTON

I want you to convert the barns in the vicinity into warehouses.

GREENE

Yes Sir.

WASHINGTON

I want you to store the food, near the eating areas, medicine near the churches. The muskets, ammunition, tents, and wagons, store together.

GREENE

Yes Sir.

WASHINGTON

Convert some of the local buildings into commissary offices. I want the camp tailors together. Blacksmiths, wheelwrights, cooks, and carpenters should be comfortable. Erect a slaughterhouse. I want Morristown to look busy. There are Loyalists living in this village. If they report anything to the British, it's going to seem as if we are a force to be reckoned with.

GREENE
Where should we house the Hessian prisoners? We have no place to put them.

Billy helps Washington buckle his sword.

WASHINGTON
General, Morristown has iron mines and not enough labor to extract the ore. They will work in the iron mines, free laborers. I want that iron to be made into cannons. By the end of the winter, we should have enough new artillery to give the British some sleepless nights.

GREENE
Yes Sir. Should I endeavor to drill the men tomorrow?

WASHINGTON
So I can set my watch by it. Tarry not.

GREENE
Sir, General Weedon asked me to give you this note.

Greene hands a note to Washington.

WASHINGTON
You may go. Tarry not.

As Washington reads the note, Greene starts to leave.

WASHINGTON

Nathaniel, hold it. This must be a joke.

GREENE

No Sir, I think he is quite serious.

WASHINGTON

Sam wants to go home and return in early summer?

GREENE

Yes Sir. He is homesick.

WASHINGTON

This isn't fun and games. This is a war. Could I stand justified, do you think, in the opinion of the public, to suffer the officers of the states to be absent so long at this most important and active part of the campaign?

GREENE

No Sir.

WASHINGTON

No man wishes to gratify officers more that I do…nor can any man feel more for their private inconveniences, because no person suffers more by being absent from home than myself. Why am I railing at you? Send Sam Weedon here immediately.

GREENE

I believe he is on the road.

Act I Scene 3   41

WASHINGTON

Then send some horsemen after him. I want him standing in front of me before this day is done. I haven't been home for two years. Send General Sullivan after him.

GREENE

Yes Sir.

Greene exits.

WASHINGTON

William, brew me some tea. I want to be clear-eyed when this dilettante shows up.

BILLY

Yes Massa George.

There is a knock at the door.

WASHINGTON

Come in.

Alexander Hamilton enters.

ALEXANDER

General, we have a problem.

WASHINGTON

Am I losing more officers?

ALEXANDER

Yes Sir. To smallpox.

WASHINGTON

God no.

Billy exits.

ALEXANDER

We've got a dying woman, Mrs. Martha Ball.

WASHINGTON

How long does she have?

ALEXANDER

Maybe a few days. We think she contracted it from one of the soldiers.

WASHINGTON

We must contain it here in this city.

Washington paces.

WASHINGTON

If we go the standard route of inoculation, it will take weeks to get it under control. Alexander, I want you to go to the ministers, most of them are doctors too. Tell them to get their churches ready. We are going to have immediate inoculations.

ALEXANDER

Sir, we can't do that. We've got over three thousand men in this town. It would be a nightmare.

WASHINGTON

I know the devastations of this disease. If we do not act quickly, we won't have an army or a town. We can't wait.

ALEXANDER

I understand General…it's just never been done this way.

WASHINGTON

Alexander, are you a gambling man?

ALEXANDER

Only when I'm sure of the odds.

Billy reenters with a tray and a pot of tea and cup.

WASHINGTON

I know the odds. I am giving orders that every soldier in this army is to be inoculated. We will allow the civilians the right of refusal. Theirs will be on a voluntary basis.

ALEXANDER

Yes Sir.

Billy pours Washington's a cup of tea.

WASHINGTON
Dismissed, get to work.

ALEXANDER
Yes Sir.

Alexander leaves. Billy hands Washington the cup of tea; then Billy brushes Washington's uniform topcoat.

BILLY
Smallpox. Sound like a pretty big problem.

WASHINGTON
My biggest problem is keeping this army together. The enlistment is up for a lot of men and they can go home. I will lose a large number of my soldiers. I must come up with a plan to make the soldiers re-enlist.

BILLY
Massa George, what would keep a man fighting when he got smallpox and he wants to go home?

WASHINGTON
Freedom is a theory right now. An ideal. The reality of their daily lives is in conflict with the dream. They must do the mundane to survive in their private lives.

BILLY
What would keep a man fighting?

WASHINGTON
There is only one carrot I can really offer.

BILLY/ WASHINGTON
Money? Money.

WASHINGTON
I just have one little problem...I am not endowed with the authority to offer any more money. Only the Continental Congress can do that. But if I don't offer them something, they will go home and work their farms and businesses and the war will end. Maybe if I can convince Robert Morris to supplement...

BILLY
You mean the little fat man with the round red cheeks? The banker?

WASHINGTON
What did I tell you about that William?

BILLY
I'm sorry Massa George. I just wanted to make sure we both talking about the same man.

WASHINGTON
Yes, that's him. Maybe I can get around Congress and go directly to Robert.

BILLY

Massa George, you got slaves fighting in place of they white Masters. Will they go home too?

WASHINGTON

Yes. There is no way for me to stop them.

BILLY

Offer them freedom.

WASHINGTON

I can't do that.

BILLY

This here a war. You can do lots of things. Offer the slaves they freedom. They puttin' they lives in danger anyway. Offer freedom and they fight for something they know. Something they want.

WASHINGTON

I'm not sure that would work.

BILLY

In a few days, they going back to they Masters. Let them re-enlist for a year, on the condition they get they freedom. What they Masters gonna do? Stop you! They want to win this war too. Small price to pay for starting another Camelot.

WASHINGTON

That is something to think about. First let me see if I can keep my army.

BILLY

How much you pay extra?

WASHINGTON

A five-dollar bonus above their wages.

BILLY

Is that enough to make a man fight for a longer time? Man gonna get shot for freedom. How much is that worth?

WASHINGTON

It's worth fifteen. But I know Morris can't raise that kind of money.

BILLY

Sound like ten.

WASHINGTON

Ten dollars. Ten dollars is a fair price.

BILLY

Ten dollars sound good to me.

WASHINGTON

William, we must toast the British for The Stamp Act.

Washington raises his tea cup to Billy, who nods.

WASHINGTON

We were no longer just second-class citizens to England. We were her slaves.

BILLY

I know what you mean.

WASHINGTON

The spirit of freedom beats too high in us to submit to slavery. We are determined to shake off all connections with a state so unjust and unnatural.

BILLY

Good reasons for a war.

WASHINGTON

Money or no money, smallpox or not, I will find a way to win this war.

BILLY

Yes Massa George.

WASHINGTON

I'm going for a ride. I need to cogitate on this situation.

BILLY

Don't think it's a good time, Massa George. Weather is pretty nasty out there.

WASHINGTON
I'll worry about the right time.

BILLY
I'll get my riding spurs.

WASHINGTON
No William, I'm going alone. How is your reading progressing?

Billy helps Washington put on his uniform top coat.

BILLY
Doin' better. What should I say to General Weedon if you're not back by the time he arrives?

WASHINGTON
Tell him to wait here for his Commander-in-Chief. Get my Bible. I want you to read the psalms.

BILLY
Yes Sir. Which ones?

WASHINGTON
All of them. When I get back from my ride…I will reprimand Sam Weedon. Then I want you to read to me.

Washington goes out to the stables as Billy walks over to Washington's desk and picks up the Bible. He sits in a chair and reads. Alexander knocks. Billy gets up and goes to the door and opens it. Alexander enters.

ALEXANDER

Billy Lee…by yourself?

BILLY

Yes Sir.

ALEXANDER

You are learning how to read. That's good. Where is his Excellency?

BILLY

He needed some thinking time, so he went riding.

ALEXANDER

In this weather?

Alexander crosses to the General's desk and is looking at the General's papers. He is snooping.

BILLY

Yes Sir.

Billy crosses to the General's chair. His red scarf is lying on the floor beneath the chair.

BILLY

This is the General's scarf.

ALEXANDER

So it is. Billy Lee, someday all Negroes will be free, just like the white man. I keep talking to his Excellency; he'll see the light one day.

BILLY

I don't know, Sir. He is more concerned with keeping his men alive.

ALEXANDER

He's a general first. This is true.

BILLY

It is too cold for him to be riding without his scarf.

ALEXANDER

Did I tell you I was raised in the Caribbean?

BILLY

Yes Sir. St. Croix.

ALEXANDER

Well, I've seen it work. Blacks and whites living together. Hell, there are free black men in New York, New Hampshire, Boston. Did you know the first man to fall in the Boston Massacre was a black freeman, Crispus Attucks?

BILLY

Yes Sir, you told me.

ALEXANDER

Well, don't you forget it. These white people have to see the light.

BILLY

Yes Sir. I think maybe I should take his scarf to him.

ALEXANDER

Well, what are we fighting for if not freedom for everyone? Do these people think that once the war is over, they are going to go back to the same old ways? Those pompous idiots like Jefferson are not going to get away with that, I promise you.

BILLY

I hope you're right.

ALEXANDER

Of course I'm right. Damn it, Billy we are fighting for equality. How can we honestly look into a black face and not see the truth of this war?

BILLY

Some people do.

ALEXANDER

The winds of change are blowing… and it's going to blow right across this country and the rest of the world. Mark my words Billy, this is just the beginning. This is the dawning of a new age, an age of enlightenment.

                          BILLY
Yes Sir.

                        ALEXANDER
When the General gets back, I need to talk to him about the farmers. They are setting two prices--one for hard cash and then they go fifteen percent higher for scrip. It's outrageous!

                          BILLY
Yes Sir.

Alexander exits the room. Billy crosses to the General's desk to see what Alex was looking at. He looks at the scarf. He takes the scarf with him as he exits the room.

Black Out.

Scene 4

In the darkness there is the sound of a horses galloping. Lights up: two days later. Washington is lying on a cot in the tavern at night. Next to the cot is a bowl filled with blood. Washington's arms are red with blood. It is obvious that they have been draining his blood into the bowl. He has a towel around his neck. He is unconscious. Greene is pacing. Billy dabs Washington's forehead with a wet rag. Alexander enters.

ALEXANDER
How is he doing?

GREENE
He is fading fast.

ALEXANDER
All this from a sore throat?

GREENE
Throat infection. He went riding in the cold. Closed-up his throat tight. The doctor has bled him... but it doesn't seem to help.

BILLY
Should someone tell Miss Martha?

ALEXANDER
She should be arriving any minute. How much longer do you think he has?

GREENE

Hours, if we're lucky. He's not going to make it. The doctor wants to bleed him some more, but I think she should be here before we lose him entirely.

ALEXANDER

If he dies now, we'll never win this war.

GREENE

Alex alert the sentries to escort her here immediately.

ALEXANDER

Yes Sir.

GREENE

Oh, and Alex…oblige me by accompanying the soldiers. I don't want any rumors leaking.

ALEXANDER

Nathaniel, I know how to be discreet.

Alexander exits.

GREENE

Billy Lee…

BILLY

Yes Sir.

GREENE

You heard the General turn over the command to me?

BILLY

Yes Sir. You're the interim Commander-in-Chief till Congress appoints someone else.

GREENE

I need to know what he was working on before he fell ill.

Billy gets up and goes over to the General's desk. Billy adjusts the papers as he talks.

BILLY

Yes Sir. He was reviewing these papers here. These dispatches had come in. I think they are about some of the spies he has in New York. He was organizing the inoculation at these churches. He wanted to set-up the iron works to build more cannons. I believe Robert Erskine is in charge of that. These are the newspapers he wanted to read and I think he was arranging a dinner for Miss Martha when she arrived.

GREENE

Billy Lee, that is very impressive.

BILLY

Yes Sir, that's why we call him his Excellency.

GREENE

No, Billy Lee, I was talking about you. I'm impressed.

BILLY

I just try to make things right for the General.

GREENE

If he doesn't make it, we will talk about your freedom and you working for the army.

BILLY

Thank you, Sir.

Martha enters with Alex and Ona. She sees Washington and crosses to him.

MARTHA

George. Oh George. He looks terrible.

Martha feels George's forehead.

MARTHA

He has a fever.

GREENE

We've been bleeding him. It doesn't seem to help.

MARTHA

George…can you talk?

Washington does not respond. He is out cold.

MARTHA
Billy Lee, Hercules is unloading the wagon. Tell him I need him.

GREENE
Who is Hercules?

MARTHA
Everybody needs a lucky charm and Hercules is mine.

ALEXANDER
Hercules is their cook.

MARTHA
General Greene, what were you doing sitting at my husband's desk?

GREENE
Quite honestly, Lady Washington, we don't think he's going to make it. *He* doesn't think he's going to make it.

MARTHA
He doesn't?

GREENE
No Ma'am. So, he has turned over the command to me in the event of his death. I was just familiarizing myself with his notes.

MARTHA

Sir, we have come too far for my husband to turn over this war to someone else's command.

ALEXANDER

It was his idea, Lady Washington.

MARTHA

Mr. Hamilton, I know you put a lot of trust in your doctors, but I know my husband. And I know Hercules. He will have the General on his feet. George, Hercules is coming and I'm going to have him make you one of his hot potables.

GREENE

Lady Washington, I'm not sure the doctors are going to approve of that.

MARTHA

Nonsense. Their methods are not working. We're going to try something I know will work.

Hercules enters.

HERCULES

Yes, Missus Martha?

MARTHA

Hercules, I need you to make one of your medicinal drinks for Master Washington. I think... *Zeus's Blood* should do the trick.

HERCULES

Yes, Ma'am.

MARTHA

Just tell Billy Lee what you need. He'll get it.

HERCULES

Billy Lee, I need half dozen onions, some molasses, and a big pot.

BILLY

Right away, Herk.

Billy exits.

HERCULES

Ona get me my gunny sack from the wagon. The one with the herbs and the High John the Conqueror Root.

ONA

It's done.

Ona exits.

MARTHA

Gentlemen, let us leave them to their work.

She ushers Alex and General Green towards the door.

MARTHA

I will sit up with my husband.

GREENE

But, Lady Washington…

MARTHA

Please General Greene, give us a few hours. There will be plenty of time for you to look over my husband's notes.

Alexander and General Greene exit.

MARTHA

Hercules, this is very important, what you're doing. The fate of a new nation rests in your hands.

HERCULES

Now Missis Martha, when you know me not to do my best?

MARTHA

You're right. You're right. It's just that I've never seen him this ill before. Take off your hat.

Hercules takes off his hat. Martha rubs the top of his head.

MARTHA

For luck.

HERCULES

Don't worry Missus Martha, by the time I get done…those British ain't gonna know which George to bow to. King George the III or General George Washington.

Martha laughs. Hercules attends to Washington. Martha goes to her purse and pulls out George's military glove. She clutches it to her breast; she stares at George for a moment then sits next to him.

Fade to Black Out.

Scene 5

Music cue: Mozart Cosi Fan Tutte, Overture. Lights up: Billy Lee sits in front of a fireplace on the first floor of the Tavern. It is night. The light of the embers of a dying fire reflect on his face. He reads Le Morte D'Arthur. Hercules comes into the room with a bowl of potatoes to peel and sits next to him.

HERCULES

What you doin'?

BILLY

Readin'… about a man named Lancelot.

Music fades.

HERCULES

Good man?

BILLY

French.

HERCULES

He teach you to read?

BILLY

Makes it easier for me to organize his papers. You know letters, newspapers, maps.

HERCULES

Oh. Where is Ona?

BILLY

Sitting with Miss Martha. They are at his bedside.

HERCULES

Yeah, Miss Martha is a strong woman. She gonna make sure he see tomorrow.

BILLY

You think he's gonna make it?

HERCULES

I did my best. He'll make it. All Miss Martha got to do is keep his blood in his body.

BILLY

Bleeding, don't make no sense to me.

HERCULES

White folks, what 'cha gonna do? (*beat*) I can't wait to get back to Mount Vernon. (*beat*) How bout you Billy?

BILLY

Herk, I don't think I'm gonna stay with him much longer. Live or die…I'm running away.

HERCULES

No. You can't.

BILLY

Yes, I can. I have to.

HERCULES

But you've been with him since before the war.

BILLY

Herk, I want to be free.

HERCULES

Where would you go?

BILLY

New Hampshire. They've got favorable laws there.

HERCULES

New Hampshire, huh.

BILLY

Yeah…New …Hampshire.

HERCULES

When?

BILLY

That's what I'm waitin' on… the right time.

HERCULES

New Hampshire. You've been faithful, Billy. Why the change of heart?

BILLY

Herk, I've listened to these white folks talk about freedom. Talk about the tyranny of the British. I feel the same way they feel…but they don't see it. We're invisible to them Herk.

HERCULES

Yeah, guess that's true.

BILLY

I try to hint to his Excellency…while he's freeing the colonies, he could be freeing us too.

HERCULES

I know he ain't happy to hear that.

BILLY

Well, he's got enough problems holding these white folks together. He don't want to add no more to his list of things to do.

HERCULES

How you goin' to get gone?

BILLY

I don't know yet. I just know I've got to do it. I want to be free as much as they want to be free. Think I'll wait till we're farther North.

HERCULES

Want some of that red pepper.

BILLY

For what?

HERCULES

The dogs. Put that red pepper in your shoes. Once those dogs sniff that pepper, they won't be able to find a squirrel in a walnut tree. 'Cause you know he won't stop till he find you.

BILLY

Not if I'm gone during one of those battles. He's got enough to worry about. He'll forget all about me.

HERCULES

(*laughs*) You believe that if you want too, but I know better. He makes everybody call him Excellency. White folks got pride. He'll send out one of his best generals to bring you back... Benedict Arnold or somebody like that. Oh, no Billy Lee, you his favorite.

BILLY

Well, if he don't make it, it'll be a lot easier.

HERCULES

(*laughs*) Billy Lee, he's gonna make it. 'Cause I did my best. You should have told me this earlier, I could have been less skillful. Now? Well, now it's too late.

BILLY

Hercules, I wouldn't want you doing less than your best. I work out my own troubles.

HERCULES

He's gonna live to a ripe old age, unless he catch a musket ball.

BILLY

Come with me, Herk.

HERCULES

No Sir. I got it good Billy. Eat whatever I want. Stay in the house. Nice clothes. No Sir, I ain't goin' no where. I'm living a good life for a slave. I just hope Miss Martha don't make this a habit. I hate leaving Mount Vernon.

BILLY

Herk, ain't you been listening to what freedom is all about?

HERCULES

I don't pay no attention to those white folks. I'm just trying to get by as best I can. I like cooking. It's something I'm really good at.

BILLY

Well, you can keep slavery. It gives me a pain. As soon as I see a chance to get gone…I'm headed for New Hampshire.

HERCULES

All I got to say is two things, Billy Lee…good luck, and… good luck.

Black Out.

Scene 6

In the darkness birds sing. Music cue: Mozart, Clarinet Concerto in A, Adagio. Lights up: three days later on the second floor of Jacob Arnold's Tavern, Martha enters with a mug of Zeus's blood. She gives it to George. Billy Lee is sewing a button on the General's coat. Washington sips the blend.

MARTHA

Feeling better?

WASHINGTON

Much better. That Hercules is a magician.

MARTHA

A couple of more days and you'll be back on your feet.

WASHINGTON

Ahh, Martha, what would I do without my valiant Martha?

MARTHA

It's part of my vows sweetheart.

WASHINGTON

You came to my rescue.

MARTHA

I will always ease your discomfiture.

Music fades.

WASHINGTON

I've so much to do. For a while, it looked as if I would have to pass this mantle off to someone else. Thank God for you.

MARTHA

George Washington, remember this, if nothing else…my love for you is as prodigious as the Atlantic Ocean.

WASHINGTON

I return my love to your soul a hundred fold.

She kisses him.

MARTHA

Is there anything that I can help with here in Morristown?

WASHINGTON

No Martha. What's left are army matters. Decisions I have to make.

MARTHA

If you are in a quandary, I might add counsel to your thoughts.

WASHINGTON

No, I think not. I'm faced with a shortage of weapons. Farmers who want hard cash instead of Congressional scrip, desertions from homesick officers…and a Congress that makes promises, but is failing on the assumption of their duty.

MARTHA

Papa, I think I might have the proper course of action for one of your dilemmas.

WASHINGTON

I'm listening.

MARTHA

You are encamped here in Morristown for the winter?

WASHINGTON

We're fighting smallpox, freezing weather, and an ailing general. Most assuredly, we are here for the winter. That is correct.

MARTHA

Why not ask your officers to send for their wives, Papa?

WASHINGTON

Wives? What would they do here?

MARTHA

A woman's touch is certainly in order here. I could start a sewing circle. That would be useful…

WASHINGTON

Martha…

MARTHA

The wives could nurse their ailing husbands back to health. Help some of the other sick soldiers…and when more of the men are back on their feet, we could have some dinner parties. Good for the morale.

WASHINGTON

Martha…

MARTHA

Papa, I see a few things around this camp that could benefit from a woman's touch.

WASHINGTON

Martha, I may be ill, but I do recognize a splendid idea. You must with all due speed implement this strategy. I'll summon Alexander Hamilton. He will draw up the orders and make sure the officers know they have benefits.

MARTHA

Good Papa, I want to send a note to Governor Livingston. He is living in Lord Stirling's Basking Ridge Mansion. It may be time for those walls to hear the sound of laughter and music. I should think his palate would also enjoy what Hercules' talents can do with mutton.

WASHINGTON

I leave you to your designs.

MARTHA

Billy Lee, make sure the General finishes his drink.

BILLY

Yes, Ma'am.

Martha kisses him, then exits.

WASHINGTON

William, let me have a newspaper.

BILLY

Virginia Gazette, Weekly Mercury, or the *Connecticut Journal*?

WASHINGTON

I prefer the *Gazette*.

Billy hands him the Gazette. *Billy sits down and reads the* Pennsylvania Magazine. *There is a moment of silence as both men enjoy their papers.*

BILLY

Massa George, why do you keep this *Pennsylvania Magazine*?

WASHINGTON

There is a poem in it that I like.

BILLY

Oh, I read this...*His Excellency George Washington* by Phyllis Wheatley. You know her?

WASHINGTON

She's a patriot.

Billy reads the poem. George reads his paper, in silence then...

BILLY

I like this line:

"And so may you, whoever dares disgrace

The land of freedom's heaven defended race!"

Master George, she a good poet, she has a gift.

WASHINGTON

You're reading much better William. Did I tell you she is a Negro?

BILLY

Is she free?

WASHINGTON

No. Very talented, though. I sent her a note of thanks.

BILLY

I'm glad you keep it.

WASHINGTON

I could do with a smoke.

BILLY

Too soon. Strict orders from Miss Martha.

There is more silence between the men as they read.

BILLY

This newspaper has got it all wrong.

WASHINGTON

Got what all wrong?

BILLY

Says here…your army is forty thousand men, strong and true.

WASHINGTON

The *Gazette* says fifteen thousand.

BILLY

Journalist…can't trust a word they write.

WASHINGTON

No, we started those rumors. They wrote exactly what I wanted them to write.

BILLY

But it is all wrong.

WASHINGTON

And it is exactly the kind of information I want the enemy to have.

BILLY

You want them to get it wrong?

WASHINGTON

If the British really knew our strength, they would be relentless till they crushed us. It's a lie. But it is a lie for the good.

BILLY

It's a good lie.

WASHINGTON

Exactly. Congress has the power to appoint generals. So I am fighting using the untalented… the vagaries of friendships. Congress also believes in short term enlistments. An army of citizen soldiers. My hands are tied. So I must be inventive in my endeavors for success.

BILLY

Master George, everyone respects you. Don't you have the power to change their minds?

WASHINGTON

I can only ask for so much. My hand must be hidden. So I make alliances. The alliances make entreaties to the Congress without them knowing it is really coming from me.

BILLY

A hidden hand.

WASHINGTON

The unfortunate policy of short enlistments is daily and hourly exemplified. If the troops which were enlisted a few months ago had been engaged for the war even for a year, I could with them have driven the British army out of Jersey. But a three-month enlistment is ludicrous.

BILLY

Therefore the good lie. Instead of letting the enemy know you just have three thousand men, you have misled them.

WASHINGTON

Before this conflict is over William, you will know all there is to know about fighting a war.

BILLY

I sit at the feet of the Master, his Excellency.

Black Out.

Scene 7

In the darkness the sound of a solitary fife can be heard. The tune is melancholy. Music cue: Mozart Clarinet Concerto in A, Adagio. Lights up: Ona and Billy are sitting by the fireplace at Jacob's Tavern. It is night. He is reading a book and she is sewing.

ONA

What is it called?

Music fades.

BILLY

Le Morte D'Arthur. It means the death of Arthur.

ONA

How come you not reading the Bible?

BILLY

Finished it. 'Sides white folks don't pay the Bible no mind. They can quote it but they don't live by it. I believe in it more than they do. This Arthur book means more to him than the Bible. He lives by this.

ONA

No. Miss. Martha ain't like that. She lives by the Bible.

BILLY

I know, but there is things said in this book about soldiering, about honor, about the law…seems to mean more.

ONA
Why you want to read and write?

BILLY
Been doin' it for a while now.

ONA
Why?

BILLY
Something I overheard Massa talkin' about. Want to be able to read it for myself.

ONA
What you want to read?

BILLY
His friend, Jefferson, wrote the Declaration of Independence. I want to read that…for myself. I'm thinking of making my own declaration.

ONA
Declaration of Billy's Independence.

BILLY
That Overseer Taylor still messing with you?

ONA
I think he's waitin' for a year to come and go.

BILLY

A year?

ONA

Yeah. Told me, then I be ripe. He wants to add some more babies to the Washington household.

BILLY

He can't do that. You just a child.

ONA

Don't make him no never mind. Overseer Taylor see what he wants and usually gets it. Right now he interested in Lucy…but I know my time is coming.

BILLY

Little girl you need your liberty. You need to walk in the sunlight.

ONA

Moonlight's fine by me.

BILLY

No Oney. That's always during the cover of darkness. The night holds secrets. The day holds the truth. Good or bad…daylight shines so everyone can see. You a smart child. I hate seeing you grow up as a slave. You needs to be free.

ONA

You so silly. We can only be free in the night, Billy Lee. The night is our friend. The night gonna hide me from Overseer Taylor.

BILLY

I want to walk as a free man in the day and the night.

ONA

I want to be courted. Want to be free--want to meet a man and have him write me love letters…then I'll be a lady.

BILLY

White man wants freedom. I want it too. That's what this war is about.

ONA

Billy Lee, this war is about money.

BILLY

No Oney, this war is about the white man being free. Being able to look an English man in the eye, in the daylight and say, "I am a man." I been reading they books.

ONA

You so silly. This is a war about taxes. About them white folks keepin' they money. I heard Miss Martha talkin' about it.

BILLY

What she say?

ONA

You know she was one of the richest widows in Virginia when he married her?

BILLY

Yeah, so?

ONA

So the mother country put them so far in debt; seem like there was no way out; Jefferson too. All the planters, they wanted the taxes to stop. So they told them boys in England to forget it. They ain't paying no more. No stamp tax, no tea tax. Dress up like Indians to make a point. Everybody knows Indians don't drink tea. What they care about some tea? No, Sir, these white folks was making a point… and using the Indians to do it. No more taxes!

BILLY

Now that's why I'm learning to read. I want to make my point.

ONA

You want to make a point to these white folks?

BILLY

Yes, I do.

ONA

Then let's get free together.

BILLY

You want me to take you away from all this fine living?

ONA

Yes I do.

BILLY

Who do you think I am--Sir Galahad?

ONA

Sir who?

BILLY

Galahad. He was a knight…a soldier, and he would save a damsel in distress.

ONA

What is a damsel?

BILLY

A damsel is a pretty brown-skin gal. Got delicate hands and all her teeth. Skin is smooth and eyes flash like the coals in a tavern's fireplace.

Ona laughs.

BILLY

She got a laugh that shames the singing birds.

ONA

That's me ain't it?

BILLY

I'm gonna take you to the land of New Hampshire.

ONA

Will I be safe from Overseer Taylor in New Hampshire?

BILLY

Oh, yes. There are laws that old dragon Taylor cannot conquer.

ONA

Then, I meet me a man that can court me. We sit and talk… and he won't be bored neither, cause I know how to keep a conversation going.

BILLY

We must be ever vigilant. Ready to leave on a moment's notice. I will give you a list of things to do. Be ready, for when I call on you…we can not hesitate or the dragon will win.

ONA

Oh Galahand, you are my knight, and I believe that you will save me from that evil, nasty smelly, rotten-tooth dragon.

BILLY

It is the code of something called chivalry. And as a knight I must obey.

Billy takes her hand and kneels before her. Ona curtseys.

Black Out.

Scene 8

Music cue: Mozart Symphony No. 4, Jupiter Molto Allegro. Lights up: Six weeks later, Washington is sitting in a chair and being shaved by Billy Lee at the Tavern. It is daytime. Alexander is holding some papers to be signed.

ALEXANDER
Today, Your Excellency, is the day of the executions.

WASHINGTON
The eight deserters?

ALEXANDER
Yes Sir. Are we to proceed?

WASHINGTON
Examples are to be made. Which papers do I sign?

ALEXANDER
These Sir.

As the music fades, Alexander lays some papers before Washington and he signs them.

ALEXANDER
Thank you, Sir.

WASHINGTON
Tarry not.

Alexander does an about-face and leaves.

BILLY

Master George, can I ask a question about soldiering?

WASHINGTON

Certainly William.

BILLY

Couldn't you spare some of those soldiers' lives?

WASHINGTON

They were deserters William. I need soldiers to understand that during a time of war, we cannot afford to have men desert. They will be hung in front of their comrades. This will provide an object lesson to the others.

BILLY

So all eight men must die?

WASHINGTON

That's right.

BILLY

Who was the leader of the deserters?

WASHINGTON

A soldier named Mythias Smith.

BILLY

What if you just hung *him*?

WASHINGTON

They were tried and all found guilty. I must maintain discipline in this army.

BILLY

If the seven other men were following that man Smith, they might not know how bad a trouble he was getting them in.

WASHINGTON

I think they understood the consequences of their actions. If not, they will pay the ultimate price and their fellow soldiers will benefit from the knowledge.

BILLY

Some of those men did some good fighting. Now they are all being hung for following the wrong man.

WASHINGTON

The court has delivered its sentence.

BILLY

Remember Cambridge and Colonel John Glover's Marblehead regiment getting into a fight with the Virginia Militia?

WASHINGTON

You are referring to the time the White Virginia Militia was upset that Glover had so many black free men fighting for the cause?

BILLY

Those Virginians got into fisticuffs. There were easily a thousand men fighting.

WASHINGTON

We rode right into the center of that melee.

BILLY

I will never forget the look on the faces of the two men when you leaped off your horse and grabbed them by their throats and lifted them off the ground.

WASHINGTON

It had to be done. End the fighting without blood shed. We needed every man for the battle ahead.

BILLY

Those black sailors were tough sailors. They helped you evacuate the troops out of Brooklyn. Didn't lose a man. Some of them Virginians.

WASHINGTON

I know what you are implying, but I am in an ingenuous position politically. Being the general, I cannot move on this issue.

BILLY

Those black sailors helped nine thousand men retreat. Didn't lose a man. Seem like a waste of seven good lives. Seven men that could hold a rifle are gonna be swinging from a tree. Seven more chances to stop an Englishman are gone. You got an army and you lying about the size to make the enemy think you got more than you got. And now you not even losing the men to musket fire, you losing 'em to your own rope. I know you smarter than me Master George, but seem like those seven men might never run away again if they see the leader go and they stay.

WASHINGTON

If I wanted to, I could grant a reprieve to some of the men.

George looks at some of the papers.

BILLY

Bet those men that get a reprieve would think twice about running away from an Englishman. Bet they maybe even fight harder, cause they know they could have been dead anyway.

WASHINGTON

This report says that two of the soldiers fought well at Fort Ticonderoga.

BILLY

Maybe they would fight well again.

George writes a quick note.

WASHINGTON

Of course, this would only be an experiment. A way to test my theory.

BILLY

Yes Sir. No need to try this more than once. You know what they say, "A singed cat may make a good mouser."

WASHINGTON

Spare me the proverb.

BILLY

Is it worth a chance?

WASHINGTON

It's worth a chance. Take this note to Alexander Hamilton. Tarry not.

Billy grabs the note and is out the door.

WASHINGTON

We don't want these boys swinging before it's their time to die.

Washington smiles to himself.

Black Out.

Scene 9

In the darkness, the sound of one drum beating a death march, then one man gagging from the rope around his neck. Music cue: Mozart Violin Concerto No. 3, Adagio. By the light of the fireplace at night in the tavern, Billy is reading a newspaper. Hercules is polishing silverware. Music fades.

HERCULES

Read it again.

BILLY

"All men are created equal."

HERCULES

They have to mean us too.

BILLY

I don't think so.

HERCULES

But it says all men. They got free black men fighting in this war. What they think they fighting for?

BILLY

Yes, but a Virginian wrote it. And not just any Virginian. Jefferson has a lot of slaves.

HERCULES

It don't make sense anyway else.

BILLY

It's a point. Sometimes it seem white folks only see what they want to see.

HERCULES

Read the whole sentence.

BILLY

"We hold these truths to be self-evident that all men are created equal."

HERCULES

I don't see how they cannot mean everybody. They don't say all white men. They say all men…that includes us.

BILLY

Bet they don't mean Indians too. I don't trust them. I'm running.

HERCULES

You're crazy. You've got it good.

BILLY

Herk, if I don't run now, it will be harder when the war is over. Lots of confusion. It's the perfect time.

HERCULES

Billy, I say give the white man a chance. Lots of Northerners are abolitionists. When the war is over, Washington will make them Southerners see the light. Washington's a Virginian too.

He's seen black folks fight this war. He's seen black folks on the battlefield. He knows what we can do.

BILLY

Honestly, I don't think he believes we deserve the right to be free.

HERCULES

Even though we helping him to win this war?

BILLY

Even though black folks are helping him to win this war.

HERCULES

That don't make no good sense at all. Rhode Island is talking about forming an all-Negro regiment.

BILLY

Rhode Island may never happen. That's just talk. Hercules, it just ain't right. I sit and listen to them in the meetings. They want our help, but they don't want to help us.

HERCULES

Billy, we got to give them a chance. They will come around. They have to.

BILLY

You know sometimes the general sends me on errands in the dead of night. I know that's when he be having his secret meetings. He don't want me to listen, but I know…

HERCULES

Secret meetings. What kind of secret meetings? With the other generals?

BILLY

They ain't all generals. Everybody be shaking hands and talking strange. Talking in riddles…and they wear these funny-looking lambskin aprons.

HERCULES

Next time, you should hide out and see what they be doin'.

BILLY

I don't want to have nothin' to do with it. I just want to get me some place where I can be my own man. Breathe free air. Take Ona with me.

HERCULES

Gonna marry that gal?

BILLY

Naw, she just a child… I'm just gon' help her get free.

HERCULES

Now that's a dream. Read it again.

Lights fade slowly.

BILLY

"That they are endowed by their creator with unalienable rights; that among these rights are life, liberty, and the pursuit of happiness."

HERCULES

They *got* to mean us.

BILLY

I'm running tomorrow.

HERCULES

No, you ain't.

BILLY

Gonna be free by tomorrow night.

Black Out.

Scene 10

Music cue: Mozart Symphony No. 41, Jupiter, Rondo. Music fades. In the darkness, the sound of a horse galloping and cannon fire. Billy Lee is brought into the tavern at night. His right leg is hurt and he is moaning in great pain. He is leaning on Alexander Hamilton and Ona Judge. Hercules is in the room and stops what he is doing.

ALEXANDER
Put him on the couch.

HERCULES
What happened?

ALEXANDER
I think he shattered his knee.

HERCULES
Oh, no.

ALEXANDER
Billy Lee, you are going to be all right. We'll get a doctor. Hercules, quick go find Doctor Craik.

Hercules exits.

HERCULES
Yes Sir.

BILLY
(*in pain*) Thanks Mr. Alexander.

Washington enters the room.

WASHINGTON
Billy Lee, what the hell were you doing out there?

BILLY
Just trying to make things better.

WASHINGTON
You had no business being on that side of the camp. You could have been killed.

BILLY
Didn't know they was gonna be testing cannons.

WASHINGTON
Why were you riding Nelson? You know I don't allow any one on Nelson?

BILLY
Just wanted to stretch his legs.

WASHINGTON
In the middle of the night?

ALEXANDER
When he reared up like that I thought you were dead for sure.

WASHINGTON

You're lucky he just fell on one leg. You could have been crushed.

BILLY

Don't look like I'll be dancing anytime soon.

Washington examines Billy's leg.

WASHINGTON

You'll be lucky if you end up walking with a cane. This leg is in pretty bad shape. I'm afraid we may have to cut it off.

BILLY

No. No Master George, don't let them cut off my leg!

WASHINGTON

I may not have any say so over this. We'll let Doctor Craik look at it and see what he says.

ALEXANDER

I sent Hercules to get the doctor.

WASHINGTON

Ona, what were you doing with William? Why weren't you with Martha?

She looks at Washington, then Billy, and runs out the room sobbing. Billy grabs Washington.

BILLY

Master George, don't let them take my leg. I need my legs. Don't let them cut me. Don't let them take my leg.

WASHINGTON

It doesn't look good, William. We'll leave the final decision to Doctor Craik. But I think it's going to have to be amputated.

As the lights fade, Hercules returns with Doctor Craik.

BILLY

Please Master George, they listen to you…I want my legs. I WANT MY LEGS!

Music cue: Beethoven Symphony No. 9 Overture, Coriolan.

Black Out.

END OF ACT I

Gordon Goodman and Adam Clark

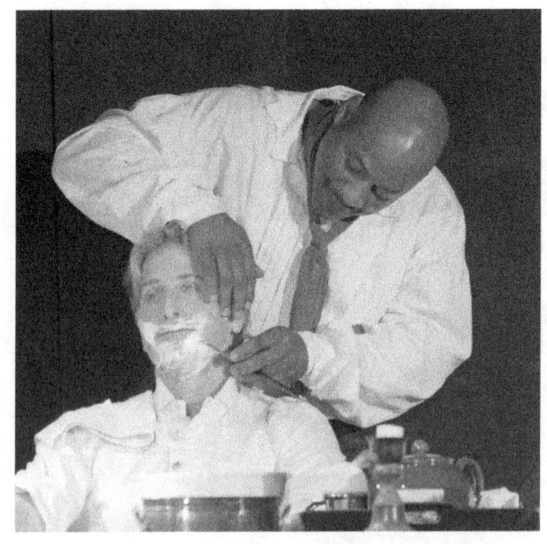

Gordon Goodman and Adam Clark

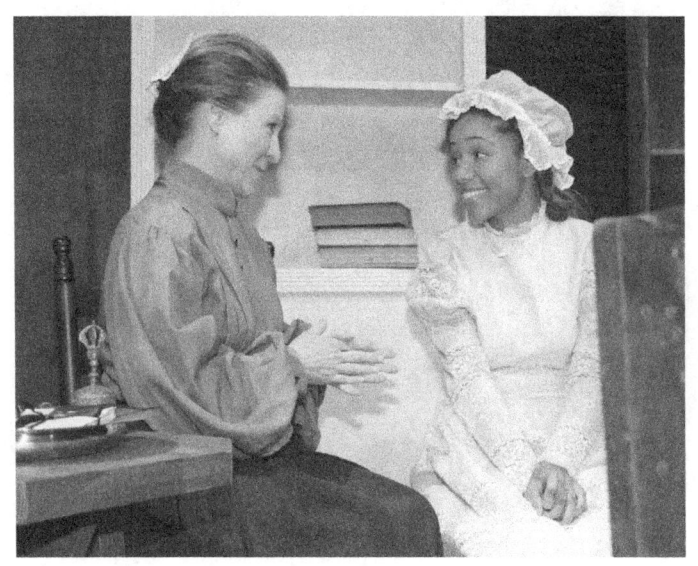

Connie Ventress and Chrystee Pharris

Adam Clark and Ken Sagoes

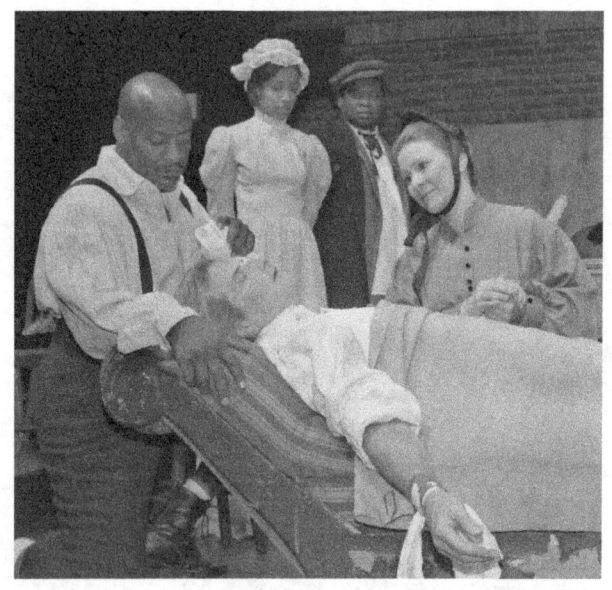

Left to right: Adam Clark, Gordon Goodman, Chrystee Pharris, Ken Sagoes, and Connie Ventress

Gordon Goodman and Connie Ventress

Gordon Goodman and Ken Sagoes

Chrystee Pharris and Adam Clark

Robert Pine and Chrystee Pharris

Trisha Mann and Adam Clark

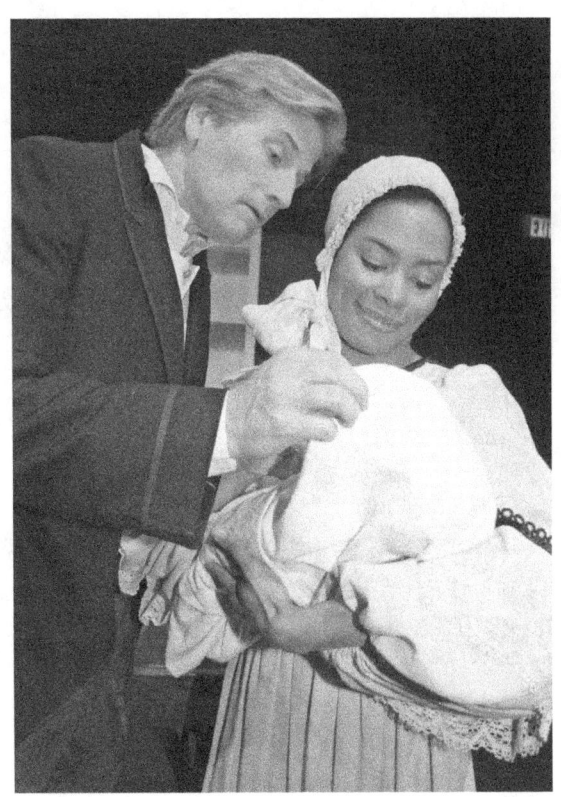

Gordon Goodman and Tiffany Adams
Photos by Mary Lange

ACT II

SCENE 1

Music cue: Mozart Piano Concerto No. 21, Adante. Lights up: Washington's Office, New York; fourteen years later, February 1790. Washington is sitting at his desk; he is trying to eat his breakfast, but the food is awful. Venus, a slave, pours his tea. Martha and Ona are sitting in chairs sewing. Ona is much older; she is a woman. Music fades.

WASHINGTON
Martha, I refuse to eat another breakfast from those so-called cooks. I want them relieved of their duties. I am going to hire someone else.

MARTHA
Hire someone else? Who?

WASHINGTON
I don't know at this moment. These people cannot broil fish. They overcook it. I have repeated myself more than I care to. How difficult is it to broil fish?! They burned my corncakes. Their cat-head biscuits are dry. I just want a simple breakfast.

Billy enters using a cane. He is carrying a book. He returns it to a bookshelf.

MARTHA

Let me bring Hercules here. We won't have to pay him and he's a wonderful cook.

WASHINGTON

We can't.

MARTHA

Why pray tell?

WASHINGTON

He's not a mulatto.

MARTHA

And what difference does that make?

WASHINGTON

I'm President now. Our slaves reflect who we are. We must put our best foot forward. I only want mulattos living in the residence.

MARTHA

Yes, but Hercules has skills.

WASHINGTON

I am not sure if Hercules would be comfortable here in the city.

MARTHA

Papa, tell that to your stomach. I'm sure your appetite doesn't care who prepares your food as long as it's palatable.

WASHINGTON

Martha, I warrant that…

MARTHA

Venus, clear those dishes and follow me.

Venus clears the dishes from Washington's desk.

VENUS

Yes, Missus.

MARTHA

Take this Oney.

Martha hands her sewing to Ona.

ONA

Yes, Ma'am.

Ona puts her sewing and Martha's sewing in a basket.

MARTHA

You will not get an argument from me, George. But just remember the next time you're sitting in a meeting and you're nursing the disorder in your stomach.

WASHINGTON

Martha, send for Hercules.

MARTHA

Thank goodness, your sense of taste has overruled your sense of protocol.

Martha, Ona, and Venus exit.

BILLY

Massa George, how come you only want mulattoes working here?

WASHINGTON

There are many different values on the implementation of this new way of life. We must put our best face on. My slaves reflect me. You are no ordinary slave. You represent me. You are not a common slave nor do I treat you as such.

BILLY

Yes, Massa George.

WASHINGTON

I don't dress you like a common slave. You read, you write, you can use reason. You know words. I don't want you stammering for a meaning of a word. You are my right hand William. You have shared with me more lethal experiences than most white men, who think they know me.

BILLY

It cannot be denied. But don't you think all slaves desire freedom? The dark slave as well as the light slave?

WASHINGTON

William, slavery is woven into the fabric of this land. I fear that if I try to unravel the threads of slavery, we risk destroying the whole cloth. No more talk of this, I have other matters to attend to.

Washington sits at his desk and goes over his papers.

BILLY

Massa George, you think the Abolitionist Bill will pass?

WASHINGTON

How do you know about that?

BILLY

Rumors.

WASHINGTON

It is not very likely.

BILLY

Even with Mister Ben Franklin leading the cause?

WASHINGTON

He's what?

BILLY

Mr. Ben signed a petition for the Congress to abolish slavery.

WASHINGTON

That is unfortunate. William, we are in a very tenuous position as a nation. It's like birthing a baby. If we are not careful the baby could die. Abolishing slavery would mean certain death to the Republic. You must be patient.

BILLY

The Constitution says that slavery cannot be addressed till 1808. You mean I must wait eighteen years before we can even talk about it? You had black soldiers fighting for liberty.

WASHINGTON

Yes, but some of them where already free men.

BILLY

And what of the slaves that fought that were not free? What were they fighting for?

WASHINGTON

They fought because their Masters wanted them to fight.

BILLY

I believe they thought they were fighting for their own freedom. You freed those that re-enlisted. You know the other masters. You can make them see the plight of the Negro people.

WASHINGTON

William, it is impossible for me to ask other slave owners to consider that. This is a truth, I think you know.

BILLY

I know that other slave owners are beasts.

WASHINGTON

That is not true. The majority of planters are trying to work a business. More importantly, they are not your Master. I am your Master. The dilemma of other slaves does not affect you.

BILLY

You don't understand, do you? You are a great man. You are the architect to building this new country…during the war you were called General, others called you Excellency, and now you are called President, but I must always call you Master. There are Negroes that have fought in the war and they are now free. I don't understand your heart.

Billy hobbles out of the room.

Black Out.

Scene 2

Music cue: Mozart Piano Concerto No. 21, Andante. Lights up on Martha as she enters Washington's office. Washington is studying a map. As she puts a shawl on his shoulders, the music fades.

WASHINGTON
Martha, I want you to take Hercules with you when you return to Mount Vernon.

MARTHA
I thought you liked his cooking?

WASHINGTON
I do. However …I have a plan to move the seat of government from here in New York to Philadelphia, but there are a few little problems I want to avoid.

MARTHA
Papa, don't talk in riddles.

Hercules starts to enter the office but stops in the door way. He is holding a tray of food.

WASHINGTON
Attorney General Randolph has made me aware of a Pennsylvania law that allows any slave to demand their emancipation who is a resident there for six months or more.

MARTHA

Papa, Hercules has been in our family for years. You don't trust him?

WASHINGTON

It is not a matter of trust. I want to take some precautions. I have Tobias Lear looking into the law to determine if the six-month rule can be gotten around by moving Hercules and the other slaves to Mount Vernon before the time has expired, then returning them to Philadelphia to start the clock again.

MARTHA

What about our other slaves? Billy Lee, Paris, Oney?

WASHINGTON

I need you to set up a rotation schedule.

Hercules enters.

HERCULES

Excuse me sir, Massa George. I been standing in the hall with your supper and I sorta overheard everything you just said.

WASHINGTON

Hercules, I told you to bring me that later.

Hercules sets the tray of food down on Washington's desk.

Act II Scene 2   115

HERCULES

Massa George I was worried about you. You ain't been eatin' proper lately. Good thing too; otherwise, I'd have never heard what you got planned.

WASHINGTON

This is for your own good Hercules and the good of the Washington household.

HERCULES

Yes, Sur, Massa George, I know it is not my place to say nothin' but I must say something.

WASHINGTON

This was a private conversation Hercules and although it concerns your future, I must act for the well being of my house. Our home.

HERCULES

I need to tell ya…why I am glad you is my Massa. I know you think I may be like other slaves and want my freedom. But I's happy to serve you. I would never stop serving the President. I's seen how other slaves been treated by they Massas. You is fair. You is honest.

WASHINGTON

It pleases me to hear that, Hercules.

HERCULES

I am your cook. I tries to make food that gives you strength to lead your army, to lead this new country, too. Food that will serve you as I serve you. Other Negras may think being in Philadelphia is a chance for them to get gone. But I'se here for you. I served you all during the war.

WASHINGTON

Yes you did.

HERCULES

And now as President, I think you gonna do great things. You are a great man, but how can a man as great as you not trust the one cook that helped to keep him fed. Made sure there was no poison in his food.

MARTHA

Poison? Everyone loves George, Hercules. Who would ever try to poison him?

HERCULES

Thomas Hickey, tried and failed.

MARTHA

Thomas Hickey? Your bodyguard?

WASHINGTON

It was during the war Martha. It's over.

MARTHA

You never told me about this.

WASHINGTON

I didn't want to worry you.

MARTHA

Worry me? You were riding into battles. How could it not worry me?

HERCULES

Massa George was eating a meal here in New York at Queen's Head Tavern. Thomas Hickey poisoned his green peas.

MARTHA

Outrageous. How dare he!

HERCULES

Sam Fraunces' daughter Phoebe warn Master George.

MARTHA

Black Sam's daughter?

HERCULES

Yes Ma'am.

MARTHA

You wait till I see Thomas Hickey. I'm going to serve him bitter words.

WASHINGTON

You can't.

MARTHA

I certainly can.

WASHINTON

He's dead. Died in the war.

MARTHA

Prison camp?

WASHINTON

No. I hung him.

MARTHA

Oh dear.

HERCULES

Missus Martha, that's when he send for me. I make sure his food was safe and taste good. Now, you, this same great man don't trust the one slave that trust and believe in him?

WASHINGTON

Liberty is a very tempting prize.

HERCULES

Massa George, I had many chances to run off during some of them battles. I had a chance to go to the other side. I ain't like Deborah Squash. I had a chance to more than once get the best of bad situations. But I stayed right here by your side… cooking beans, making corn pone, roasting possum, broiling your breakfast fish.

MARTHA

He has a point Papa.

WASHINGTON

Martha, please.

HERCULES

You even started eatin' green peas again. I want you to know I would never use the laws of Philadelphia against the President.

WASHINGTON

You're asking me to believe that you would rather serve me than be free.

HERCULES

I'se happy to serve you, Massa George.

George thinks for a moment.

WASHINGTON

Okay, Hercules. I am trusting that you are going to keep your word. You can stay.

MARTHA

Oh, Papa.

WASHINGTON

And I want you to promise me not to tell the other slaves about this law.

HERCULES

I promise. And a promise is a promise. I'se gonna bake you the sweetest cherry pie you ever tasted. A cherry pie to remind you of this day. I ain't tellin' no lies.

Hercules exits. Washington checks his watch.

WASHINGTON

Negroes…he's not smart enough to want his freedom. Martha, you must excuse me, I have a meeting with Tobias Lear. We're going over some maps of the Potomac.

MARTHA

Yes sweetheart. When do we leave for Philadelphia?

WASHINGTON

Within the month. You might get Oney and Venus to help you pack. Think about the things you want to bring.

MARTHA

Yes sweetheart. I will make the appropriate plan right away.

She leaves.

WASHINGTON

Cherry pie.

Lights fade to Black Out.

Scene 3

Music cue: Mozart Clarinet Concerto in A, Adagio. Lights up: Billy's room, Philadelphia, Pennsylvania. Billy is reading a book and sipping some wine. There is a knock at the door.

BILLY

That door is open.

The music fades as Margaret, a beautiful brown-skinned woman, opens the door. She is close to Billy's age.

MARGARET

Excuse me, I'm looking for a gentleman named William Lee.

BILLY

And what would you want with that so-called gentleman?

MARGARET

I understand he is very knowledgeable about horses.

BILLY

Why I would have to agree with that assumption. I don't know no man, white or black, know more about horses than William Lee. But why would a slave like yourself need his services?

MARGARET

Oh...I ain't no slave. I'm free.

BILLY

You a free woman?

MARGARET

Yes Sir. My name is Margaret Thomas and I am one hundred percent free. You gonna find a lot of free blacks here in Philadelphia. This is the "City of Brotherly Love."

BILLY

Well, Margaret, my name is Billy Lee, but you can call me William.

MARGARET

Are you as good as they say?

BILLY

Better. What you need?

MARGARET

I have a friend who wants to buy some horses…but he don't know a good horse from a mule. He's a city boy. Sometimes white folks take advantage of Negroes. We would like a little guidance on our side.

BILLY

Is this friend your man?

MARGARET

No.

BILLY

No?

MARGARET

I ain't got no man.

BILLY

Pretty woman like you ain't got no man? Free woman too?

MARGARET

This is a new day Mister Lee. Ain't nobody told you, I don't have to be lovers' with no man I don't want. I choose who I want and who I don't want. I ain't no breeder. I'se free.

BILLY

Don't be mad. I'm just teasing.

They sit down at Billy's table.

MARGARET

You free?

BILLY

I am the personal valet to the President of the United States.

MARGARET

Personal valet?

BILLY

Yes Ma'am. That just means I'm his slave. Master George just don't like to use that word…but it means the same thing. Personal valet, body servant, it all equals slave.

MARGARET

Oh. Can you help me?

BILLY

Most certainly I can try. May I ask who your friend is? Is he free too?

MARGARET

Yes, Mister Lee, he's free too. I am here as a representative of Reverend Richard Allen.

BILLY

The Abolitionist?

MARGARET

The very same.

BILLY

And what can I do for Reverend Allen?

MARGARET

He wants to buy some horses for our church.

BILLY

Mother Bethel Church?

MARGARET
Yes, do you know where it is?

BILLY
Of course I do. Every Negro free and bound knows about Reverend Allen.

MARGARET
Odd. I've never seen you at service.

BILLY
There is a first time for everything. Maybe I'll show up for service this Sunday?

MARGARET
Would that be all right with the President?

BILLY
He trust me. Some of the slaves in our household are pretty much free to walk about Philadelphia when our work is done. Our cook often goes for evening strolls.

MARGARET
Can you come by the church this Saturday at noon and pick out some horses?

BILLY
Don't see why not.

MARGARET

Reverend Allen will have the horses there and you can pick the ones he should buy. He can pay you a small fee for your services.

BILLY

Sounds fair. And if I choose to go to church on Sunday will you be there?

Margaret stands.

MARGARET

I haven't missed a Sunday yet.

BILLY

Praise Jesus.

Billy shakes her hand. There is a moment when their eyes connect.

BILLY

See you on Saturday…and I can't wait for Sunday.

MARGARET

Noon.

BILLY

Noon.

MARGARET

Saturday.

BILLY

Indeed.

They like each other. He is holding her hand just a little too long. Hercules pokes his head in the door.

HERCULES

Want anything while I'm out?

BILLY

What…oh. Where are you going, this time of night?

Hercules enters dressed in a fine suit of clothing with a cane.

HERCULES

To the theatre.

MARGARET

I should be going. Goodbye Mister Lee.

BILLY

See you on Sunday.

MARGARET

Good bye Hercules.

HERCULES

Goodbye Margaret.

BILLY

You know Margaret?

HERCULES

How you think she found you? I go to church.

BILLY

Where you get money to go to the theatre?

HERCULES

I didn't tell you 'bout my agreement?

BILLY

What agreement?

HERCULES

Me and the President made an agreement.

BILLY

You and Master George?

HERCULES

Billy Lee, you have to be enterprising in this white world or people will treat you just like an Indian. I may be a slave but, I watch how the white man works. And I think he likes it when a Negro is enterprising. Even if I is a slave, I figure out ways to work some things to my advantage.

BILLY

And you learned a new word. Enterprising, who told you that word?

HERCULES

The President. Right after we made our agreement.

BILLY

Which is?

HERCULES

He let me sell leftovers from the meals I prepare for him to the citizens of Philadelphia…and I get to keep the money.

BILLY

How'd you do that?

HERCULES

Charm, Billy Lee, just plain ol' Southern charm. I get him to let me rent out my cooking skills to his friends and I keep that money too.

BILLY

How much you saved?

HERCULES

(*laughs*) Oh, I ain't tellin'… but I buys these here clothes I got on my back and this here walking stick. And I am gonna get my picture painted.

BILLY

(*laughs*) Who gone paint your picture?

HERCULES

You ain't the only Negro to get his picture painted. Who painted your picture?

BILLY

I know you ain't got enough money to have Edward Savage paint your picture.

HERCULES

He paint that one with you and the general and the horse?

BILLY

No, that was John Trumbull. He painted the one with me and the family. You know the Custis children and Master and Missus.

HERCULES

Edward Savage. Hmmm, I got a painter named Gilbert Stuart. He gone paint a picture of me in my chef clothes. Gone be a picture of just me. No President, no President's wife, no spoiled children. In fact… ain't gone be no white folks in my picture at all. Gone be a picture of just me.

BILLY

That's called a portrait.

HERCULES

Well, that's what it's gonna be. A portrait.

BILLY

You be sure to let me see this.

HERCULES

You'll be the first.

Ona knocks and enters.

ONA

Billy we got to talk. Oh Hercules, I'm sorry. I'll come back.

HERCULES

No need, I am on my way out the door.

ONA

You look nice.

HERCULES

Oney Judge, I always look nice. I am an enterprising man.

Hercules leaves.

ONA

Billy it's gon' be tonight. I'm gonna run. You comin'?

BILLY

Run? Look at my legs. I can't even walk.

ONA

All we gotta do is get to the docks. I got a sloop.

BILLY

Oney, I ain't going nowhere.

ONA

Billy, we got to go tonight. Missus Martha is on her way back to Mount Vernon. I know if I go back to Virginia, I'll have to be with Overseer Taylor again.

BILLY

Oney, don't wait on me. Run. You run now.

ONA

Billy Lee, don't you want your freedom?

BILLY

You get on that sloop, forget about me.

ONA

I'll wait there till you come.

BILLY

Hear me good, Oney. He ain't no ordinary Master now. He the head of a whole country.

ONA

I know.

BILLY

White people love him. He's the father of this new country. Run and don't look back.

ONA

Our country.

BILLY

Not yet. Not till they make us all free.

ONA

I ain't never getting no freedom 'less I take it. Miss Martha told me when she die, she ain't gone free me. She gon' give me to someone else. I got to run.

BILLY

You need someone here to make sure he don't know where to look. You get to that sloop. I'll make sure that the docks the one place he don't think to look.

ONA

Billy Lee, I'm on my way to breathe some of that free air and be a lady. You get away, you come find me.

BILLY

Now you listen to me and you listen to me good, I ain't going nowhere. I'm his slave, Oney Judge. I'm his slave and I'm makin' do with what I got.

ONA

No, Billy, you my knight.

BILLY

I was your knight.

ONA

No Billy. I'm gonna talk to Captain John. He'll come back and get you.

BILLY

My leg ain't in no shape for what has to be done. You make a new life…be a lady, find a gentleman…and live a free life. Now go.

ONA

If 'n you change your mind…you remember, Captain John Bowles, from *The Nancy*…

BILLY

Don't wait, 'cause I ain't coming. I want you to be like Lott. When you leave this room, don't you look back. Now go.

Ona gets up and crosses to the door. She stands in the doorway. She wants to turn around but she knows she shouldn't. She leaves without a last look at Billy's face. He gets up and hobbles as he crosses to a small wine bar and pours himself a drink. He takes a nice good swig.

Lights fade to Black Out.

Scene 4

In the darkness, there is the sound of a ship sailing through the water, sails catching the wind. Music cue: Mozart Violin Concerto No. 3, Adagio. Lights up: Washington is sitting at his Presidential desk, Philadelphia, Pennsylvania. Billy is close by organizing his mail and newspapers. Music fades as Martha enters. She is holding Ona's sewing basket.

MARTHA

Papa, it's Ona.

WASHINGTON

Is she ill?

MARTHA

No. She's gone. She's run away.

WASHINGTON

That doesn't sound like her. Are you sure?

MARTHA

Yes I'm sure. Her trunk is gone. All of her clothes. And some of my hats. We were going to leave for Mount Vernon this morning. Her bed has not been slept in.

WASHINGTON

What did you say to her?

MARTHA

Nothing. I haven't done a thing. We must put an ad in the paper, to bring her back.

WASHINGTON

No, Martha we can't.

MARTHA

Why not? She's my favorite slave…and her mother and sister are expecting her back at Mount Vernon.

WASHINGTON

If she took a trunk… she is gone. And she is probably wherever she wants to be by now.

MARTHA

We can't advertise for the return of my slave?

WASHINGTON

Martha, I am President. How would it look if I advertise that I couldn't hold on to one of my slaves? William, do you know anything about this?

BILLY

If she gone, she gone.

MARTHA

I don't care how it looks. She's valuable.

WASHINGTON

I will get her back I promise you. But I will not advertise. I have too many enemies. The abolitionists would rejoice at this. Not to mention the Northerners who are on the fence with this issue. No Martha, we are not going to advertise, but I will have someone search for her.

MARTHA

What if we start a rumor that someone lured her away? She fell in love with a Spaniard or a Frenchman or someone else exotic.

WASHINGTON

Martha, I have another alternative. Don't worry, we'll find her. So you know nothing about this?

Billy picks up a pair of the President's shoes and starts to polish them.

BILLY

I think you right. If her bed ain't slept in, she gone. Ain't no getting her back now.

MARTHA

Papa, how long will I be without Oney?

WASHINGTON

Let me find Tobias Lear. I'll have him to look into this.

Washington exits the room.

MARTHA

Billy, you must stop what you are doing. I want to talk to you.

He sits in a chair. He sets the shoes on the floor.

BILLY

Yes, Miss Martha.

MARTHA

I want to ask you a question and I expect honesty in your answer.

BILLY

Yes, Miss Martha.

MARTHA

Do you think I treat my slaves well?

BILLY

Better than most.

MARTHA

I think so too. You thirsty?

BILLY

Ma'am?

MARTHA

I could use a glass of Madeira.

BILLY

Don't mind if I do.

MARTHA

Let's not tell George.

Billy gets up and brings a decanter of Madeira and two wine glasses to the desk.

BILLY

I won't if you won't.

MARTHA

You know he needs you. Sometimes more than he needs me.

BILLY

To comb his hair and shine his boots.

MARTHA

You have a bond that goes beyond your servitude.

Billy pours the wine.

MARTHA

It's what I feel for Ona. Why do you think she ran?

BILLY

Maybe, she was in love.

MARTHA

Love? What does a slave know of love? For goodness sake. Even if she thought she was in love, she could have told me and we could have purchased the young buck.

BILLY

She ain't in love with no man. She in love with freedom. Love it more than she love Mount Vernon.

Martha takes a sip of wine.

MARTHA

I have a secret Billy Lee…and I will share it with you…but you must keep my confidences.

BILLY

What kind of secret?

MARTHA

Family secret. I know you know where Ona Judge is. I want her back. I know you can convince her to return to me and if she does …things will be different.

BILLY

Not sure what you mean.

MARTHA

As you know, I was married before I met George. I was a widow…married to Daniel Custis.

BILLY

Yes, Ma'am, before that you were a Dandridge.

MARTHA

Very good Billy Lee. What you don't know is that the Dandridge family and the Custis family were not very fond of each other. But that did not stop Daniel and me from falling in love. I was seventeen and he was thirty-eight. His father thought my motives were driven by monetary considerations.

BILLY

Because Mr. Daniel was much older?

MARTHA

Yes Billy Lee. Another consideration was that he was not his father's favorite son. John had sired a second child, a boy named Black Jack Custis.

BILLY

Never heard of him.

MARTHA

That's because Black Jack was a mulatto.

BILLY

He was a slave?

MARTHA

And I don't mind telling you he was the apple of his father's eye. I dare say that John loved that black child more than he loved Daniel. That's when I hit on an idea. I enlisted the aid of a friend of mine, attorney James Power. I had him deliver a roan horse to Black Jack, with a brand new bridle, and a saddle crafted in Williamsburg.

BILLY

Expensive.

MARTHA

I was young and determined to be Mrs. Daniel Custis. I had Attorney Power deliver a note to the elder Mr. Custis, stating that Daniel had made the purchase for his younger brother, and he wished all good things to his sibling.

BILLY

Did that help?

MARTHA

Indeed, that gesture softened the rocky heart of John Custis and his eldest son's desires became his biggest concern. He blessed our forthcoming nuptials and after John died, Black Jack lived with us. In the house.

BILLY

Black Jack moved in with you?

MARTHA

Lived like he was family. Well, he was family now wasn't he? I don't mind if you pass that story on to Ona Judge.

BILLY

Don't know where she is Miss Martha.

MARTHA

I knew you were going to say that, but tell her I look on her as one of the family. And I don't want my family feeling they have to run.

BILLY

What happened to Black Jack? How come we never see him?

MARTHA

Very unfortunate. A year after he came to live with us, he was taken ill and died… just twelve years old. Well, I must go see what Hercules has planned for this evening's supper.

BILLY

I know whatever it is, it'll be good. I wish I knew Massa George's heart.

MARTHA

I'd be lost without Hercules. No one truly knows my husband, Billy Lee. He is becoming a legend…and only you and I can keep him on compass. I am comforted to know that you will never run. It would break his heart…and Billy Lee don't pick up the bottle.

She leaves. Billy finishes her glass of wine.

Black Out.

Scene 5

In the town of Portsmouth, New Hampshire, there is the sound of seagulls. Lights up on the home of Joseph Whipple. He is white and elderly. He is playing chess by himself. There is a knock at the door. Ona Judge enters. She is wearing Martha Washington's bonnet.

ONA

I'm here to see Mr. Joseph Whipple.

WHIPPLE

Ah, yes, my dear. Come in, come in. Sit down.

Ona stands.

ONA

Ya'll need a maid?

WHIPPLE

Yes, this is true. Sit, sit, sit, please, sit down.

Ona sits in a chair. Uncomfortable at first she grows to like it.

WHIPPLE

Just someone who can do a little light house work, nothing really difficult. Dusting, scrubbing the floors, washing my clothes, maybe some cooking now and then. I am a widower. Lost my wife during the war. Hessian pigs. Lovely woman. I loved her deeply. Well, that's neither here nor there now is it? May I see your letters of reference?

ONA

No Sir. I'm new to this here city.

WHIPPLE

No letters of reference. Well, that does put me in a quandary now doesn't it? So tell me, how would I know if you are a good maid or a bad maid? You might steal from me…pilfer any number of things from my home right under my very nose?

ONA

Well Sir, you could give me a week to prove my usefulness. Then check the silverware and see if anything is missing.

WHIPPLE

Can you tell me who you worked for prior to your coming to this wonderful city of Portsmouth?

ONA

Yes Sir. I could tell you…but they so far away. It might be better for you just to rely on my skills as a maid and you on your skills of seein'.

WHIPPLE

How far away? Say Virginia? You do look like you are from Virginia, maybe a little stop over in New York? Yes, yes, I can see I am hitting close to the mark, now aren't I? I might even hazard a guess that you worked for some lady from the Mount Vernon Plantation. Oh, yes. Very warm now aren't I?

ONA

Sir, do I know you?

WHIPPLE

No Ona Judge…

ONA

You seen my face before?

WHIPPLE

No, not I, Ona Judge…you were seen by the lovely Miss Elizabeth Langdon. She saw Lady Washington's hat, here in Portsmouth, and you were seen under that hat. Elisabeth sent a letter to Lady Washington not sure of your status. One thing led to another and I was finally contacted to retrieve you and send you back…and that I will do.

ONA

Mr. Whipple, you own any slaves?

WHIPPLE

Oh, no, my dear. Not exactly my cup of tea.

ONA

So you don't know what it is like to own a person?

WHIPPLE

No, not really.

ONA

It ain't what you think. You don't really know what slavery is like.

WHIPPLE

I know your mistress. She is very distressed. She is fond of you, not just as a slave, but she likes you as a person too. Of course I cannot say if I am in agreement with her assessment as we just met, but I must admit you have a certain countenance. Pleasant. But of course that is neither here nor there. Suffice to say I am instructed to tell you that Lady Washington wants you back.

ONA

If I go back, Missus gonna give me away when she die. I ain't got no chance at freedom.

WHIPPLE

That's her right, now isn't it? She owns you. Course from what I understand she treats you fair and well.

ONA

Ain't talking about her. Talkin' about who she want to give me to when she die. Mean lady. Miss Eliza Custis.

WHIPPLE

Oh, goodness gracious.

ONA

She does mean things to white people what you think she do to a slave? Don't have no quarrel with Missus Martha. Just don't like the future she got planned for me.

WHIPPLE

Yes, I know Lizzie. She doesn't have the softest heart. I remember one time I was at a ball given by Patrick Henry and Eliza poured red wine on my new silk white shirt. She said it was an accident, but I knew better. She poured it on my shirt, she did not spill it. I know the difference. She was jealous that I was talking to Cynthia Larkin. Cynthia is a lovely girl. Sweet disposition and the tiniest little feet. But I am rambling aren't I?

ONA

Yes Sir.

WHIPPLE

Maybe I can be helpful. Let me write to the President.

ONA

What you say?

WHIPPLE

I'll say you want to return…

ONA

Be a slave again?

WHIPPLE

I will negotiate.

ONA

Negotiate?

WHIPPLE

Yes, yes, yes. We will get you back to the Washington family on the condition that in the event of her death…you are to be freed. How's that? Lady Washington must provide for your manumission. It will be in her will and you can be free legally. Right now anyone who finds you, can return you.

ONA

You think Missus will agree to that? You think she let me go free when she die?

WHIPPLE

She will be dead…and really who cares if Lizzie Custis is happy or not. By the by, do you know how to get red wine stains out of a white silk shirt? Convince Lady Washington, hmmm well, that shouldn't be too hard to do. You have made a reasonable request…of course, that is neither here nor there.

Ona takes off her hat.

ONA

Here, you give her back this here hat. Don't want no parts of it. Guess it's bad luck to borrow someone else's hat. You think he say yes, too?

WHIPPLE

You let me do this. I know how to handle the President.

Whipple walks her to the door.

ONA

Yes sir. You still need a maid? I promise not to borrow nothing from you.

WHIPPLE

Heavens no, my dear! It was just a ruse. A little trifle of a deception, for the benefit of our new President. But I will contact you in a few weeks with his answer. Don't worry leave everything to me.

She exits.

Light fade to Black on Whipple.

Scene 6

Music cue: Mozart Symphony No. 41, Jupiter, Rondo. Lights up: Billy's room, Philadelphia, Pennsylvania. Billy Lee is sewing a button on the President's coat. There is a glass of wine on the table. The music fades as there is a knock at the door.

BILLY

I'm almost done. Tell the President to give me a few more minutes.

The door opens. It is Margaret. She is carrying a basket.

MARGARET

I'm not here for the President. I'm here for you.

BILLY

Margaret, come in.

MARGARET

This is just a little gift the church wanted to give you as a *thank you* for your help.

BILLY

Wasn't necessary.

MARGARET

You don't like cat-head biscuits?

BILLY

Love 'em. I'm sure the person from your congregation meant well, but it's just that... you can't get a much better cook around here than Hercules.

MARGARET

I baked these myself.

BILLY

Well, that certainly deserves a taste, don't it?

Billy gets a biscuit and takes a bite.

BILLY

You know I never realized something till this moment.

MARGARET

What's that?

BILLY

Hercules is the second best cook in Philadelphia.

MARGARET

(*laughs*) You flatter me William Lee.

BILLY

No, Margaret Thomas, you truly flatter me.

MARGARET

I talked to a friend of mine about your knee. She thought this salve might be helpful.

She pulls out a small metal container from her purse.

BILLY

Ain't necessary. I'm stuck with this limp no matter what happens.

MARGARET

She's from Louisiana. Says there is powerful medicine in it. I'm told this may relieve some of you discomfort.

BILLY

Is it worth a try?

MARGARET

Should I put some on now? And we can see?

Billy hobbles over to a chair. Margaret rolls up his pants leg. He is wearing a leather brace. She undoes the brace and applies the salve to his knee.

MARGARET

How do you know so much about horses?

BILLY

Raised on a plantation in Westmoreland County that bred horses. I spent more time in the stables than I did in the slave quarters. I like to ride.

MARGARET

I bet you are really good.

BILLY

Was really good.

MARGARET

How does that feel?

BILLY

Warm. The General likes to ride. Can't most people keep up with him, 'cept me. He's pretty good in the saddle...but I showed him a few things when he first bought me. After that, we rode all the time together.

MARGARET

You miss it?

BILLY

Margaret, nothing like it in the world...feel a horse under you. Listen to his breathing...feel the beat of his heart. Feel his power and you... running together. You a part of that horse and that horse a part of you.

                    MARGARET

Like a centaur.

                     BILLY

What's that?

                    MARGARET

That's a man that's part horse, part man. There all done.

She rolls down his pants leg and gets up.

                     BILLY

How you know a word like that?

                    MARGARET

I can read William. Most Negroes that are free can. It's not a luxury, it's a necessity.

                     BILLY

What do you like to read?

                    MARGARET

I like the Bible. Shakespeare. Greek Mythology.

                     BILLY

King Arthur?

                    MARGARET

I haven't read him.

BILLY

I've read some Shakespeare.

MARGARET

What have you read?

BILLY

Romeo and Juliet.

MARGARET

"Two households both alike in dignity."

BILLY

"In fair Verona, where we lay our scene."

MARGARET

What is your favorite part?

BILLY

The part where his hand touches her hand and it is like a kiss, and the kiss is like a prayer.

Billy's hand touches her hand. Their hands come together as if they are praying together.

MARGARET

A kiss?

BILLY

Yes. I know for a fact that Romeo liked Juliet's cat-head biscuits, but what he really wanted was a kiss.

MARGARET

What if Juliet does not kiss well?

BILLY

Only one way to find out.

He kisses her.

BILLY

I really do feel like Romeo, 'cause we got the same problem they got.

MARGARET

My family doesn't hate you.

BILLY

No, I mean you're free. I ain't.

MARGARET

You are a man…I am a woman. Everything else can be worked on.

BILLY

Margaret Thomas, I like you a lot. You have no idea how much.

MARGARET

Sure I do. You said I was a better cook than Hercules. Man got to like a woman a whole lot to tell that lie.

BILLY

How can we be together when the world is made for us to be apart?

MARGARET

You sound like Romeo. But remember he took a chance.

BILLY

You think we can get around our situation?

MARGARET

That is a question we must answer later. Right now, your Juliet wants you to answer this.

She kisses him.

Lights fade to Black.

Scene 7

Music cue: Mozart Symphony No. 41, Jupiter, Rondo. Lights up: the President is at his desk reading the Bible. Music fades as Venus, a beautiful young black girl enters. She is carrying a letter.

VENUS
Massa George, Missus Martha ask me to bring you this here letter.

WASHINGTON
Thank you Venus.

He reads the letter. An awkward moment of silence passes between them.

VENUS
Want me to wait? For an answer?

WASHINGTON
This is outrageous. Whipple is negotiating with a slave.

VENUS
Yes Sir.

There is a knock at the door.

WASHINGTON
Come in. Thank you, Venus…that will be all.

She exits. Washington writes a letter. Margaret and Billy Lee enter. He is walking with his crutch.

BILLY

General, you remember Margaret Thomas?

WASHINGTON

Why of course. We met after my meeting with Benjamin Banaker. How are you?

MARGARET

Fine Sir.

BILLY

General, Margaret and I would like your permission to marry.

WASHINGTON

William, you know that I cannot purchase any more slaves. You are a lovely young woman Miss Thomas, but my finances prohibit such a venture. In addition, I have sworn not to buy any mores slaves, as I feel the controversy of this issue seems to be growing.

MARGARET

President Washington, I'm free.

WASHINGTON

Free?

MARGARET

Yes Sir.

WASHINGTON

You know that William is my slave? And when I am done with my work here, I am returning to Mount Vernon with him?

BILLY

She knows General. I told her. But we want a life together as husband and wife.

MARGARET

Because I am free…I can go anywhere. Here are my papers.

Margaret hands Washington her papers and he examines them.

BILLY

Reverend Richard Allen of the Mother Bethel Church has agreed to perform the marriage rites.

WASHINGTON

Isn't that the church where free Negroes worship?

MARGARET

Yes Sir. Freemen and slaves. All are equal in God's eyes.

Washington hands the papers back to Margaret.

WASHINGTON

William, I do not own a slave…that I trust more than you…but being married to a free woman may lead you into a temptation for your liberty.

BILLY

General, I love Margaret…but my first duty is to you. You own me, that is why we come to you to ask for your permission.

WASHINGTON

You think that if you are married to a free woman, you would not want to run away? You think you can live for me and her?

BILLY

Yes Sir.

MARGARET

President Washington, you are a powerful man. I know if William and I ran away, you would not rest till you found us.

WASHINGTON

This is true. I am dealing with the situation of one of my dower slaves. Martha's favorite.

MARGARET

I am free Sir. I don't want to live my life as a fugitive. I don't want to be looking over my shoulder. I'm in love with William Lee. I want to be his wife. I want to share my days and nights with him. Slave or no slave…he's the man I love.

WASHINGTON

I don't know you Miss Thomas…but I do know William. I trust you William. I just need some assurances.

BILLY

Sir? What kind of assurances?

Washington goes to his desk and gets the Bible. He hands the Bible to Billy.

WASHINGTON

Swear.

BILLY

Swear?

WASHINGTON

Swear on this Bible that, "I will remain his faithful slave."

BILLY

I swear to George Washington I will remain his faithful slave.

WASHINGTON

And I swear that if I run, may my soul be damned for all eternity.

BILLY

You want me to swear to that?

WASHINGTON

You love her don't you?

BILLY

And I swear that if I run, may my soul be damned for all eternity.

WASHINGTON

Amen.

BILLY

Amen.

WASHINGTON

William, you have taken an oath. It is a promise that cannot be broken.

BILLY

Yes Sir.

WASHINGTON

This Oney Judge problem has forced me to consider simple matters in a different way.

BILLY

I understand General…but I still want to hear you say you give us your blessings.

WASHINGTON

I give my blessings. Margaret when you come to stay at Mount Vernon. I will make sure there is a special place for you and William in the slave quarters. It will be my wedding gift to you.

MARGARET

You are a generous man President Washington.

BILLY

Come Margaret, let us find the Reverend Allen and make our plans. Thank you General.

WASHINGTON

William, I am happy for you.

BILLY

Thank you, Sir.

Margaret and Billy start to leave.

MARGARET

Better than Romeo and Juliet.

Washington finishes writing his letter.

Black Out.

Scene 8

Music cue: Mozart Piano Concerto No. 21, Andante. Lights up: Joseph Whipple's home. Whipple is holding a letter in his living room. There is a knock at the door. He answers the door. Ona Judge is standing in his door way.

WHIPPLE
Come in, come in, Ona. This is most upsetting. Very upsetting indeed. I've just gotten a letter from the President. We have a great problem… or rather *you* have a great problem.

ONA
Maybe I ain't goin' back.

WHIPPLE
Oh no, you have to go back. I promised the President.

ONA
But I didn't promise nobody nothin'.

WHIPPLE
Ona Judge, you are a fugitive. Living here in New Hampshire cannot…wait, wait, wait…you look to no longer be a maiden.

ONA
Can you tell?

WHIPPLE
You have a certain glow.

ONA

Yes sir. Thank you sir. Met a man.

WHIPPLE

Is the Frenchman the father?

ONA

Frenchman?

WHIPPLE

Yes, yes, yes. The Frenchman. The President said you were influenced to run away with a Frenchman.

ONA

No Sir. Don't know nothin' about no Frenchman. That's a lie.

WHIPPLE

My dear Ona, are you insinuating that the President of the United States would tell a lie?

ONA

No Sir.

WHIPPLE

Good.

ONA

I just know that ain't the reason I run. I'm gettin' married. Soon as he come back from sailing. He big, he black, and he free.

WHIPPLE

If he's free…how do you know he's coming back? You may never see him again.

ONA

Oh, I'll see him again. I just ain't carrying our child…HE COURTED ME!

WHIPPLE

Courted you? I can't believe my brother Mason would lie to me.

ONA

And he gave me this.

She is wearing a sailor's whistle around her neck. She pulls it out.

WHIPPLE

What is that?

ONA

Looks like a sailor's whistle, but it's really a token. A token of how he feel about me.

WHIPPLE

What's his name?

ONA

Now I ain't tellin' you that. Don't you know, I know, what you can do with a man's name? That Mister Whipple is my secret… 'cause if I got to run again, I ain't gon' make it easy.

WHIPPLE

Married. My, my, my, that certainly complicates things now doesn't it? The President lied to me. I think I am over my head in this endeavor. Try to do a favor for someone and suddenly I am involved in criminal activity. This is terrible.

ONA

Mr. Whipple, you ain't never heard of the Declaration of Independence?

WHIPPLE

Heard of it? My brother William is one of the men to sign it.

ONA

Well, I'm making the declaration of Ona's independence. I'm free…gonna stay free.

WHIPPLE

Ona Judge you are not legally free.

ONA

Don't know nothin' about that. Don't care neither.

WHIPPLE

What am I to tell the President?

ONA

Tell him I know how he feels. I know how it feels to get up in the morning when I want to get up. I know what it's like to work and get money for my work. Tell him I know what the sun feel like when it shines on my face and I ain't got to worry about no Master wanting something. I can take my time cause it's my time…because I am my own master. Tell him I know what it feels like to be free and I ain't never letting this feeling go. Tell him I know just how he feels.

WHIPPLE

I can't tell that to the President.

ONA

Then tell him I'm gone.

WHIPPLE

Oh, dear.

She exits.

Black Out.

Scene 9

Music cue: Mozart Symphony No. 40, Allegro Molto. As the lights come up in Washington's office, Billy Lee is sneaking a drink. Venus enters the President's office with a tray. She is six months pregnant.

VENUS

He finished with this tea?

BILLY

Yeah, he's done.

VENUS

Need to talk to you.

Music fades.

BILLY

Go right ahead.

VENUS

They gone for a while?

BILLY

Won't be back anytime soon.

VENUS

Got to ask you somethin' first.

BILLY

Ask.

VENUS

Why you never run?

BILLY

It ain't over. I could run tonight.

VENUS

No, you ain't runnin'. I watch you.

BILLY

You watch me?

VENUS

Yes. I watch you Billy Lee and you ain't runnin' nowhere. Why is that?

BILLY

My reason for running is gone.

VENUS

How can a reason for being free…go?

BILLY

Just did. 'Sides maybe these white folks will come to they senses and free all the black folks.

VENUS

(*laughs*) Oh, they ain't never gon' to do that. Massa George doin' this President business for seven years. I listen. I know they ain't about to give no Niggers they freedom. We stuck, unless we run. Now…why ain't you run Billy Lee?

BILLY

Just don't see the need.

VENUS

You love Margaret and she live here…ain't that it?

BILLY

Little girl, what you know about love?

VENUS

Look at my belly. I know somethin'. I love me somebody…and I got me a secret.

BILLY

You ain't love nearly as strong as I love. I love so much I gave up the one thing a slave should never give up. I ain't free, but I'm happy with my life. You thinking about running?

VENUS

Not sure.

BILLY

Why you not sure?

VENUS

Don't know what it's like out there. So I ain't sure 'bout where to go.

BILLY

Oh, I can help you with that.

VENUS

Won't be easy cause I'm carrying. I'm wondering about my baby being born free or born a slave.

BILLY

You wondering?

VENUS

Yeah, I'd like to go out West, to the Ohio Valley. That's the future.

BILLY

You sound like Master George. Out West, that's how he talk.

VENUS

Is he wrong?

BILLY

No, he ain't wrong.

VENUS

It's all wilderness out there. I want my baby born healthy and safe. I know I can get that here. After he born, maybe then I'll run.

BILLY

If you don't run now you may never run. Nobody know that better than me.

VENUS

You stop that drink…you could do it.

BILLY

I like the taste and it kills the pain.

VENUS

I see you and Massa George together. He let you get away with a whole lot of things. He don't treat no other slave like he treat you.

BILLY

We was in the war together. I carried his spy glass. We seen things at the same time.

VENUS

You his boy… *ain't cha?*

BILLY

We seen the same things at the same time. I may have been looking over his shoulder, but I seen them. You gonna run?

VENUS

I don't know. Got to think about it some more.

BILLY

You can't go west right away…but, we can get you there eventually. Let me know I'll help you.

VENUS

I will, Billy Lee, I will.

BILLY

Who's the daddy?

VENUS

Now Billy Lee, that's a secret…and it gone stay a secret.

BILLY

Venus, you a strong little girl…*ain't cha*?

VENUS

(*laughs*) Stronger than most Billy Lee, stronger than most.

Black Out.

Scene 10

Music cue: Mozart The Magic Flute, Overture. Lights up in the President's Office. Alexander is standing in front of Washington. Billy Lee is standing next to Washington. Washington is signing some papers.

ALEXANDER
This saddens me.

Music fades.

WASHINGTON
It's time Alexander. I need a rest. It's time for me to retire.

ALEXANDER
You would have been re-elected to a third term if you wanted it.

WASHINGTON
Two is enough. Quite enough.

Washington takes off his wig and hands it to Billy Lee. He exits.

ALEXANDER
I just can't stand the idea of Adams succeeding you.

WASHINGTON
Better choice than Aaron Burr. Adams will do an exemplary job.

ALEXANDER

He's not you. He doesn't look like a President. He's short and rotund, balding, he's lost all his teeth, and he lisps when he talks.

WASHINGTON

The President needs a sharp mind and Adams has that. I miss Mount Vernon. I want to walk the land.

Washington hands the papers to Hamilton.

ALEXANDER

It's your farewell address. The end of the adventure.

WASHINGTON

No Alexander, now begins the real adventure. Will our experiment work? Can our colleagues sustain what we started?

ALEXANDER

The United States of America. It's working so far, we've got a good chance…but can Adams lead us?

Venus knocks on the door then enters. She is holding her baby.

WASHINGTON

That will be the enduring question to the next generations. Their ability to pick the right man for the job. That will be all.

ALEXANDER

Yes sir.

Alexander leaves. Washington looks at Venus's baby.

WASHINGTON
Have you picked out a name?

VENUS
West. I like the name West.

WASHINGTON
West Ford. Good strong name.

Washington takes the baby in his arms.

VENUS
Maybe someday he see the West?

WASHINGTON
Maybe.

VENUS
You happy?

WASHINGTON
Venus, you have made me very happy.

Washington then coos to the baby. Venus smiles.

Slow fade to Black Out.

Scene 11

Music cue: Mozart Violin Concerto No. 3, Adagio. Lights up in Billy Lee's room. Billy Lee shines Washington's shoes. His crutch is by his side. Music fades as Hercules enters.

HERCULES

Billy Lee, where's that book tells you all the meaning of the words?

BILLY

You talking about… *Johnson's Dictionary*?

HERCULES

That's it, *Doctor Sam Johnson's Dictionary*. Want you to look up a word for me.

BILLY

What word?

HERCULES

Freedom.

BILLY

Freedom? Hercules, why you want that word? You already know its meaning.

HERCULES

Just look it up Billy Lee. I want to see what the white man say 'bout that word.

Billy Lee puts his hand on the book but doesn't open it. He recites the definition by heart.

BILLY

"Freedom. From Free; Number one, Liberty; exemption from servitude. Independence." Here's a quote, "The false enfranchisement with ease found. Slaves are made citizen by turning round." Dreyden. Number two, Privileges...

HERCULES

That's enough. Don't need no more.

BILLY

What are you thinking Herk?

HERCULES

"Slaves are made citizens by turning round." I like the sound of that Billy Lee. It gon' be tonight.

BILLY

You running?

Hercules puts his index finger to his lips to schuss then nods his head yes.

BILLY

Why now?

HERCULES
He's retiring. Two terms. I kept my word. I told Massa George I would never run… as long as he was President. I ain't going back to Mount Vernon. This is your last chance. You coming with me?

BILLY
Wish I could. I'd just slow you down.

HERCULES
I got some of that red pepper. By the time his hounds get their noses back, we'll be deep in Pennsylvania.

Hercules pulls out a sack of red pepper from his pocket.

BILLY
No, Herk. One thing you don't want that white man to do is, be looking for two runaways together. Especially if one is a cripple. Too easy to find.

HERCULES
I'm leaving the General one of my pies.

BILLY
Not cherry.

HERCULES
Wouldn't be right leaving nothin' else.

BILLY

He won't be laughing this time.

HERCULES

That's gonna be the last good cherry pie, he'll ever eat. And the last pie I baked as a slave. You know he gonna heap some mess on you 'bout me leaving.

BILLY

Don't you worry 'bout me. I know how to get around the Ex- President.

HERCULES

If he catch you with me, you can demand your freedom. That's the law in Pennsylvania.

BILLY

I'm workin' on him giving me my freedom when he die. He gonna do right by me. He knows, passing me on to someone else, after all these years… ain't right.

HERCULES

He knows? All Massa George think about is how to make a profit. What's good for his cash box.

BILLY

He's a proud man, but he ain't no fool. My wife is free and he gone free me. I just got to make sure I outlive him.

                    HERCULES
Billy, I'm gonna miss you. Ain't nobody in this world like you.

They shake hands.

                     BILLY
You just make sure you get gone.

                    HERCULES
Hell, if Oney Judge can do it, I can do it.

                     BILLY
I don't want to see them dragging your sorry behind back to Mount Vernon.

                    HERCULES
This is the last you'll see of me.

Hercules exits.

Black Out.

SCENE 12

In the darkness, there are the sounds of hound dogs barking, then squealing. They have lost the scent. Music cue: Mozart Symphony No. 41 Jupiter, Molto Allegro. Lights up at Mount Vernon, December 14, 1799. George Washington is on his death bed. He has been bled. There is a bowl full of blood next to the bed. He has a woolen scarf around his neck. His hair is unkempt. Martha stands by the bed. Venus is applying a cold compress to his head. Doctor James Craik leans over Washington. Music fades.

WASHINGTON

Doctor, I die hard, but I am not afraid to go. Lafayette knew that. He fought with me in our war.

MARTHA

I wish I knew where Hercules ran off too. I remember the time this happen to George at Morristown. He brewed his *Zeus' Blood* and George recovered.

DOCTOR CRAIK

That was most likely luck. You can't depend on home remedies.

MARTHA

Whatever it was he did worked. His herbs or our prayers, all I know is that Hercules was my lucky charm.

There is a soft knock at the door.

MARTHA

Come in.

Billy Lee enters the room.

DOCTOR CRAIK

Well, we've tried ammonium carbonate, the vinegar gargle, the sage tea, a few prayers certainly wouldn't hurt now.

BILLY

Master George, you wanted to see me?

WASHINGTON

Yes, William, my hair is a mess.

BILLY

Yes Sir.

Billy goes to the fire place mantel and gets the ornate wooden box holding the brushes and combs.

WASHINGTON

Martha, would you get my will from the top drawer of my desk?

Martha goes to the desk and gets the will and comes back to George.

WASHINGTON

Doctor, have you ever seen the key that unlocked the door to the Bastille in France? Thank you, Martha.

DOCTOR CRAIK

No Sir.

WASHINGTON

It was a gift from Lafayette. When the Bastille fell, the French stepped into our world. Martha, would you show the kind doctor my treasure.

MARTHA

But George I don't want to leave you...

WASHINGTON

I'll be all right, I'm here with William. Take Venus with you.

MARTHA

George, I don't think...

WASHINGTON

Martha, I promise not to die till you get back.

MARTHA

What a thing to say. Come Doctor, let me show you George's key to the future of the world.

They leave. Billy combs Washington's hair.

WASHINGTON

William, sometimes I lament that I never had children.

BILLY

What about Venus's child?

WASHINGTON

West?

BILLY

Yes, West. West Ford.

WASHINGTON

A good lad. Smart, industrious, stoic, but...

BILLY

But the boy's half black.

WASHINGTON

No, William, that is not what I was going to say...but certainly he is at a disadvantage.

BILLY

You are the one person that can insure that he has an advantage.

WASHINGTON

He is my son, all be it not the legitimate son I longed for...and I will make sure he is provided for. He will carry with him a legacy that I don't necessarily desire to be revealed.

BILLY

He's your secret…and I live my life knowing your frailties and enduring an unjust existence.

WASHINGTON

I know we have had a lot of adventures together. Some good, some not so good. I know you may hate me for some of the tribulations we had to endure together. But as I lie here dying I hope that you will forgive me for some of my miscalculations.

BILLY

I don't hate you. I hate what this country you've created has become. This ain't no Camelot. You stood at the threshhold of greatness and you yielded to the avarice and gluttony of others. I as a black man have borne the scars of a land where its white citizens function from a platform of duplicity. So now you lie on your death bed, asking for my forgiveness and you feel perfectly justified in your request…I have walked into danger with you, stood by you at your lowest moments, but in your precious history books will they talk of the adventures we shared? No. Why? Because I am a slave. I have lost strong friendships because they prized their freedom, and had the courage to take a chance. I stand before you in your eyes not as a man, not as a compatriot, not even as a servant. I'm a cripple, drunken, fellow traveler in bondage to you. A slave who watched you free yourself from the bondage of your mother country. Do you think I did not have thoughts of my own freedom when you and your friends talked of yours? Where is my justice? When you meet our Lord what will you say to him? In your heart you know the truth of our journey together…

and the eye of God can see into your soul. Your judgment day is at hand, Master George. What will you say to the almighty creator?

WASHINGTON
Throw this will into the fire.

BILLY
What?

WASHINGTON
Take this will from my hand and throw into the fireplace.

Billy takes the will and throws it into the fireplace.

WASHINGTON
William, go to my desk. Pull open the center drawer. In the back of that drawer, push the center panel. Pull out the papers from that compartment. Bring them to me.

BILLY
The Last Will and Testament of George Washington.

WASHINGTON
Find your name in the fourth paragraph.

BILLY
And to my Mulatto man, William, calling himself William Lee, I give immediate freedom…you're freeing all of your slaves.

                    WASHINGTON
William, we did have a friendship. I just didn't realize it. You wanted freedom…now it is yours.

                    WASHINGTON
Now go get the Martha, I feel myself going.

Billy crosses to the door, stops, he wants to turn back to Washington.

                    WASHINGTON
William…never look back.

Billy exits through the door. A beat, then Martha and the Doctor run into the room. George fades. Music cue: Mozart, Violin Concerto No. 3: Adagio.

                                                    Black Out.

END OF PLAY

Bibliography

Baker, Houston A., ed. *The Narrative of the Life of Frederick Douglass, An American Slave.* New York: Penguin Books, 1986.

Berline, Ira & Leslie M. Harris. eds. *Slavery in New York.* New York: The New Press, 2005.

Blackaby, Anita D. *Washington and the American Revolution.* Washington: The Council of American Revolutionary Sites, 1986.

Blockson, Charles L. *The Liberty Bell Era: The African American Story.* Harrisburg: RB Books, 2003.

Blumrosen, Alfred & Ruth. *Slave Nation.* Naperville: Source Books. Inc. 2005.

Brookhiser, Richard. *Founding Father Rediscovering George Washington.* New York: Free Press, 1996.

Buchanan, John. *The Road to Valley Forge.* Hoboken: John Wiley & Sons, Inc., 2004.

Callahan, North. *Thanks, Mr. President.* New York: Cornwall Books, 1991.

Carretta, Vincent. D. *Unchained Voices*. Kentucky: The University Press of Kentucky, 1996.

Chadwick, Bruce. *George Washington's War.* Naperville,: Sourcebooks, Inc., 2004.

Douglas, Frederick. *Narrative of the Life of Frederick Douglass.* New York: Dover Publications, Inc., 1995.

Ellis, Joseph J. *Founding Brothers: The Revolutionary Generation.* New York: Vintage Books, 2000.

Ellis, Joseph J. *His Excellency George Washington.* New York: Alfred A. Knopf, 20004.

Flemming, Thomas. *Washington's Secret War.* New York: Harper Collins, 2005.

Flenmer, James Thomas. *Washington the Indispensable Man.* Boston: Little Brown and Company, 1974.

Fox-Genovese, Elizabeth. *Within the Plantation Household.* Chapel Hill: The University of North Carolina Press, 1988.

Griffin, Juith Berry. *Phoebe The Spy.* New York: Scholastic Inc. 1077.

Hirschfeld, Fritz. *George Washington and Slavery.* Columbia: The University of Missouri Press, 1997.

Kaplan, Sidney & Emma. *The Black Presence in the Era of the American Revolution*. Amherst: The University of Massachusetts Press, 1989.

Kitman, Marvin, & General George Washington. *George Washington's Expense Account*. New York: Harper & Row, 1988.

Knoblock, Glenn A. *Strong and Brave Fellows*. Jefferson: McFarland & Company, 2003.

Langguth, A.J. *Patriots, The Men Who Started the American Revolution*. New York: Simon & Schuster, 1989.

Lengel, Edward G. *General George Washington*. New York: Random House, 2005.

Lindlsley, James Elliot. *A Certain Splendid House*. Morristown: The Washington Association of New Jersey, 2000.

Mackesy, Piers. *The War for America 1775-1783*. Lincoln: University of Nebraska Press, 1993.

Martin, Joseph Plumb. *A Narrative of a Revolutionary Soldier*. New York: A Signet Classic, 2001.

Martin, William. *Citizen Washington*. New York: Warner Books, 1999.

McCullough, David. *1776*. New York: Simon & Schuster, 2005.

McKissack, Patricia C. *A Picture of Freedom: The Diary of Clotee, a Slave Girl.* New York: Scholastic Inc. 1859.

Mitnick, Barbara J., ed. *George Washington: American Symbol.* New York: Hudson Hills Press, 1999.

O'Brian, Patrick. *Master & Commander.* New York: W.W. Norton & Company, 1970.

Randall, Willard Sterne. *George Washington: A Life.* New York: Henry Holt & Co. 1997.

Ridley, Jasper. *The Freemasons.* New York: Acrcade Publishing, 2001.

Rinaldi, Ann. *Taking Liberty.* New York: Simon Pulse, 2002.

Schwarz, Philip J., ed. *Slavery at the Home of George Washington.* Mount Vernon: Mount Vernon Ladies Association, 2001.

Smith, Richard Norton. *Patriarch George Washington and the New American Nation.* Boston: Houghton Mifflin Company, 1993.

Taylor, Yuval, ed. *I Was Born a Slave.* Chicago: Lawrence Hill Books, 1999.

Weintraub, Stanley. *General Washington's Christmas Farewell.* New York: Free Press, 2003.

Wiencek, Henry. An *Imperfect God.* New York: Farrar, Straus and Giroux, 2003.

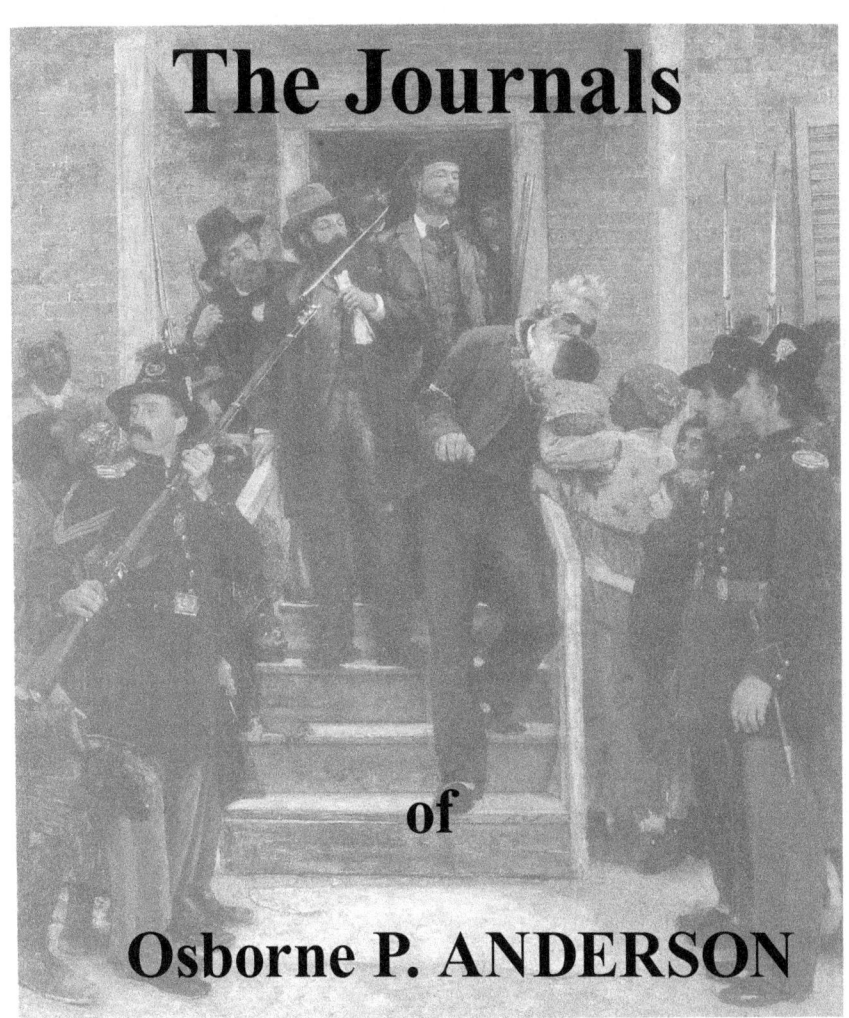

The Journals of Osborne P. ANDERSON

The Last Moments of John Brown, 1882-84. Thomas Hovenden

Dedicated to

My Brother,

Michael Finley Lange

Thanks to

Tom Whayne

Rhone Fraser

Barbara Morrison's Performing Arts Center

The Leimert Park Vision Theatre Consortium

Fernando Pullum and the Fernando Pullum
Community Arts Center

The Journals of Osborne P. Anderson opened on May 15, 2015, at Theatre, Theater, Los Angeles, California with the following cast:

JAMES DOYLE	Paul Messinger
DRURY DOYLE	Stephen Spiegel
ALBERT HAZLETT	Jason Galloway
	Steve Ducey*
JOHN BROWN	Gordon Goodman
OSBORNE P. ANDERSON	Thomas Anthony Jones
HARRIET NEWBY	Chrystee Pharris
	Sahlima*
SHIELDS GREEN	Adam Clark
	Ken Sagoes*
FREDERICK DOUGLASS	J.D. Hall
	Lou Beatty, Jr.*
JOHN COPELAND	Boise Holmes
	Ted Lange*
DANGERFIELD NEWBY	Kareem Grimes
DELILAH COPELAND	Starletta DuPois
LEWIS WASHINGTON	Bruce Cervi
	Jeff Murray*
JEB STUART	William Reinbold
JOHN WILKES BOOTH	Michael Proctor
CAPTAIN JOHN AVIS	Daniel Kucan
	Camron Robertson*
JUDGE RICHARD PARKER	Drew McAuliffe
	Bruce Cervi*
LASWON BOTTS	Paul Messinger
SILAS SOULE	Stephen Spiegel
GEORGE STEARNS	William Reinbold
CONDUCTOR	Kareem Grimes
	*Alternate

Director:	Ted Lange
Set Designer:	Micheal Ricks
Costume Designer:	Mylette Nora
Lighting Designer:	Micheal Ricks
Sound Designer:	Veronica Mullins
Stage Manager:	Sahlima
Producer:	Mary Lange
Wardrobe Master:	Wendell Carmichael

The Journals of Osborne P. Anderson opened on August 4, 2015, at the Hanesbrand Theater-Milton Rhodes Center for the Arts, Winston/Salem, North Carolina at the National Black Theater Festival with the following cast:

JAMES DOYLE	Paul Messinger
DRURY DOYLE	Stephen Spiegel
ALBERT HAZLETT	Steve Ducey
JOHN BROWN	Gordon Goodman
OSBORNE P. ANDERSON	Thomas Anthony Jones
HARRIET NEWBY	Chrystee Pharris
SHIELDS GREEN	Adam Clark
FREDERICK DOUGLASS	Lou Beatty, Jr.
JOHN COPELAND	Boise Holmes
DANGERFIELD NEWBY	Kareem Grimes
DELILAH COPELAND	Starletta DuPois
LEWIS WASHINGTON	Bruce Cervi
JEB STUART	William Reinbold
JOHN WILKES BOOTH	Michael Proctor
CAPTAIN JOHN AVIS	Camron Robertson
JUDGE RICHARD PARKER	Bruce Cervi
LASWON BOTTS	Paul Messinger
SILAS SOULE	Stephen Spiegel
GEORGE STEARNS	William Reinbold
CONDUCTOR	Kareem Grimes

Director:	Ted Lange
Set Designer:	Micheal Ricks
Costume Designer:	Mylette Nora
Lighting Designer:	Micheal Ricks
Sound Designer:	Veronica Mullins
Stage Manager:	Mary Lange
Producer:	Mary Lange
Costumer:	Wendell Carmichael

The Setting

Act I

On May 24, 1856, John Brown and his men visit the Drury home in Kansas. The end result of this visit is the Pottawatomie Massacre. In 1859, John Brown and Frederick Douglass meet at a stone quarry in Pennsylvania and confer on a plan to free the slaves. Brown and his raiders meet at the Kennedy Farm in Maryland. They formulate their strategy for the attack and get to know each other. They storm Harper's Ferry which results in death and capture.

Act II

Opens in the Charlestown jailhouse. The town prepares for the trial and hanging of John Brown and his raiders. Osborne travels north to avoid capture and plans his escape to freedom.

Author's Notes

I first wrote *The Journals of Osborne P. Anderson*, the second play in my trilogy, in 2007, but set it aside as I realized that it had too many characters. I needed to find a way to tell the story of Harper's Ferry, not lose the thrust and immediacy of the incident, and focus on the black characters without making it a four-hour marathon. So, it stayed in the wings and I wrote and produced the third play in my trilogy, *Lady Patriot*. In 2013, Rhone Fraser had heard about my history plays and wanted to do a reading of one of my plays at Malcolm X Park, in Philadelphia. I gave him the two plays I had already produced, *George Washington's Boy* and *Lady Patriot,* as well as *Osborne,* even though it had only been done as a reading not as a staged play. Rhone read the plays and wanted to do all three. So, I flew to Philadelphia for the reading of *Osborne* as I thought I might gain some insights on how to make it stage ready. Malcolm X Park was not the easiest venue for a play reading. There were many distractions: kids playing basketball, dogs barking, children playing tag, helicopters, fire engine sirens--I think you get the picture! As the reading started, we had a small but interested audience. As the play unfolded, more and more people stopped what they were doing and listened. By the end of the reading, we had a large, attentive, and mixed (black and white) audience. I was excited about reworking the play and staging it in Los Angeles. On Saturday, August 30, 2014, I did another reading in Los Angeles at Barbara Morrison's Performing Arts Center for the Leimert Park Vision Theatre Consortium. This reading crystalized how I needed to shape and cut the play to bring it to the stage and my wife gave me a complete dramaturge of the play on the ride home! I started rewriting immediately!! The rest, as they say, is history…it still has a large cast, but several of the roles may be double cast.

The Journals of Osborne P. Anderson

Synopsis

John Brown and nineteen men stormed Harper's Ferry in 1859 and all were killed or captured except for one—the black raider Osborne P. Anderson. In his journals, Osborne chronicled the events at Harper's Ferry including the little known participation of four other black men: Dangerfield Newby, John A. Copeland, Shields Green, and Lewis Leary. Harper's Ferry is considered by many the catalyst for Southern secession which ultimately led to the Civil War. Based on historical fact, *The Journals of Osborne P. Anderson* combines Lange's signature drama and comedy as it peels away traditional stereotypes prevalent in the South before the Civil War.

Cast of Characters

James Doyle is a middle-aged farmer living in Missouri.

Drury Doyle is James's son.

Albert Hazlett is a white abolitionist.

John Brown is an abolitionist, who it tall and thin.

Osborn P. Anderson is a black freedman and printer.

Harriet Newby is a slave and Dangerfield Newby's wife.

Shields Green is a fugitive slave.

Fredrick Douglass is a black orator and abolitionist.

John Copeland is a former Oberlin College student and a free black man.

Dangerfield Newby is a freeman and Harriet's husband.

Delilah Copeland is a free woman and John's mother.

Lewis Washington is a middle-aged plantation owner and George Washington's great grand-nephew.

Jeb Stuart is a bearded, U.S. Marine who wears a hat with a feather in it.

John Wilkes Booth is a Virginian soldier and an actor.

Captain John Avis is a Charles Town jailer.

Judge Richard Parker is a Virginia barrister.

Lawson Botts is a Virginia lawyer.

George Luther Stearns is white man and one of the secret six.

Silas Soule is a Yankee abolitionist.

Conductor is an abolitionist, working for the Underground Railroad.

Parts that may be double cast:

James Doyle & Lawson Botts

Drury Doyle & Silas Soule

Dangerfield Newby & Conductor

Lewis Washington & Judge Richard Parker

ACT 1

SCENE 1

James Doyle, a father, and Drury, his son, are in the Doyle farmhouse. James' voice is heard as Lights slowly fade up.

JAMES

There is nothing on God's green earth lower than a nigger. I may be poor…but at least I ain't a nigger.

DRURY

I know, Daddy. Seems like you tell me that every day.

JAMES

That's because I love you son. Did I tell you, I'm gonna get me a nigger?

DRURY

Yes Sir.

JAMES

Work his black ass till he learns the value of being white in this world!

DRURY

Yes, Daddy. Give me five points.

They are playing dominoes. James is drinking whiskey from a shot glass. He has a mason jar full of whiskey and pours shots into his shot glass as he talks. The sound of two bull dogs barking in the yard can be heard. James hands a piece of paper to Drury so he can write the score.

JAMES

Trust me, Drury, I know what I'm doing. Dutch Henry's gonna help me get a nigger. Knows where I can get one cheap. He promised. We own us a slave, we can turn this farm around. I ain't left Tennessee just to be another poor white man. We got friends here in Kansas and those friends are gonna see to it, that we prosper. Dutch Henry is an important man.

DRURY

I think he's mean, Daddy.

JAMES

Mean? You too young to understand how to handle folks. I wish I could handle those free soil idiots like Dutch.

DRURY

I miss my friends back in Tennessee, Daddy. Mama says, this ain't our fight. We don't own any slaves. Me and William are doing all the work with you. Mama says, pro-slavers should do their own dirty work. Give me ten.

Drury slams down a domino. The sound of two bulldogs barking, suddenly stop. Drury writes the number on the piece of paper.

JAMES

Now, Drury, that's just the problem with women. They don't got no foresight. No vision. They can't see the future of America. Niggers are in our future. Someday I'm gonna own me a whole passel of slaves. This little farm is gonna grow and we gon' be rich. I promise you, son.

There is a knock at the door.

JAMES

Damn awful time for a soul to be knocking at a man's door.

Who's there?

The voice of Albert Hazlett is heard from behind the door.

HAZLETT

Sir, I am lost.

JAMES

Lost? Damn right you're lost.

HAZLETT

May I come in?

DRURY

(*in a whisper*) Daddy, please… don't open the door.

JAMES

You should know better than to make an uncivil noise at my door at this hour.

HAZLETT

I was on my way to Allen Wilkerson's house, and somehow I got lost.

JAMES

Wilkerson's house? You are lost.

James opens the door. Standing in the doorway is Albert Hazlett. He wears a hat and has on a baggy coat two sizes too big for him.

HAZLETT

I am terribly sorry Sir. I don't have any idea of where I am?

JAMES

Allen Wilkerson…you're half a mile away.

HAZLETT

I hate to stop and ask for directions, but I really am lost.

JAMES

You gotta go west, you'll come to an old oak tree, then go south. You'll see a pond…

HAZLETT

It's dark out tonight. Everything looks the same. I have to get my bearings. May I come in? Would you draw me a map? Maybe put some landmarks on it?

JAMES

Drury, look in on your brother, Come in, young man. Come in.

James lets Hazlett into his home.

DRURY

What about our game?

JAMES

I'm tired of dominoes, boy. Look in on your brother.

DRURY

You always find an excuse when you're losing, Daddy.

Drury goes into another room.

JAMES

What's your name young man?

HAZLETT

Albert Hazlett, Sir.

JAMES

Sir...well, well, ain't you the fancy one. A young gentleman with manners. I'm James Doyle.

                          HAZLETT
Good evening, Mr. Doyle.

                           JAMES
Call me James…Albert.

                          HAZLETT
Yes Sir. Are you the same James Doyle that served on the court at Dutch Henry's crossing?

                           JAMES
What?

                          HAZLETT
I'm with the Northern Army, sir.

                           JAMES
Hazlett…I know you Hazlett? Who are you Albert Hazlett?

                          HAZLETT
Mr. Doyle, I'm a soldier.

                           JAMES
A soldier, huh?

Hazlett crosses to the door and opens it. John Brown and Dangerfield Newby enter.

HAZLETT

Yes Sir. I am. Under the command of Captain John Brown and The Army of the North…and I am here to inform you…that you are our prisoner. We have a half dozen men outside your home and you are leaving with us, sir.

BROWN

Mr. Hazlett get his sons.

HAZLETT

Yes, Captain Brown.

Hazlett exits the room. James looks at Newby then Brown.

JAMES

What are you doing? We are white men. Surely you do not place the value of a nigger above your own kind.

BROWN

It is a new day Sir…and your conviction will be the birth of our revolution.

JAMES

Surely you don't think you're going to get away with this? If you kill me…my death will be avenged.

BROWN

Mr. Doyle…you misunderstand. I want your friends to know. We're sending a message. You try and make Kansas a slave state…it will cost you dear.

Black Out.

Scene 2

Lights slowly fade up on Osborne P. Anderson's Home. Anderson is writing in a journal at a desk. Anderson stops writing, makes a correction, and writes another sentence.

ANDERSON

Boston, in the year of our Lord 1861. My sole purpose in publishing the following narrative is to save from oblivion the facts connected with one of the most important movements of this age, with reference to the demise of American slavery.

The lights come up full on Anderson. He stops reading, crosses out a word, and writes in a new word.

ANDERSON

With reference to the *overthrow* of American slavery.

Anderson pauses.

ANDERSON

There weren't that many of us at Harper's Ferry…and we all had different reasons for being there. One fellow named Dangerfield got a letter.

Lights go to half on Anderson and Lights up on Harriet Newby. Harriet is in her slave quarters writing a letter.

HARRIET

Dear husband, I's wan' you ta buy me as soon as possible, for if'n you do not get me somebody else will…de las' two years has been like a troubled dream ta me. It is said Massa is in wan' of money. If so, I know not what time he may sell me and den all my bright hopes of de future are blasted, for dere has been one bright hope to cheer me in all my trouble, dat is ta be wid you.

Black Out.

Scene 3

Lights up on Anderson. Anderson is still reading at his desk, he puts down the journal and checks a page that he has handwritten and reads.

ANDERSON

Another fellow was recruited in Chambersburg Pennsylvania, the year was 1859. The Rock Quarry is quiet as a colored man. Shields Green enters.

Lights fade up at the Rock Quarry. Shields Green enters and checks out the area. He signals for another man to enter.

ANDERSON

He is the body guard to a second colored man, Fredrick Douglass.

Frederick Douglass, enters. They look around. They are waiting to meet someone. The two men say nothing to each other. John Brown enters carrying a fishing pole and a creel.

BROWN

Douglass.

DOUGLASS

Captain Brown.

The two men shake hands. Shields steps back.

                    BROWN

Good to see you again.

                    DOUGLASS

And you too. How long have you been fishing?

                    BROWN

Since I came out of Kansas. Fishing for freedom.

                    DOUGLASS

Here you'll find plenty of fish. Not much freedom.

                    BROWN

Think I might find both.

                    DOUGLASS

I like your beard, nice touch.

                    BROWN

I think it adds an air of stateliness. You bring any money?

                    DOUGLASS

Compliments of Reverend Gloucester and his lovely wife.

Douglass hands him a ten-dollar bill.

                    BROWN

Ten dollars. Not enough to raise an army, but just enough to raise my spirits.

DOUGLASS

As you see I brought Shields Green with me as you requested.

BROWN

Ah, yes. Emperor, good to see you again.

Green nods his head. Brown goes to him and shakes his hand.

DOUGLASS

I have informed him of your plans to hit and run.

BROWN

Times change Mr. Douglass, times change…and with the changing times, one must change one's plans.

DOUGLASS

Change in what way?

BROWN

Mr. Douglass, this is 1859. Slavery should have ended in 1783 with the American Revolution. Seventy-six years, Mr. Douglass, it has been seventy-six years. How long do you think your people should wait?

DOUGLASS

That answer Captain Brown is in God's hands.

BROWN

I know your heart. You are not just a Christian…you are a Calvinist.

DOUGLASS

I never thought of my Christian beliefs as that specific.

BROWN

Mr. Douglass, a lot of Christians like to talk about change but none are really willing to implement the tenets of the good book. Calvinists take action. When you were in captivity as a slave, you saw your situation and you acted on changing it.

DOUGLASS

Maybe I'm a Calvinist at heart?

BROWN

My point exactly...and as a man of action I want to share something with you...I have a new plan to end slavery.

DOUGLASS

A new plan?

BROWN

Mr. Douglass, you must hear me out. I know I talked of rescuing slaves from plantations and using the Blue Ridge Mountains as a shield for our escape, because of the inevitable pursuit by slave catchers.

DOUGLASS

Yes. As you know Shields is an accomplished mountain man and tracker. He escaped from South Carolina, not an easy feat.

BROWN

His skills as a man of the woods most definitely will be useful in my revised plan.

DOUGLASS

Revised in what manner?

BROWN

With one bold move from strong brave men. Men like Mr. Green here.

DOUGLASS

Captain Brown, what is this new plan?

BROWN

I am going to take Harper's Ferry.

DOUGLASS

The arsenal?

BROWN

Take Harper's Ferry. Get the word out to the surrounding plantations and slaves will come running to my door.

DOUGLASS

That is Federal land!

BROWN

Once the slaves arrive, I will arm them and with this army march through the South gathering slaves and leading them. Leading them to freedom. I will lead as Cromwell led.

DOUGLASS

Captain Brown, you attack federal property and that action will array the whole country against us.

BROWN

When I capture Harper's Ferry, it will serve as a notice to the weak, and the strong, to the old and the young, to the healthy and the infirm, that their friends have come. That the Lord has sent his Messenger. It will be like the sound of Gabriel's trumpet rallying them to his standard.

DOUGLASS

Once you arm those slaves, there will be no possible exit. By the time this new army of yours is formed, the Federal troops will surround you, then bring you in.

BROWN

It would be impossible to dislodge me. I will have all the ammunition I need…and the slaves outnumber the whites…

DOUGLASS

Captain Brown, this is not Osawatomie. Don't you see, that is the perfect steel trap. They don't have to shoot it out with you. They can wait you out. Food and water will run low. You'll be forced to exit and when you do, they will kill every last man, woman and child. Starting with the blacks.

BROWN

Contingency Mr. Douglass, contingency.

DOUGLASS

What kind of contingency, Captain Brown?

BROWN

Hostages. And here is the beauty of my plan. I will kidnap a number of prominent white citizens.

DOUGLASS

You cannot be serious?

BROWN

Deadly. Do you think the Federal Government would kill the great grandnephew of George Washington?

DOUGLASS

You rile up these Virginians and they won't care that Lewis Washington is a hostage! Rather than submit to that kind of force, they will blow Harper's Ferry sky high. Blow you, the slaves, and any unfortunate white people you happen to hold. Later they will issue a statement, saying that you killed the hostages and our cause has a major set-back. No, Captain Brown, what you've designed is a suicide mission. No good can come of it.

BROWN

Mr. Douglass, I am surprised you cannot see the logic and practicality of my new plan. Instead of freeing five or six slaves, I gather up five or six hundred. I could use a man with your influence to help me recruit other blacks.

DOUGLASS

You want me to join your army?

BROWN

Think of what we can accomplish together. You have the ear of your people. We could build an army that would force the government to address the atrocities of slavery.

DOUGLASS

I know nothing of military strategy.

BROWN

But I do. I've studied Napolean, Toussaint L'Ouverture, Cromwell.

DOUGLASS

Not good enough...to argue with you is futile, I can see that. John Brown, I will keep your secret...but I must go back to Rochester.

BROWN

Come with me Douglass, I will defend you with my life. I want you for a special purpose. When I strike, the bees will begin to swarm and I shall want you to hive them.

DOUGLASS

Captain Brown, you are a great orator…but I feel your plan is impractical. Now Shields, you have heard our discussion. If in view of it, you do not wish to stay, you have to say so, and you can go back with me.

GREEN

I b'lieve I'll go with de ole man.

DOUGLASS

You know, I think this is suicide?

Green nods.

DOUGLASS

You may not come out of this adventure alive, do you understand that?

A beat, then Green nods.

DOUGLASS

Emperor, you have a good heart. Good day Captain Brown.

BROWN

Mr. Douglass, if you change your mind, I've rented a farm house under the name Isaac Smith. It's the Kennedy Farm house in Maryland, Sandy Hook, Maryland, five miles from the ferry.

DOUGLASS

Good luck to you my friends.

Douglass shakes Green's hand and leaves. Brown checks the time on his pocket watch, then goes to his fishing creel and extracts a Holy Bible.

BROWN

Mr. Green, we will pray together…but before we do I want you to swear on this Bible. I want you to take an oath. Do you understand?

Green nods his head yes. Both men kneel. Green puts his hand on the Bible.

BROWN

I, Shields Green swear on my soul that I will do everything within my power to end this insidious institution of slavery. I promise to follow John Brown and help him any way I can in this our most righteous cause.

GREEN

I swear.

Black Out.

Scene 4

Lights up on the Kennedy Farm. Osborne P. Anderson and John Copeland are sitting on stools. Copeland has a gunny sack full of weapons and an opened book in front of him. Anderson is writing in his journal. Copeland interrupts him, he pulls a pistol out of the gunny sack.

COPELAND

You want a rifle or a gun?

ANDERSON

Already got two guns… one for each hand …what more I need?

Copeland ain't you hungry? I'm hungrier than a fat man in a bakery.

COPELAND

Here…slide this in your boot.

Copeland reaches into the gunny sack and pulls out a knife, he tries to hand Anderson the knife.

ANDERSON

Don't need a knife. Let me see that Sharp's rifle there.

Copeland refuses.

COPELAND
You a city boy, what you know about a Sharp's rifle anyway?

ANDERSON
I know somethin' 'bout somethin' college boy. What 'bout you?

COPELAND
(*laughs*) Oh, I can handle anything with a hair trigger except a sassy woman.

ANDERSON
Then I won't introduce you to Backdoor Betty.

COPELAND
I know I shouldn't ask this…but why do you call her Backdoor Betty?

ANDERSON
Cause when she's doin' it, she likes lookin' over her shoulder. (*laughs*)

Dangerfield Newby enters. He approaches Anderson and Copeland.

NEWBY
Well, look at this…two strong young men. Who's Copeland and who's Leary?

COPELAND
I'm Copeland…this is Anderson. Leary is my uncle and he is with Oliver getting the pikes.

NEWBY

I'm Dangerfield. How many pikes?

COPELAND

Not sure…maybe a couple of hundred.

NEWBY

Anderson…that makes five.

ANDERSON

Five?

NEWBY

Five of us. Thought there would be more.

ANDERSON

Maybe there will be. More could show up tomorrow.

NEWBY

Tomorrow may be too late. I turn in my report to Captain Brown tonight.

COPELAND

Report?

NEWBY

I been spying for Captain Brown. I got a farm near the ferry. I'm a freeman…but my wife is a slave.

ANDERSON
That's hard.

NEWBY
Most beautiful gal you ever seen.

The lights change. Lights up on the Slave Quarters. Newby gets up and walks into the slave quarters of his wife, Harriet Newby. Harriet is holding a baby. Newby picks up a small bouquet of wild flowers.

HARRIET
Danny, Danny, he's got a tooth coming in.

NEWBY
Well, look at you, Jedidiah.

He hands her the flowers. She gives him the baby to hold. She takes the flowers and puts them into a mason jar.

HARRIET
One mo' month and I'm cuttin' him off. He's starting to bite.

NEWBY
Harriet, catch. I got the money!

Newby tosses a leather sack of money to Harriet.

HARRIET
All of it?

NEWBY

$1,500…every last red cent.

She takes the baby out of his arms and puts the baby into a basket. She leaps into his arms.

NEWBY

You gon' be mine. We take Jedidiah with us.

HARRIET

You my man Dangerfield Newby…and that is why I love you. You ain't gon' let these white men beat you.

NEWBY

I know what I got Harriet. I know white men want you. But you mine. We married. I belong to you and you belong to me.

HARRIET

Know what I'm gon' do? First minute I step off this dirt?

NEWBY

No, what?

HARRIET

I gon' kiss you just like this.

She kisses him.

HARRIET

Then when I get to our new home, I'm gon' straighten up our kitchen…'cause you know I know how you are Danny.

NEWBY

Harriet, I built us a nice house.

HARRIET

It takes more than a hammer and nails to turn a house into a home. I'm gonna wash all the pots and all the pans. Then I'm gonna find me a wild blackberry bush.

NEWBY

I know just where to look.

HARRIET

Gon' pick me a whole mess of blackberries. Then, I'm gonna cook us up a piping hot pan of blackberry cobbler.

NEWBY

Loves your cobbler.

HARRIET

Pour some fresh cream over dat. Think about it…think about it…. We gon' eat each bite slow and easy. Then you know what I'm gonna do?

NEWBY

No…tell me like you love me.

HARRIET

Well, Danny…you just guessed it didn't you. I'm gonna love you. Love you for all those days you spent working. Working to get me and Jedidiah free.

NEWBY

I ain't done. Ain't gonna stop till all our chillun is free with us.

HARRIET

Look at you. Got the world on your shoulders. I'm gonna help. I be free…my work is gonna count for something. We a team. Me and you…working on our future together. Oh, Danny. God is good. Everything is gon' be all right.

Lights fade on the Slave Quarters and Lights up on the Kennedy Farm. Newby crosses back to the men.

ANDERSON

Mr. Newby, if you got a wife and family, are you sure you want to risk your life on this endeavor?

NEWBY

That's just it Mr. Anderson. I don't have them. I couldn't buy my wife. Soon as I handed her Master the money, he looked at me and laughed. Then he doubled the price.

COPELAND

Bastard.

NEWBY

Got this letter a week ago. He ain't gone let me buy my wife and children. He's planning on selling them to someone else. I told "Old Man Brown", I got to get them 'fore he does.

COPELAND

We'll get her back. Don't you worry Mr. Newby.

NEWBY

How'd you get in dis, Mr. Copeland?

COPELAND

Helped rescue a slave named John Price

ANDERSON

John Price?

COPELAND

Yes.

ANDERSON

You a part of dat?

COPELAND

Damn right.

A beat, then Anderson picks up his journal and pulls a pencil out of his pocket.

ANDERSON

Well Copeland...just don't sit dere like a frog waitin' for a princess to kiss ya. Tell us de inside story.

COPELAND

Two United States Marshals from Kentucky were trying to ambush Price. Me and another Oberlin student...Turner Wilson, we were late for our biology class. Our professor was a horse's ass so we were in no hurry to share our afternoon with him. Professor Edward Keyes. He had a nasty habit of chewing tobacco in the classroom and spitting on your shoes if he didn't like your answers. Anyway, me and Turner were late for class. We saw these two slave catchers loading Price into a buggy. That buggy took off like a sinner being chased by an arc-angel...almost ran down a mother and her child.

Anderson is still writing.

NEWBY

Black?

COPELAND

No...white. So you know they must have been in a hurry...if they didn't care about a white woman.

ANDERSON

Bet if she was a Virginian woman, dey would have fed her dinner and made her dessert.

COPELAND

Osborne, If you keep interrupting…you're gonna miss the good part.

ANDERSON

Tell it. Two slave catchers load Price in a buggy and dey take off like a hungry hound after a Thanksgiving turkey.

COPELAND

They headed south, to catch the afternoon train from Wellington. We followed them and saw 'em go into the Wellington Hotel. Then, we ran to the station to find out when the next train was leaving. We had some time. I knew a few abolitionists nearby. Turner and me banged on some doors, ran into the businesses of a few merchants. Hell by the time Turner and me were done, we had rounded up close to three hundred people.

ANDERSON

Damn, Copeland, dat's good.

COPELAND

Not bad for two tardy students. We had some other Oberlin students, local farmers, shopkeepers, even Professor John Monroe showed up.

NEWBY

Yo biology professor be dere too?

COPELAND
Hell no! I told you he was a horse's ass.

NEWBY
Oh.

COPELAND
We had the main body of the residents stage a diversion, in front of the hotel. Then me, Turner, Earl Johnson, Professor Monroe, Adam Clark and Sugar Bear Bailey, we broke down the back door of the hotel, found John Price tied up in the hotel attic, cut his bonds, and put him on our own railroad train. It went straight underground.

ANDERSON
Good work Copeland. I'm impressed.

COPELAND
I took him to Canada. My sister Katherine lives in Chatham, Ontario. That's where I saw you get elected as Congressman to the provisional government. Saw Brown at the convention, too. Saw him become Commander-in-Chief.

ANDERSON
It was a great day.

COPELAND
Thirty-seven men from that day in Wellington were caught, indicted, and served time for breaking the Fugitive Slave Law.

ANDERSON

Bad luck!

COPELAND

I don't believe in luck. I believe in destiny. It was my destiny to be walking down that street and see what happened to John Price. Just like I believe it is my destiny to be here now.

Anderson sets down his journal. He reaches into his pocket and pulls out a silver dollar.

ANDERSON

I believe in luck. Tryin' to make sure mine don't run out. See dis here silver dollar? Found it in Chatham, just before I was elected Congressman.

COPELAND

You think that silver dollar is going to bring you luck?

ANDERSON

Found it face up!

NEWBY

Face up means good luck.

COPELAND

Face up or tails up--what difference does it make?

ANDERSON

Face up…good luck. Tails up…no luck at oll…den it's just a dollar, right Mr. Newby?

NEWBY

Right.

ANDERSON

Face down…you got money in yo pants, but ain't no luck comin' your way. You just another nigger.

COPELAND

Osborne you are only a nigger if you believe the white man's lie.

ANDERSON

Copeland I know a nigger when I see one.

COPELAND

Do you know that America has many products? Cotton, tobacco…

ANDERSON

Yes I know.

COPELAND

But America's greatest product is niggers.

NEWBY

How so?

COPELAND

It's our history, Mr. Newby. Some Europeans go to Africa, and they capture some Africans. They put the Africans on a boat and ship them to America. When the Africans get off the boat they are no longer Africans…they are niggers. Now…how did that happen?

Anderson and Newby take a moment to think about it.

ANDERSON

How did it happen??

COPELAND

First of all these Europeans are from a country that speaks Spanish.

ANDERSON

Spain.

COPELAND

Muy Bueno. Now in the Spanish language there is a word for black. It is Negro. So instead of calling their cargo Africans, they use the term blacks…the blacks…Los Negroes. It is better to look at the cargo as less than human. So, the Spanish just say Negro.

ANDERSON

That doesn't explain a nigger.

COPELAND

The Spanish drop these Negroes off in Virginia. The white folks there don't particularly like the Spanish and they have no intention of learning their language. "You're in America now…speak English." They take that word Negro…bastardize it…figuratively and literally…and it becomes nigger. Now they have rightly insulted the Spanish and at the same time disavowed a whole race of people. A nigger is one of the most valuable products made in America. Better than cotton, better than tobacco. It is the gift that keeps on giving. It's versatile and can reproduce better than any crop grown in the ground. It can entertain you and actually feed you. Oh, this is a wonderful product…owning a nigger. And the only place you can get a nigger is in America.

ANDERSON

Is that what an education can do for you?

COPELAND

You just keep writing down what I say and you'll sell a lot of books.

Both men laugh. Brown enters with Green.

BROWN

Mr. Copeland, Mr. Anderson…have you met Mr. Green?

COPELAND

No, Captain Brown.

BROWN

It's about time that you did. I see you met Mr. Newby.

COPELAND

Yes sir.

BROWN

Well, Mr. Newby...you ready to give me your report?

NEWBY

Yes, Sir.

ANDERSON

Cap'n Brown, when's supper?

BROWN

Soon Mr. Anderson, very soon.

Brown and Newby exit. Green joins Copeland and Anderson.

ANDERSON

Have a sit down.

COPELAND

John Copeland.

Green and Copeland shake hands.

GREEN

You can call me Emperor. Dat yo' book?

COPELAND

Yes it is.

GREEN

What's it called?

COPELAND

Henry the Fifth.

ANDERSON

It's Shakespeare Emperor. Dat means dere's a whole lot of fancy soundin' words dat rhyme and takes ten minutes to figure out what de guy meant and by de time you figure dat out he done said another bunch of rhymin' words.

GREEN

Oh.

A beat, then Green Looks at Anderson as he's not exactly sure what he meant.

GREEN

It jus' us?

ANDERSON

You mean colored?

Green nods.

COPELAND

No…there's Lewis Leary. He's my uncle…and you met Mr. Newby.

ANDERSON

He's owns hisself.

COPELAND

Himself, Anderson, he owns himself. You a runaway?

Green nods.

COPELAND

From where?

GREEN

South Carolina.

ANDERSON

Dat's a hell a lot of runnin'.

Green shrugs his shoulder.

COPELAND

Pistol, rifle or knife?

GREEN

Pistol.

Copeland hands him a pistol. Green checks it.

ANDERSON

Can you read?

GREEN

Learnin'.

ANDERSON

Do ya know about Chief Justice Roger Taney's ruling on Dred Scott?

GREEN

Said we ain't got no rights.

ANDERSON

When we take over 'dis here country, we putting in a new constitution. I'm not goin' over the whole thin'…but I wants you to hear dis. It's really good.

Anderson reads from his journal. Copeland hands Green another pistol.

COPELAND

For your left hand.

Green puts the first pistol in his belt. He has no holster. Green checks the second pistol.

ANDERSON

Emperor, listen to dis. Whereas, slavery throughout its entire existence in the United States, is none other than the most barbarous, unprovoked, and unjustifiable war on one portion of its citizens upon another portion…

COPELAND

I think we all understand that.

ANDERSON

Copeland please…I'm tryin' to make a point. Where was I? Okay…most barbarous, unprovoked, and unjustifiable war on one portion of its citizens upon another…

COPELAND

Meaning you and me and every other black soul in America, Emperor.

Emperor laughs.

ANDERSON

Copeland!! Please….don't rub my dick in the dirt. I'm trying to tell the man something.

COPELAND

Sorry, Anderson. You go on and tell it.

ANDERSON

The most barbarous, unprovoked and unjustifiable war on one portion of its citizens upon another portion…

Anderson stops. Waits.

ANDERSON

You ain't got nothin' to say?

COPELAND

Why would I?

ANDERSON

Oh, I don't know. Thought maybe dat highflutin' Oberlin college education might think I missed somethin'.

COPELAND

You're reading. I don't have a problem with your reading. It's your vocabulary that needs improving.

ANDERSON

Copeland, I ain't studying you. Unprovoked, and unjustifiable war on one portion of its citizens upon another portion. The only conditions of which are perpetual imprisonment and hopeless servitude or absolute extermination; in utter disregard and violation of those eternal and self-evident truths set forth in our Declaration of Independence. Therefore...

COPELAND

Here for your boot.

Copeland hands Green a knife. Green puts the knife in his boot.

ANDERSON

Copeland, do you mind?

COPELAND
We're listening.

ANDERSON
I'm tryin' to read somethin' to de man.

COPELAND
No problem. I just wanted him to be armed in case of an emergency.

ANDERSON
Ain't nobody to shoot at 'round here.

COPELAND
There *isn't* anyone to shoot around here. Emperor…this guy worked as a printer up in Canada, you'd think he's have a better command of the language. You never know Osborne, there are spies everywhere.

ANDERSON
Don't pay any attention to him Emperor, he's from Ohio.

Hazlett walks into the room and over to the men.

HAZLETT
Hey, anybody here know how to heal a blister on the bottom of your foot?

ANDERSON
Yeah. Let's see.

Hazlett takes off his shoe and rolls back a dirty white sock. Anderson examines his foot.

ANDERSON

Hummm. Um, um, ummmm.

HAZLETT

Well, how...

ANDERSON

Don't walk on it.

HAZLETT

Thanks a lot. You guys are a big help.

Anderson, Green, and Copeland all laugh. Hazlett limps away.

ANDERSON

Where was I? Oh, here. Therefore: We, the citizens of the United States and the oppressed people who, by a recent decision of the Supreme Court are declared to have no rights which the white man is bound to respect.

GREEN

Linseed.

ANDERSON

What?

GREEN
Linseed oil. Good for a blister.

ANDERSON
Emperor, dis is important. Dat bad foot ain't gonna kill him... but dis here is somethin' every colored person should know about.

COPELAND
Go ahead Anderson, finish reading, we're listening.

ANDERSON
Together with all of the people degraded by the laws thereof, do, for the time being ordain and establish ourselves the following Provisional Constitution and Ordinances, the better to protect our persons, property, lives and liberties; and to govern our action. That's pretty good, huh?

Green nods.

ANDERSON
When this new government is implemented, I'm gonna be a congressman.

Green nods.

ANDERSON
Emperor you catch my drift?

Green nods.

ANDERSON

Ya know Emperor, I'm starting to notice somethin' bout you…. you don't talk much.

GREEN

You ah nigga, tellin' me… another nigga, somthin' ev'ry nigga in 'merica already know. Slavery ain't right. I'm ah runaway. Ah'm here to help utters nigga's run away. Don't need no utter reason to fight.

ANDERSON

Copeland, why don't you explain a nigger to Emperor?

COPELAND

Emperor, don't pay any attention to him. Anderson will talk enough for the both of us. I think he's been around white people too long. He'll sit up and argue with a white man about which is more profitable, going to Pike's Peak for gold or hunting for silver in the Comstock Lode.

ANDERSON

Gold at Pike's Peak.

COPELAND

Who cares!

ANDERSON

Jus' sayin', it's closer. Easier to get to.

COPELAND

Negro, you may be dead in a week, so what difference would it make?

ANDERSON

You don't know dat. Might change my mind right now. Might go dig for gold.

COPELAND

What do you think Emperor?

Green shrugs.

ANDERSON

Oh, you gonna ask silent Sam here.

COPELAND

That's what I like about him. He's quiet. He knows how to keep a secret.

Lights change. Lights down at the Kennedy Farm. Lights up in Delilah Copeland's Dining Room as Copeland gets up and walks over to his mother's dining room.

COPELAND

That was delicious Mama. Nobody bakes a duck like you.

DELILAH

Not too much cayenne?

COPELAND

Perfect.

He checks his pocket watch.

DELILAH

I packed some leftover duck, bread, and cheese, to take on the train.

She hands him a tin box wrapped in a cloth.

COPELAND

Train leaving in a little while. I've got to go.

Delilah takes the tin back.

DELILAH

Junior…you don't have anything to tell me?

COPELAND

No Mama, I'm all packed and ready to go.

DELILAH

Boy, don't you know I know when you are holding a secret.

COPELAND

What kind of a secret?

DELILAH

I don't know. I'm waiting for you to tell me.

COPEAND

Mama, I don't have any secret.

DELILAH

John Anthony Copeland Jr., don't you leave this house with a lie on your lips…to your Mama. What if this is the last time I see you? Now Junior, I know you up to something and I know you aren't going to Canada.

COPELAND

How do you know I am not going to Canada?

DELILAH

I went through your pockets. I found your train ticket. The ticket said Chambersburg, Pennsylvania. Why are you travelling South--when you should be going North?

COPELAND

Oh Mama…

Copeland sits.

DELILAH

Boy…my mama didn't raise anybody's fool. You're my son and I love you. And if you love me back…you'll wipe that lie off of your lips and spit out the truth.

COPELAND

Shoot. It's about Uncle Lewis, Mama.

DELILAH

What about him?

COPELAND

I promised him I wouldn't tell.

DELILAH

That's not a good promise, that's a foolish promise. You've run this far…finish the race. Tell your Mama, what's so important that you and Lewis have to lie?

COPELAND

(*beat*) We're going to help John Brown.

DELILAH

Lord have mercy.

COPELAND

We are going to help him liberate some slaves.

DELILAH

Son, that's dangerous work.

COPELAND

I know Mama, that's why it's a secret.

DELILAH

Does Mary know?

COPELAND

He didn't want to worry her.

DELILAH

They just had a baby. That baby isn't six months old.

COPELAND

I know, I know. We are just going to liberate some slaves and we'll be right back.

DELILAH

I'm proud…and distressed at the same time. I can see you've got your mind made up.

COPELAND

Yes Mama.

DELILAH

Junior, whatever you do in this life good or bad…I don't want you lying to me…you understand?

COPELAND

Yes Ma'am.

Look out for you uncle…he's two years older, but that doesn't mean he's smarter. He's got a quick temper. You best be looking out for that.

COPELAND

I know Mama.

DELILAH

Now, tell me you love me and give me a hug…

He gives her a hug. The lights change. Lights down in the Dining Room. Lights up at the Kennedy Farm as Copeland walks back over to the other men.

COPELAND

Not everyone understands the value of keeping a secret, Anderson.

Brown enters with Newby. He is checking his pocket watch for the time.

BROWN

Men we're getting close. Almost time to leave. I want you men to know that you are the key to this endeavor. I do not want you to underestimate your importance to what we are trying to accomplish.

He puts away his watch.

ANDERSON

So Cap'n Brown…is it time to eat?

BROWN

First things, first, Mr. Anderson. I'm going to give everyone their assignments. Then we will feast like kings.

ANDERSON

Turnips in dat feast?

BROWN

With hot water cornbread. Ann and Martha baked some sweet potatoes. We've got gruel of French barley, plenty of buttermilk, ham sliced cold, and a big pot of black-eyed peas.

NEWBY

All dat sound good to me.

ANDERSON

Me too.

BROWN

Come, gentlemen. Let us join the other men.

ANDERSON

Cap'n Brown. I really want to hear our orders. But I really rather hear dem on a full belly.

COPELAND

Captain Brown, I think what Mr. Anderson is trying to say, is that it will be easier for him to retain the information if he is not listening to you and the grumbling in his stomach.

Brown pauses and looks around at the black men.

BROWN

Listen, men…let's eat.

Black Out.

Scene 5

Lights up on the Washington Plantation. Shields Green and Anderson are rummaging through a room in the Washington Plantation. Lewis Washington enters the room. He sees the two men.

WASHINGTON
Here, here, what do you think you're doing?

Anderson turns to face Washington.

WASHINGTON
You're not one of mine.

ANDERSON
Perceptive.

WASHINGTON
Nigger, who do you belong to?

ANDERSON
Myself.

Anderson draws his pistol on Washington. Hazlett enters with a box.

HAZLETT
Osborne, I found the pistols.

WASHINGTON
What do you think you're doing?

ANDERSON

Where is the sword?

HAZLETT

Couldn't find it.

WASHINGTON

That is an heirloom.

Anderson holsters his pistol, opens the box, and stares at the contents. Shields Green exits.

ANDERSON

Pistols from the Marquis De Lafayette.

WASHINGTON

You will put that box down and get your black ass out of my home before I…

ANDERSON

Shut him up and sit him down.

Hazlett pushes Washington into a chair.

WASHINGTON

You're talking to a white man, boy.

ANDERSON

Mr. Washington…you are my prisoner. I am confiscating these pistols.

WASHINGTON
That was a gift to my great grand uncle from…

ANDERSON
I said shut him up. I'm not finished talking.

Hazlett backhands Washington with his gun. The force snaps his head back.

ANDERSON
Now, Mr. Washington, nod your head if I have your attention.

Washington nods.

ANDERSON
At this moment, your slaves are being rounded up…we are going to free them. Those that want to join us…can. Those that choose to leave…will. You Mr. Washington are my prisoner. I am taking you to my Captain.

WASHINGTON
May I speak?

Anderson nods.

WASHINGTON
Are you going to kill me?

ANDERSON

That depends on you. Your fate is in the hands of my Captain Isaac Smith. If I report to him that you have been cooperative it will be helpful...but if you continue to act in an obstinate manner, it will not be helpful to your situation. Have I made myself clear?

Washington nods.

WASHINGTON

Can I offer you a drink? I've got brandy, or whiskey. Would you like some whiskey?

ANDERSON

If I want a drink...I'll take it. I'm not thirsty...and if you think getting a black man drunk is an opportunity for you to take advantage...you are going to have to rethink your present situation. I am not a runaway. I'm a freeman.

WASHINGTON

When I get nervous, I get hungry. Right now I could use a drink.

Shields Green enters carrying a sword.

GREEN

Found da sword.

ANDERSON

Oh, this is a beaut.

WASHINGTON

Careful with that. It was a gift.

HAZLETT

How did you find it?

GREEN

His wife, she seen de light.

WASHINGTON

You didn't harm her?

GREEN

I ain't about hurtin' no women and chillun.

WASHINGTON

That sword, once belonged to Frederick the Great of Prussia. It was given to my great grand uncle.

ANDERSON

And now it is going to be worn by a black man.

Anderson primps as if he is in front of a mirror.

WASHINGTON

I am sorry if I appeared to be ungrateful. You've been a gentleman. You want my slaves? Take them. You don't need me. You want my…the Lafayette pistols…take them. Hell, I give them to you. Take the sword. I won't report them missing. It's worth a lot of money. Just leave me and my family alone.

ANDERSON

Oh, we are going to leave your family alone....but you are coming with us.

WASHINGTON

Me? You don't need me. I said you can have my slaves. I'll sign paper. Just leave me.

ANDERSON

Mr. Washington you're always trying to impress people about how important you are...you and your great lineage. Well, you are very important to my captain and our plan.

WASHINGTON

I've got money. Let me give you money.

ANDERSON

The only thing I want from you is your time. And you are going to share your time with my captain. Let's get him out of here. Let's go.

WASHINGTON

But I have a family, they need me...

HAZLETT

Not another word or I'll shoot you now and deliver a body to my captain.

ANDERSON

Who's your neighbor?

Washington doesn't answer.

                    HAZLETT

John Allstadt.

                    ANDERSON

How many slaves does he have?

                    HAZLETT

He has twelve slaves.

                    WASHINGTON

(looking at Hazlett) Traitor.

                    ANDERSON

He *had* twelve slaves. Let's go show them what freedom looks like.

Washington is silent as they lead him out.

Black Out.

SCENE 6

Lights up on the Slave Quarters. Harriet Newby talks to her children. She addresses the audience as if they are her children. She is holding her baby, Jedidiah.

HARRIET

Chillun, come here, come here. I think I got good news. Yo' father sent me a message. He's comin' ta rescue us. He gon' take us ta freedom. He got an army of good men, strong men. Dey comin' for us. We gon' walk in dat freedom light. Gon' see Ohio. Jedidiah, you gon' grow up free. Yes sur, you my little man, and you gon' see all de things little white boys get ta see....and you ain't gon' have a care ta worry 'bout. (*laughs.*) I'm laughin' cause I'm de happiest woman in de world.

Black Out.

Scene 7

There is the sound of gunshots in the darkness. Lights up on Harper's Ferry. Brown is guarding his hostages. Anderson arrives with his prisoners. Anderson and Hazlett bring in their hostage, Lewis Washington. Shields Green holds his gun on Washington.

ANDERSON
Captain, I have the pistols from Lafayette.

BROWN
Let me see them.

ANDERSON
Yes sir.

Anderson hands him the box. He opens the box and looks at the pistols.

BROWN
George Washington's pistols. Let those bastards think of the magnitude of this.

There is the sound of more gunshots.

BROWN
Anderson, take some men and liberate the next plantation.

ANDERSON
Yes Sir. Come on Albert.

BROWN

Be careful...we got militia showing up. Anderson I need soldiers. Bring me black men ready to fight for their liberty.

ANDERSON

Yes Sir.

Anderson draws his pistol ready to shoot his way out. More gunshots sound as he and Hazlett exit.

WASHINGTON

Are you going to kill me?

BROWN

You are my hostage; I am not a barbarian. I am doing God's will.

WASHINGTON

God's will?

BROWN

Moses said to Pharaoh, "Let my people go."

WASHINGTON

These are not your people; they are the half-monkey race. I'm your people.

GREEN

Should I shoot him?

BROWN

Hold on! Slavery is the sum of all villainies. It must be abolished, if not…human freedom and republican liberty will soon be empty names in these United States.

WASHINGTON

You don't make any sense. Smith, where are you from? I know you're a Yankee?

I hear it in your voice.

Brown crosses to Washington and bends down to him so they are nose to nose.

BROWN

Mr. John Brown to you Sir.

WASHINGTON

Oh, my God, Osawatomie Brown! I heard what you did in Kansas.

BROWN

I taught a few border ruffians the meaning of justice.

WASHINGTON

Justice? You kidnapped, shot and killed ol'man Doyle…went to the Wilkinson farm, killed him … hacked to pieces his two sons. The Pottawatomie Massacre. You think we Southerners are ignorant of your lawlessness?

BROWN

I did not raise the sword that took their lives.

WASHINGTON

They died at your hands and now you want to kill me too.

BROWN

I want you for the moral effect it would give our cause having one of your name and history, as my prisoner.

WASHINGTON

My God, man!! You're crazy! Lord, I'm so hungry.

BROWN

I do not expect you to understand, since you are the manifestation of what is evil in this land. Your greed has blinded you to the light. I am but a candle and tonight I will take you from the darkness and lead you to the path of righteousness.

WASHINGTON

That is insane. You are insane.

BROWN

They called Cromwell a mad man.

WASHINGTON

This isn't England. We're in Virginia!

BROWN

Good ol' George Washington is blessing this event from his heavenly perch.

There is the sound of more gunshots.

BROWN

Emperor, you catch up with Mr. Anderson. Help him with his assignment.

Green exits, as Copeland enters.

COPELAND

Captain Brown, we lost Dangerfield Newby.

BROWN

Lost? Dead?

COPELAND

Yes sir. He was helping your son hold the Potomac Bridge. He got shot in the neck. Militia… I think he was dead before he hit the ground.

BROWN

Ahh…Mr. Newby…strong soul, he is the first of our men to die.

COPELAND

These Virginians are savages. They cut off his ears and genitals. They are poking sticks into the bullet wound. More militia is showing up. We got the wagon loaded…we should leave.

BROWN

Mr. Anderson is bringing reinforcements. We must wait for the slaves to rise up.

WASHINGTON

It'll never happen.

COPELAND

We have Allstadt's slaves guarding him. They can't seem to stop smiling either.

We need to get back there with the ammunition, and take the slaves we got and head for the Blue Ridge Mountains.

BROWN

No, Mr. Copeland, I said we wait! I'll get some men and camouflage that wagon. We must make sure the militia does not capture it. Mr. Copeland…keep an eye on Mr. Washington.

Brown exits. Washington is tied up. Copeland checks his bonds. Washington is secure. The sound of more gun shots. Copeland goes to a window to check for the position of the enemy.

WASHINGTON

Hey nigger, come here.

COPELAND

Mr. Washington, I will respect you, if you respect me. My name is Copeland.

Mr. John Copeland to you.

WASHINGTON

I ain't never called a nigger mister in my life.

COPELAND

Where's your pistol?

WASHINGTON

Ain't got no pistol.

COPELAND

Well, maybe you better address me as Mr. Copeland. You aren't talking to a slave. You aren't talking to an ex-slave. I'm a free man. Went to college, Oberlin College. I can read. I can write… and I can pull a trigger on a pistol…faster than you can spell your name. I joined this cause to fight for the freedom of those poor souls who you have enslaved. Now… I knew I might have to kill some white people to bring about justice. I just didn't realize that the first white man's blood on my hands would be yours. So…before I disobey Captain Brown's orders and we have twenty-nine live hostages and one dead one, I'm gonna give you a chance.

WASHINGTON

Nigger, do you know who you are talking to?

COPELAND

I am talking to one dead peckerwood…unless he calls me by my proper name.

Copeland aims the gun at Washington's head.

WASHINGTON

Nigger you have lost your mind, don't you threaten me.

Washington stares at Copeland.

COPELAND

Mr. Washington, don't look at my black face, look into my eyes. I am going to count to three…and if you don't call me by my proper name…Mr. John Copeland…these eyes are going to be the last thing you see before meeting your maker.

WASHINGTON

I am a white man goddamn it. I ain't gonna kowtow to no nigger. You must think I'm blind, cripple and crazy.

COPELAND

One.

WASHINGTON

Nigger, I am the great grandnephew of America's first President.

COPELAND

Two.

Copeland cocks his pistol.

WASHINGTON

Mr. John Copeland may I please have something to eat?

COPELAND

That wasn't as hard as you thought it would be…now was it?

WASHINGTON

I'm sweaty, I'm tired, I'm hungry. Today has been a trying day. I feel like a baby hounddog sucking on a dry titty. I would just like a little food in my belly.

COPELAND

Today, Mr. Washington is a new day. We are gonna drag you Southerners into a world of equality. I can see this isn't gonna be easy for you…but it's time for you to live up to the words that you and your great grand uncle so eloquently used to free yourself from your mother country, "With liberty and justice for all."

WASHINGTON

My God, the world is coming to an end.

John Brown enters with the rope, that he used to camouflage the wagon. Copeland exits.

WASHINGTON

Osawatomie Brown, I'm hungry…what have you got for a starving white man?

BROWN

Air. How often did you feed your slaves?

WASHINGTON

I was good to my slaves. I treated them fair.

BROWN

Then tell me Lewis…why have so many of your slaves joined me?

WASHINGTON

You have swayed them with lies and deception.

BROWN

God's hand is guiding me.

WASHINGTON

Like it guided you in Bleeding Kansas?

BROWN

My children were being threatened. I prayed. God answered my prayers with the Old Testament.

WASHINGTON

God did not ask you to do what you did.

BROWN

And the Lord said to Saul, "Go out and slay the Philistines."

WASHINGTON

So the Lord's voice told you to go out to Kansas?

BROWN

And slay the border ruffians. Philistines…border ruffians.

WASHINGTON

This is Virginia. You are not in Kansas anymore.

BROWN

Open your ears Lewis. If you listen you can hear freedom rising over them Blue Ridge Mountains.

WASHINGTON

I'm hungry Brown. Where is your Christian charity?

BROWN

I believe it is shackled to my black brothers. When these slaves rise up and smote the evils of slavery…then you will see my Christian charity…and God's mercy.

And God said, "The meek shall inherit the earth."

WASHINGTON

Brown, you are using the words of the Bible to further your own demented ends.

BROWN

Now ain't that the pot calling the kettle black. If you can chew on that idea for a while maybe it will take away your hunger pains.

WASHINGTON

You're a son a bitch, Brown.

BROWN

No, I'm just a white man who understands how a white man's mind works.

Copeland returns with a bucket of water. Washington dips his head in the bucket of water. Brown stops Copeland.

BROWN

That's enough of that.

Copeland stops and looks at Brown, takes the bucket of water, and goes back the way he came in. The sound of more gunshots getting closer.

BROWN

Let's move everyone to the Engine house. I think I'll have your slaves guarding you. See if that clears your mind.

The men grab the hostages and run for cover.

Lights fade to Black.

Scene 8

Lights up on Anderson sitting at a writing desk. He is writing in his journal.

ANDERSON

There was plenty of confusion that night. Why did Brown move to the Engine House? I didn't understand. He was vulnerable there. Why isn't Captain Brown seizing the rest of the weapons from the arsenal?

Lights change to the hillside overlooking the ferry as Anderson leaves his desk to join Shields Green. There is the sound of distant guns.

ANDERSON

If we take our hostages, run now across the bridge to the school house, pick up the other weapons, get Owen and the others from the Kennedy farm, we can still raid more plantations before sun-up. Take those slaves and hostages into the Blue Ridge Mountains…they'll never find us. Let's get out of here.

GREEN

Who gonna tell him… slaves ain't comin'?

ANDERSON

It is foolhardy to go back in there. Look at all those militia.

GREEN

You think there's no chance Osborne?

ANDERSON

Not one.

GREEN

And the ol' captain can't get a way?

ANDERSON

No…

GREEN

Well, I believe I'll go down with de ol' man.

Green stares at Anderson then walks off in the direction of Brown and the others.

ANDERSON

That's crazy…

GREEN

I swore an oath.

ANDERSON

Damn… Damn you Emperor.

There is the sound of more gunshots.. Hazlett enters using the Prussian sword as a cane. He crouches next to Anderson.

ANDERSON

I don't understand… what he is doin'?

HAZLETT

You're not going down there are you?

ANDERSON

I don't know.

HAZLETT

That is suicide Anderson. This endeavor is a failure. Run away and fight another day.

ANDERSON

Maybe we can rescue him.

HAZLETT

Or maybe not. There is enough militia down there to fill up Pennsylvania. The United States Marines are probably on the way. We got two guns, me and you. I don't like that arithmetic. Run away… fight another day.

Hazlett runs off in the opposite direction of the firing. Anderson pauses, then takes his lucky dollar out of his pocket. He flips the coin and looks at how it has landed, then decides to join Hazlett. He picks up his coin and runs.

Black Out.

Scene 9

Lights up on the two huge white doors of the Engine House at Harper's Ferry. There is the sound of gunshots. Green is at the door looking out. Brown is reading a Bible.

GREEN
Captain Brown…white flag.

BROWN
Hold your fire. Let him in.

Jeb Stuart, a U. S. Marine, enters with a white flag of truce. He has a red plumed feather in his hat and wears it cocked to one side. Green keeps his pistol trained on Stuart.

STUART
Smith, I've come to parley for the United States Marines.

BROWN
I could wipe you out like a mosquito.

STUART
So I see…but a lot of good that will do ya. I bring a note from my superior, Colonel Robert E. Lee. He wants you to surrender.

Brown's back is facing Stuart as he reads a passage from the Bible. Stuart cannot see his face. Stuart tries to hand the note to Brown. Green stops him takes the note and starts to hand it to Brown.

BROWN

Tear it up.

Green crumbles the note then puts it in his mouth and chews on it.

BROWN

I've got hostages and I want safe passage across the Potomac for me and my men; then, I will release my hostages.

Green spits out the wad of paper at Stuart's feet. Brown closes his Bible, turns and faces Stuart. His face is clearly visible.

STUART

Well, I'll be damned. Old Osawatomie Brown.

BROWN

You know me Lieutenant?

STUART

Jeb Stuart, Mr. Brown. I was in Kansas, cleaning up the sour stench of your mess.

BROWN

You got one more job to do Lieutenant.

STUART

Ain't no escape this time, Mr. Brown. This ain't Kansas, we're Virginians.

BROWN

You tell Lee, either I go or these hostages die.

GREEN

Wan' me ta do it?

WASHINGTON

Jeb, you get me out of this alive.

STUART

Easy, Mr. Washington. Maybe you should rethink your position Mr. Brown. You may have made Kansas bleed, but right now you are not in an advantageous position to be giving orders on what you want. Believe me when I tell you…my Commander is not a man to be taken lightly.

BROWN

So you want the blood of these hostages on your hands?

WASHINGTON

Jeb!

STUART

It ain't up to me to decide. I'm a soldier. I take orders.

WASHINGTON

No!

STUART

My orders right now is to tell you to surrender.

BROWN

I got eleven hostages.

STUART

You had thirty…but nineteen got away, because you are not a soldier. You're a misguided zealot. Maybe I should explain your position, Mr. Brown. The Virginia Militia is using the body of one of your men, Will Thompson, for target practice. I see you got a wounded man over there.

BROWN

That's my son. My other son Watson, he was shot down too…shot under a white flag of truce. Animals, slave-holding animals. If you treat a white man like that, God knows what atrocities you've heaped on black men. You are disgraceful.

STUART

That was not the U. S. Military, Sir, who did that…that was the Virginia Militia.

BROWN

A white man is a white man.

STUART

Oh, and they took care of that darky Leary and your friend John Kagi. Both shot dead trying to cross the Shenandoah River …but we captured Copeland. He's alive.

WASHINGTON

Good! I want to see that smart-ass coon hanged.

STUART

I said, easy, Mr. Washington.

BROWN

Careful, I might decide that you don't need to see the light of day. Just might let the lieutenant have ten hostages. Let Mr. Green here shoot you in the head. Shoot you in the head.

GREEN

Can I do it now?

BROWN

Not yet.

STUART

You cannot escape. Harm a hostage and it will go worse for you. I hope you have a sense of your situation, I want to know…will you surrender? That just requires a simple answer, Mr. Brown, yes or no.

Stuart walks to the door.

GREEN

Wha' ya think Cap't Brown?

BROWN

By my God in heaven, I will not surrender.

STUART

Osawatomie Brown, you just made my job real easy.

Stuart walks to the door then takes off his hat and waves it. That is the signal Brown will not surrender. Stuart rushes out.

WASHINGTON
Jeb, don't you leave me here with this mad man. Jeb!

Start of Special effect: The following happens with black outs and tableaus. Lights up on Brown and his men shooting. Black Out. Lights up on more shooting and soldiers rush the engine room. Brown, and Green fire their weapons. Black Out. Lights up on the Soldiers and Brown's men fighting. Black Out. Red Lights up on the figure of a soldier stabbing Brown with his sword. Black Out. Lights up on a soldier with his sword standing over Brown, who is now on the floor, John Wilkes Booth points his rifle at Brown. Black Out. Lights up to normal. John Wilkes Booth is taking aim with his rifle.

WASHINGTON
Shoot him, he's Osawatomie Brown.

John Wilkes Booth levels his gun at Brown.

BOOTH
Get out of the way soldier and let me send this Yankee to hell.

Just as he is about to fire, Captain John Avis, using his rifle, knocks the rifle out of the hands of Booth, deflecting the shot intended to kill Brown.

                    WASHINGTON

Avis, what are you doing? He was gonna kill Osawatomie Brown.

                    AVIS

Wilkes-Booth, no more killing today. He's gonna live to stand trial.

                    WASHINGTON

Then I'll see that son of a bitch hang.

                    AVIS

Suit yourself.

Stuart unties Washington.

                    STUART

You were with him for hours--how was he?

                    WASHINGTON

I hate to admit this but…he was the coolest and firmest man I ever saw in defying danger and death.

                    STUART

How do you feel?

                    WASHINGTON

Feel? Why I feel as hungry as a hound and as dry as a powder-horn; for only think of it, I've not had nothing to eat for forty-odd hours and nothing better to drink than water out of a horse bucket.

STUART

A shot of whiskey will put the roses back in our cheeks. Captain Avis, I want you to escort the prisoner to jail.

AVIS

Yes Sir.

STUART

I am putting you in charge of him. Make sure he lives.

AVIS

Yes Sir.

Avis leads Brown out.

STUART

Wilkes Booth...

BOOTH

Yes Sir.

STUART

Get your no-acting ass over here.

BOOTH

Yes Sir.

STUART

Listen to me very carefully, John. I want you to run and get Judge Richard Parker. You think you can do that?

BOOTH

Yes Sir.

STUART

On the double then. Run.

WASHINGTON

What's gonna happen now?

STUART

They're all goin' to meet American justice…Southern style.

The song, Dixie plays.

Black Out.

End of ACT I

Thomas Anthony Jones

Cast in North Carolina

Cast Photo in Los Angeles

**The South - Back Row, Left to Right: William Reinbold, Drew McAuliffe, Michael Proctor, Paul Messinger
Front Row, Left to Right: Bruce Cervi, Daniel Kucan**

Kareem Grimes and Chrystee Pharris

Stephen Spiegel and Paul Messinger

Gordon Goodman and J.D. Hall

Boise Holmes and Starletta DuPois

Left to Right: Adam Clark, Paul Messinger, Stephen Spiegel, William Reinbold, Michael Proctor, Gordon Goodman

Left to Right: Bruce Cervi, Stephen Spiegel, Daniel Kucan, Adam Clark, Michael Proctor, William Reinbold Front: Gordon Goodman

Drew McAuliffe and Paul Messinger

**Left to Right: Jason Galloway, Bruce Cervi,
Adam Clark, Thomas Anthony Jones**

The North - Back Row, Left to Right: Thomas Anthony Jones, J.D. Hall, Gordon Goodman, Adam Clark, Boise Holmes
Front Row, Left to Right: Jason Galloway, Kareem Grimes, Stephen Spiegel

ACT II

SCENE 1

In the darkness, Lights fade up slowly on Judge Parker's Chambers. The Judge is napping. There is a bottle of whiskey on his desk and an empty glass. John Wilkes Booth runs into the room.

BOOTH

Wake up Judge! Judge, wake up! Judge Parker, Smith is really Brown!

JUDGE

Brown? Wilkes Booth, talk sense.

BOOTH

Harper's Ferry! Issac Smith was an alias. We got that nigger lovin' John Brown in jail.

JUDGE

John Brown, thank you Jesus! Hand me my shawl.

The Judge picks up his riding crop from his desk and crosses to the door. Booth hands the Judge a tan-colored shawl.

BOOTH

They want you down there now.

JUDGE

What's the hurry?

BOOTH

We want to try him and hang him before his northern lawyers get here.

JUDGE

Don't you worry, Wilkes Booth. They can bring a battalion of Yankee lawyers…that son of a bitch ain't walking out of my courtroom alive. Hell, I'll put a bullet in his brain my damn self before he reaches the Goddamn door.

Black Out.

Scene 2

Lights up on Anderson sitting at his writing desk.

ANDERSON

The interrogation of Brown and his men was not going to be easy. I think it was the first time some of these Southern white men had ever met an educated Negro. And talking to Brown was no easy task. He could be pig headed…just like a Virginian.

Lights go down to half on Anderson's desk. Lights up in the Jailhouse. Judge Parker wears a tan shawl over his shoulders and has his riding crop. He, Booth and Jeb Stuart are questioning John Brown. Brown, who is injured, is lying on a cot. He has a bandage around his head and he bleeds from his side. He is in pain but tries to answer the questions as best he can.

JUDGE

Can you tell us who furnished money for your expedition?

BROWN

I furnished most of it myself: I cannot implicate others. It is by my own folly that I have been taken. I could easily have saved myself from it, had I exercised my own better judgment rather than yielded to my feelings.

JUDGE

You mean if you had escaped immediately?

BROWN

No. I had the means to make myself secure without any escape, but I allowed myself to be surrounded by a force by being too tardy. I should have gone away, but I had thirty-odd prisoners, whose wives and daughters were in tears for their safety, and I felt for them.

STUART

But you killed some people passing along the street quietly.

BROWN

Well, sir, if there is anything of that kind done, it was without my knowledge. I did not allow my men to fire when there was danger of killing those we regarded as innocent persons, if I could help it.

BOOTH

That is not so. You killed an unarmed man at the corner of the house over there at the water-tank and another besides.

BROWN

See here my friend, it is useless to dispute or contradict the report of your own neighbors who were my prisoners.

STUART

If you would tell us who sent you here, who provided the means…that would be information of some value.

BROWN

I will answer freely and faithfully about what concerns myself…I will answer anything with honor…but not about others.

Judge Parker walks out of Brown's cell across the stage to Copeland's cell, as lights go down to half in Brown's cell and lights come up to half in Copeland's cell. Judge Parker is in the cell with Copeland. Avis sits on a stool smoking a pipe.

JUDGE

Don't worry about the others, nigger. All I want to know is who sent you?

COPELAND

Do not disrespect me and I will answer all your questions.

JUDGE

Dis… respect?

COPELAND

Yes sir. I am not a nigger.

JUDGE

Well, you look like a nigger to me.

COPELAND

Then you sir are a very poor judge of character. What do you do for a living?

JUDGE

Well, I'll be damned...now you gonna ask me the questions. Nigger--just tell me who sent you?

COPELAND

I am not a nigger. My name is John A. Copeland. ...and I will not answer any questions till you address me as such.

The judge raises his hand with the riding crop to strike Copeland. He is stopped by Avis.

AVIS

Judge, my orders are to make sure nothing happens to the prisoners.

JUDGE

Avis, I'm sure Colonel Lee wasn't referring to this black som' bitch.

AVIS

Don't know if he was. Don't know if he wasn't. What I do know is... I can't let you lay a hand on my prisoner.

JUDGE

God damn it, Avis...I'm a white man.

AVIS

Yes Sir.

JUDGE

Damn it Nigger who sent you?

COPELAND

My name is Mister John A. Copeland.

JUDGE

Mister? Will you listen to this…well. Mr. John A. Copeland… who sent you?

ANDERSON

John had a way of irritating white folks…just like he irritated me.

Lights out on Anderson.

COPELAND

This is the end of the world as you know it. I will tell you this, no one sent me. I joined Osawatomie Brown. I am a soldier in his army.

JUDGE

Oh, we got him here too. He got hisself a backache and a headache. Four gashes in his head and a punctured kidney. But we are gonna make sure he lives to see a fair trial… then we gonna hang him. Just like we gonna hang you. Now, Copeland…you know anything about those Northern abolitionists?

Lights go down to half in the Copeland's cell. Lights go up in Brown's cell.

STUART

How do you justify your acts?

BROWN

I think my friend, you are guilty of a great wrong against God and humanity…I say it without wishing to be offensive…and it would be perfectly right for anyone to interfere with you so far as to free those you willfully and wickedly hold in bondage. I do not say this insultingly.

STUART

I understand that.

BROWN

I think I did right, and that others will do right who interfere with you at any time and at all times. I hold that the Golden Rule, "Do unto others as ye would that others should do unto you," applies to all who would help others to gain their liberty.

BOOTH

But don't you believe in the Bible?

BROWN

Certainly I do.

Lights stay at full in Brown's cell and lights come up full in Copeland's cell.

JUDGE
Killing is a sin.

COPELAND
I came here to free my brothers and sisters who are unjustly in bondage.

JUDGE
How many were in your band? How did you hope to succeed?

COPELAND
We are fighting Virginians…not the smartest people in the South.

JUDGE
You'll pay for that remark.

Lights go to half in Copeland's cell.

STUART
Have you had correspondence with parties in the North on the subject of this movement?

BROWN
I have had correspondence.

STUART
Do you consider this a religious movement?

BROWN

It is, in my opinion, the greatest service man can render to God.

STUART

What?

BOOTH

Do you consider yourself an instrument in the hands of Providence?

BROWN

I do.

STUART

But why take the slaves against their will?

BROWN

I never did.

STUART

Suppose you had every slave in the United States, what would you do with them?

BROWN

Set them free.

STUART

What?!

BOOTH

Your intention was to carry them off and free them?

BROWN

Of course.

BOOTH

To set them free would sacrifice the life of every man in this community.

BROWN

I do not think so.

BOOTH

I know it. I think you are fanatical.

BROWN

And I think you are fanatical. "Whom the gods would destroy they first make mad," and you are mad.

STUART

Was it your only object to free the Negroes?

BROWN

Absolutely our only object.

Lights go to black in Brown's cell. Lights up full on Copeland's cell.

JUDGE

Not all the slaves left the plantations; some at the ferry ran back home.

COPELAND

Some slaves saw just white faces and believed they were being kidnapped to be taken and sold further South. That was one of the reasons Captain Brown wanted myself and other Negroes in his Army. To allay those fears.

JUDGE

"Allay those fears." You are one smart-talking darky. Are you aware of his constitution?

COPELAND

I am.

JUDGE

Did Brown read it to you?

COPELAND

I read it myself.

JUDGE

Ya'll can read?

COPELAND

I graduated from college. I can read; I can write and I can recognize that the sentence, "Ya'll can read"…is improper grammar.

JUDGE

Well, Copeland…you may know proper grammar, but you've come to the end of the line on this one. We're gonna have a fair trial…but it don't look good for you and your friends. Looks like you put your faith in the wrong white man.

COPELAND

If we are mark'd to die, we are enough
To do our country loss; and if to live,
The fewer men, the greater share of honor.
God's will, I pray thee wish not one man more.
By Jove, I am not covetous of gold,
Nor care I who doth feed upon my cost;
It earns me not if men my garments wear;
Such outward things dwell not in my desires.
But if it be a sin to covet honor,
I am the most offending soul alive.
That he which hath no stomach to this fight,
Let him depart, his passport shall be made,
And crowns for convoy put into his purse.
We would not die in that man's company
That fears fellowship to die with us.
From this day to the ending of the world,
But we in it shall be remembered--
We few, we happy few, we band of brothers;
For he to-day that sheds his blood with me
Shall be my brother.

JUDGE

Oh, ain't you the fancy one.

COPELAND

Don't you read?

JUDGE

One smart uppity little black som' bitch. I know the Bible when I hear it.

COPELAND

That's Shakespeare.

JUDGE

Which play?

COPELAND

Look it up.

JUDGE

It's gonna be a pleasure to see you hang.

Black Out.

Scene 3

Lights up in a Pennsylvania Wilderness. Hazlett and Anderson find a place to rest. Hazlett is using the Washington sword as a cane, to help his walking.

HAZLETT
Osborne, I've gotta rest.

ANDERSON
We should keep movin'.

Hazlett sits on a rock.

HAZLETT
Give me a minute. It's my feet. Blisters.

ANDERSON
Okay.

Hazlett takes off his shoes and his feet are a bloody mess.

ANDERSON
Jesus, how are you able to walk at all.

HAZLETT
Don't worry, I'll make it.

Anderson takes out his handkerchief and wraps it around Hazlett's foot.

HAZLETT

Gently, gently. Where do you think we are?

ANDERSON

Somewhere in Pennsylvania. We must be close to Chambersburg.

HAZLETT

How far?

ANDERSON

Can't be no more than ten miles. You think you can do ten more miles?

Hazlett stands on his bloody bare feet and tries to walk. He is in great pain. He collapses on the ground.

HAZLETT

This ain't gonna be easy.

ANDERSON

Put your arm around my shoulder.

The two men try to walk together again. Hazlett screams in pain. He sits again.

HAZLETT

Osborne, you've got to go on without me.

ANDERSON

Albert, we can do this. Ten miles…it's only ten miles.

HAZLETT

I'll meet you there.

ANDERSON

Meet me?

HAZLETT

My feet need the rest. You can make better time without me.

ANDERSON

Albert, I'm not leaving you. We're in this together.

HAZLETT

A black man and a white man traveling together. If you try to help me you're a dead man.

ANDERSON

We've got to pull together.

HAZLETT

Osborne, you go on without me. I want you safe. I have seen the darkest corners of a white man's heart. If they caught us together, you would never make it to trial. They will torture you…as if it was fun and games. You saw what they did to Dangerfield. Oh no, Osborne, your death would not be pretty. But if you live…if a black man gets away, it proves their lack of superiority. Osborne, you must go on without me. You must live, escape, so that I know I have not lived in vain.

Anderson takes out his silver dollar and flips it. Heads up.

ANDERSON

All right Albert, I will go to Chambersburg and wait for you. If you are not there in three days I'm goin' on to Canada. Okay?

HAZLETT

I'll try and get there but if you don't see me, don't you waste any time moving on.

Hazlett extends his hand. Anderson grabs it. They shake hands. Then without a word Anderson runs off.

Black Out.

Scene 4

Lights up in the Courtroom. Judge Parker is on the bench. Lawson Botts is John Brown's defense attorney. He rises and addresses the judge.

BOTTS

Your Honor, Mr. Brown has instructed me to inform the court that at this time I will be his sole defense attorney. He would like Charles J. Faulkner and Mayor Thomas C. Green to step down as he has expressed no confidence in their abilities.

JUDGE

So noted and so done, Mr. Botts.

The Judge bangs his gavel.

BOTTS

Thank you Your Honor. Your Honor I would like to request more time to prepare a proper defense.

JUDGE

Request denied.

The Judge bangs his gavel.

BOTTS

Your Honor, because of the severity of Mr. Brown's injuries I would like to request a few days recess so that Mr. Brown might recover from his wounds.

JUDGE

Request denied.

The Judge bangs his gavel. Botts goes into his briefcase and pulls out some papers.

BOTTS

Your Honor, one of the charges against Mr. Brown is being a traitor to the Commonwealth of Virginia. Since Harper's Ferry is on federal land and not Virginia soil, I would like to make a motion that those charges be dismissed.

JUDGE

Mr. Brown stands accused of the murder of five citizens that were standing on Virginia soil. The charge of treason against the Commonwealth of Virginia stands, as does murder and his attempt to incite insurrection. Motion denied.

The Judge bangs his gavel.

BOTTS

Your Honor, since Mr. Brown is not a citizen of Virginia I would like to make a motion that the charge of treason against the State be dismissed.

JUDGE

Mr. Botts, is Mr. Brown a citizen of the United States?

BOTTS

Yes Sir.

JUDGE

While a resident of Maryland at the Kennedy farm living under the alias of Isaac Smith, did he not come into Virginia for supplies?

BOTTS

Technically, yes, Your Honor, he did.

JUDGE

Is Virginia a part of the United States?

BOTTS

Yes, Your Honor.

JUDGE

Counselor, I think you see where I am going with this. If Mr. Brown is a citizen of the United States and the great Commonwealth of Virginia is located in those United States… and if Mr. Brown utilized the services of Virginia, then it stands to reason that Mr. Brown is a traitor to the Great Commonwealth of Virginia. Motion denied.

The Judge bangs his gavel. Botts goes into his briefcase and pulls out some papers, then, addresses the Judge.

BOTTS

Your Honor, since the insurrection was aimed at the United States Government and not at the great Commonwealth of Virginia, a federal court would have to try him on those charges of treason.

JUDGE

Don't play with me Counselor. Mr. Brown fired on the Virginia Militia and the U. S. Marines led by the gallant Colonel Robert E. Lee, A Virginian. Motion denied.

The Judge bangs his gavel.

BOTTS

At least Your Honor must concede that the charges of insurrection should be dismissed as not one slave left any Virginia plantation to join this rebellion.

JUDGE

Counselor, if I poison the well and don't drink the water, it does not mean the water is going to taste any better tomorrow. No sir, he tried to rile up our Negras and he is going to pay for that misdeed. Motion denied.

The Judge bangs his gavel.

BOTTS

Your Honor, two of Mr. Brown's men were shot and killed, under a white flag of truce, when negotiations were being considered.

JUDGE

Are your referring to those Yankee abolitionist sons, Watson and Aaron Stevens?

BOTTS

Yes Sir.

JUDGE

Mr. Botts, you do not want to try my patience. We are going to put this nigger-loving insurrectionist on trial. Now you can try and throw up any kind of legal mumbo jumbo you want, but Mr. John Brown ain't leaving the great Commonwealth of Virginia, until we have had our day. If the United States Government wants him, they must wait till we get through with him. We caught him and we mean to have the first chance at hanging him. The United States Government may take his dead body, if they so choose. Now do you have any more motions that I can deny?

BOTTS

No Sir.

JUDGE

Then you may proceed.

Black Out.

Scene 5

Lights up in Delilah Copeland's Dining Room. Delilah is sitting in a chair. She is looking at a framed picture of her son. She has been crying. She is sipping from a glass of wine. There is a knock at the door. She wipes her face with a lace handkerchief. She answers the door. Osborne Anderson is standing in the doorway.

ANDERSON
'Cuse me ma'am, I was told this might be the Copeland house?

DELILAH
It is.

ANDERSON
I'm sorry Ma'am. I'm a friend of Lewis Leary and John Copeland. I was hoping …maybe…

DELILAH
Young man, just don't stand there. Come in. Pryin' eyes are everywhere.

Anderson enters the house.

DELILAH
I am Delilah Copeland. John's Mother.

ANDERSON
Ma'am I'm in a heap of trouble. I just didn't know where else to turn.

DELILAH
I take it, you were part of the raid?

ANDERSON
Yes, Ma'am. Your son and I broke bread together, shared a laugh or two and…we even debated.

DELILAH
That sounds like Junior. You know he really is his father's son. Everything must be just so.

ANDERSON
He corrected my English on more than one occasion.

DELILAH
(*laughs*) Oh, yes, his father taught him well. "We must strive for the betterment of the race." Thank you for that. I haven't laughed in a while. You met my little brother Lewis, too?

ANDERSON
Yes Ma'am.

Anderson eyes a bottle of wine on a table.

DELILAH
Where are my manners? Glass of wine, Mister…

ANDERSON
Osborne, Ma'am. Osborne Perry Anderson.

Delilah pours a glass of wine. He gulps it down. Delilah pours another glass.

DELILAH

My son is in a Charles Town jail…but I cannot find any word on the fate of my brother. They have listed the fate of the white men, but no word on the Negroes that participated.

He gulps down the second glass of wine.

ANDERSON

I saw him too, Mrs. Copeland.

He pours himself a third glass of wine.

DELILAH

Help yourself. Did he get away? Is he on his way home?

ANDERSON

I'm sorry Mrs. Copeland, but your brother was not so lucky. Think he's …well you know.

DELILAH

Are you sure? He might have gotten away.

ANDERSON

I saw the Virginia Militia storm the rifle works, where he and Mr. Kagi and John were hold up. All three made a run for the Shenandoah. Mr. Kagi was shot first. He fell in the river… drifted down stream. Lewis was shot in the back. I saw John jump in the river and rescue his uncle. Set him on a rock in the middle of the river.

DELILAH

Did you see him die?

ANDERSON

No Ma'am. I had troubles of mine own.

DELILAH

Then it is possible he got away.

ANDERSON

Not likely Ma'am. Seem like every white man with a gun was pointed at that rock.

DELILAH

The reports are so vague...and they won't name the Negroes, lost or captured. I half expected to see Lewis walk through that door with you. He left his wife and baby to help John Brown.

ANDERSON

Yes Ma'am... Mrs. Copeland, can you help me? I need a railroad ticket.

DELILAH

What's your destination Mr. Anderson?

ANDERSON

Canada. Chatham, if possible.

DELILAH

I know a conductor. We'll get you there. You think Lewis died on that rock?

ANDERSON

Yes Ma'am.

DELILAH

God's will. My Brother's dead…and my son is in jail. Think he'll get a fair trial?

ANDERSON

Honestly?

DELILAH

Mr. Anderson, the only thing we have left is the truth.

ANDERSON

Mrs. Copeland, they're white men. John is a black man that stood up to them. One thing a Southern white man can't stomach is a black man that ain't gonna show no fear. Your son and your brother are two of the bravest men I ever met.

DELILAH

A black man who isn't going to show any fear.

ANDERSON

Ma'am?

DELILAH

Your grammar, Mr. Anderson, your grammar.

ANDERSON

Yes Ma'am.

She pours each of them a glass of wine.

DELILAH

Well, now. Two of the bravest.

They toast.

DELILAH

There it is, I guess there is some consolation in that. Now isn't there? You like rabbit stew? I can feed you.

ANDERSON

Yes Ma'am.

DELILAH

It's a little spicy. I hope you don't mind. I've got a heavy hand when it comes to the pepper.

ANDERSON

Ma'am, I'm hungry enough to eat a porcupine raw and pick my teeth with his quills.

DELILAH

Come with me young man.

Delilah leads Osborne out.

Lights fade to Black.

Scene 6

John Avis enters Brown's cell. He is carrying a box and a folded piece of paper.

AVIS

Mr. Brown...I have news for you. Your wife is here.

BROWN

Not sure I want to see her.

AVIS

Couldn't let her in tonight, anyway. Gives you time to think about it. Told her to...come back in the morning.

BROWN

Thank you Mr. Avis.

AVIS

She asked me to give you these.

Avis hands Brown the box and the folded piece of paper. Brown unfolds the paper and it is a picture drawn by a child. The picture is a white man leading armed black slaves.

BROWN

Ahhh, Annie, such a delightful child. Mr. Avis do you have children?

AVIS

Eileen, Sarah and Frances.

BROWN

Daughters...hold them close. Never let the business of being a righteous man get in the way of family.

AVIS

Wish I had a son. I am surrounded by women.

BROWN

It is harder to raise a boy into a man. A woman's life is laid out in front of her...clear as day. But the business of growing into manhood...can be quite a complicated road. Lost two of my sons on this endeavor. Two sons taken before there time. Was that God's plan?

AVIS

Don't know Mr. Brown. We are all God's children and only he has the answer to that question.

Brown opens the box. It contains his slippers.

BROWN

It is the little things that remind us of home. I wanted no more in life than to hear God's voice. I have prayed day after day... year after year hoping to hear it. Moses, Abraham, they beheld the heavenly voice. God spoke to them. They had the luxury of not having to have faith in the unseen God...yet I...I admit, when I pray, I hear nothing. No voice. No signs. I was left with the scriptures. They alone spoke to me, strong and so clear. They say this is a holy land, blighted, by the enslavement of men. And I realize how could God speak to me in a land such as that? Exodus: "And he that stealeth a man, and selleth him, he shall surely be put to death." I knew that until the vipers that spread this poison of slavery were smashed under foot, God would remain silent to me.

And without one doubt in my heart I left all I had in the world, turned away from my family and became an avenging angel… to rain down thunder and lightning upon God's enemies, laying them to waste! And I knew his power would be with me… Yes, I killed. Convinced other men to kill and die. Risked the damnation of my very soul so as to purge this blight from the earth. And now…now heaven seems to have forgotten me. I offered freedom from slavery, as surely as Moses did when he set slaves free in Egypt. My family, Lord God my family…I sacrificed two of my sons…Abraham was spared the sacrifice of just one. God sent an angel that spoke to him. I receive only silence. Mr. Avis. sometimes I wonder…I don't know…Is that faith? My cause is just. But have I failed my God… have I failed these poor black souls?

AVIS
I have no answers for you sir. Those slippers comfortable?

BROWN
Got these when Oliver was born. Now he's gone and all I have left are these…

AVIS

Someday I'm gonna buy me a watch and inscribe the names of my daughters on the inside.

BROWN

I don't regret fighting for the cause…but should I have waited and not used my family?

AVIS

Mr. Brown, you don't know the Southern white man. I feel for the colored myself…but you done caused them more trouble than they ever knowed. Folks around here ain't gonna soon forget what you done …or forgive it.

BROWN

I know it looks like failure. Now my sheep business …that was a misfire. But this situation here is bigger than one defeat in Harper's Ferry. I may not carry the torch to the end of the tunnel, but I feel like I lit the damn thing and it won't burn out any time soon.

AVIS

Mr. Brown, there are black folks suffering from your schemes. Black houses are being burned to the ground. Innocent blacks are being beaten and strung up. No relief is gonna come to the colored town folks here…till you are stone dead.

BROWN

Mr. Avis…if you think this is going to end with my death, you don't know the Northern white man.

Brown picks up the slippers. They remind him of his son. He puts on the slippers.

BROWN

When Oliver was a boy his mama taught him how to count. When he learned a few numbers he would rush in to show me his progress. He wanted to please me. I would hold up my fingers and he would count. One, two, three. One day I held up my hand. He said, "Five Daddy." To confuse him I held up my two index fingers…and waited for him to figure out the number two.

Brown holds up his two hand, then extends the index finger on each hand.

BROWN

He got a quizzical look on his face and said…"Eleven Daddy!" Well…I laughed so hard I grabbed him and we wrestled on the floor. That boy could touch my softer side.

AVIS

My daughter, Frances…she's the baby. I call her Primrose.

BROWN

Primrose?

AVIS

Yes. I was reading to her a book about fairies…and Primrose was a very prim and proper fairy. Well, my little Frances is a very prim and proper little girl. Soooo, that became her name.

We gave her the job of setting the table for supper. Primrose would want to make sure that the forks and spoons where in the right place and there should be napkins on the table. One day I came home from here, late…and I went into the girls' bedroom to kiss them good night. When I got to Primrose…I look down at her hands and they were blacker than Martin Delaney's face. I wanted to wake her and ask her what she had been doing to get so dirty…it was unlike her. My wife, Annie was standing in the door way, she waved me to come with her. Annie told me to look under our bed. And there it was…Primrose had gotten a pair of my beat-up old shoes and polished them till the shone like a brand new silver dollar.

BROWN

Before my Annie grows up, finds a man, gets engaged and marries, I will be dead. I will either end up at the right hand of God or the deepest pit of hell.

AVIS

Mr. Brown, your daughter will live. All we can do is plant the seeds of integrity and hope that it takes root and blossom.

BROWN

Mr. Avis the only thing I know for sure is…when they hang me …my feet are going to be very comfortable.

Black Out.

Scene 7

Lights up in Judge Parker's Chambers. The judge wears his tan shawl and is finishing writing on a piece of paper. John Wilkes-Booth is there waiting to receive the paper. The Judge checks what he has written and folds the paper and gives it to Booth. The Judge pours himself a drink.

JUDGE

Give these instructions to Sheriff John Campbell. It's the preparations for the hanging.

BOOTH

I want to see the hanging Judge.

JUDGE

You can't Wilkes Booth.

BOOTH

Why?

JUDGE

Look, it's real simple…we put him in a wagon…he sits on his coffin and we ride him to the gallows. We hang him. End of story.

BOOTH

Judge, this is a great moment in history. I don't want to miss it. I want a front row seat. I want to be a part of it.

JUDGE

Wilkes Booth, stick to acting. It's just another hanging. Some smart-ass Yankee comes here with evil on his mind and he's taught a lesson.

Jeb Stuart knocks.

BOOTH

Judge, I'm going to volunteer to be a part of the Jefferson Guard. That's up real close. I want to see his… "too too solid flesh melt, thaw and resolve itself into a dew."

JUDGE

Wilkes Booth…Edwin does it better…now get those instructions to Sheriff Campbell, I've got to meet with Lieutenant Stuart here.

BOOTH

I'm gone.

Booth exits, as Jeb Stuart enters.

STUART

Judge I have the final report on Brown and the insurrectionists.

JUDGE

Please Lieutenant give your report.

STUART

We killed ten of Brown's men.

JUDGE

Good.

STUART

We have Brown and four of his men in jail here in Charles Town. Edwin Coppoc, John Cook, Albert Hazlett, Aaron Stevens...and two niggers.

JUDGE

How many of his men do you think escaped?

STUART

Not sure.

JUDGE

Twenty? Thirty? How many Lieutenant? Forty? Fifty?

STUART

More like five or six.

JUDGE

We can account for fifteen men. You telling me...maybe twenty men came into Harper's Ferry and did this kind of damage?

STUART

Well Judge...some of the guns shooting at us were from your local slaves. Washington and Allstadt, their slaves were armed at the engine room. Then there were the slaves at the armory. Mayor Fontaine Beckham and Thomas Boerly are dead. We think George Turner was shot by his own slaves as he was coming to get them. About fifty slaves have run off. We think some of those are aiding the Brown men we haven't caught.

JUDGE

Is that in your report?

STUART

Yes Sir.

JUDGE

Take it out.

STUART

Sir?

JUDGE

I'm sorry Lieutenant, continue.

STUART

The slave, Ben, while recuperating from his wounds died at the hands of his guards.

JUDGE

Who were his guards?

STUART

Virginia Militia.

JUDGE

How did he die?

STUART

He was smothered with his pillow.

JUDGE

Can't say that.

STUART

I'm sorry Judge?

JUDGE

Can't say that Lieutenant. You know your report is causing me a whole lot of consternation.

STUART

Judge, the problem we have with Ben is that it's obvious he did not die from his wounds. The wounds were minor…he was going to recover and stand trial.

JUDGE

Was he scared?

STUART

Sir?

JUDGE

Was the nigger scared?

STUART

Yes sir, he knew his guards…and he fought well during the battle.

JUDGE

You know I hear tell, that when a slave is really scared, he can die of fright. Something peculiar to their race. You think that nigger died of *fright*?

STUART

Yes Sir, I do Sir.

JUDGE

Next item.

STUART

We think the insurrectionists are on their way to Chambersburg, Pennsylvania.

JUDGE

Why there?

STUART

We caught Albert Hazlett on a train headed there, he was carrying Washington's Prussian Sword…and John Cook was caught in Chambersburg, by a bounty hunter named Daniel Logan. We got men searching the roads…

JUDGE

Lieutenant Stuart…do you know who writes history?

STUART

Sir?

JUDGE

The winning side. Whoever wins gets to write how he won. A good writer can take a defeat and turn it into a victory. Inspire men to fight for a just cause. Now I do not want some Yankee abolitionists coming down here with poison in their pens… exclaiming how right they are and how wrong we are. This was a skirmish, a minor setback, and I don't want Northerners thinking they can just waltz into the South and have their way with her. She's a lady…not a whore. Do you understand me lieutenant?

STUART

Yes Sir.

JUDGE

I want that report to reflect that our niggers did not take part in any Northern-provoked insurrection. Now has anyone else seen that report?

STUART

Just my commanding officer, Colonel Lee.

JUDGE

I need to talk to your commanding officer. He's a Virginian, ain't he?

STUART

Yes Sir, lives at Arlington.

JUDGE

If he loves the South like I think he does, this report must not see the light of day. We must revise the truth. Give America a little Southern truth. We must make our case plausible. The entire country is looking at these events. Certain facts must be contained.

STUART

I understand Sir.

JUDGE

Good…very good. I want you to rethink your report…write me a new one. Keep in mind your duty as a Southern gentleman.

STUART

But Judge…I am a soldier for the federal government. I have a duty to my commanding officer…and he has already seen the report.

JUDGE

Lieutenant…this is a crucial time in our lives. One must think of one's family. One's honor. Is your allegiance to the federal government or to your home? I know you Jeb Stuart…you are a good Southerner, with a good heart. Don't let these Yankees convince you of something else. Rewrite this report.

STUART

Yes Sir.

JUDGE

I want you to ask your commanding officer to come see me. I think it's time we shared a drink and talked politics…

STUART

Yes Sir.

Stuart leaves. As he is halfway through his exits, he stops and tears up the report.

Black Out.

SCENE 8

Lights up on the Jailhouse. John Brown is in his jail cell. The guard, John Avis, opens the door. He is helping a drunk man to a cell. The drunk is Silas Soule.

SOULE

They stopped me in the middle of my story.

AVIS

You can finish your story tomorrow.

SOULE

Okay, okay, okay. But…but…I didn't finish my drink either.

AVIS

You've had enough to drink.

SOULE

You obviously have not seen my wife.

AVIS

No Sir, but you can't go home tonight anyway. You can sleep it off here.

SOULE

This place is a pigsty…filthy. If I had one more drink I wouldn't care where I slept it off.

AVIS

Not tonight friend.

Soule sees Brown. He staggers over to his cell.

SOULE

Wait a minute, wait a minute, wait just one minute…ain't that Osawatomie Brown. Yes Sir, it is ain't it? That's ol' Osawatomie Brown.

AVIS

That's not your cell. Your cell is over here.

SOULE

No Sir, put me in his cell. When I have grandchildren, I want them to know I met that son of a bitch.

AVIS

No, Sir. I'm putting you in this cell.

BROWN

That is all right Mr. Avis, you can let him share my cell.

AVIS

I don't think so Mr. Brown.

SOULE

Yes Sir, oh, yes Sir, he is right, I should share his cell. Mister you got a drink in there?

BROWN

This drunk soul could use a littler ministering. Let me save his soul before he sleeps it off.

SOULE

Good idea and I can save your soul from your Yankee demons.

BROWN

Sir, have you ever read the New Testament?

SOULE

No, but I heard it once. I was on a train from Baltimore to Williamsburg. Damn Preacher…practiced his Sunday Sermon on me. I think that's what drove me to drink.

BROWN

Mr. Avis, it will be all right. Let him share my cell.

AVIS

Mr. Brown in your hour of darkness…you have a big heart.

BROWN

There is an eternity behind and an eternity before, and the little speck in the center, however long, is but comparatively a minute. The difference between your tenure and mine is trifling and I want to tell you to therefore be prepared; I am prepared.

Avis puts Soule in Brown's cell.

####### AVIS

Mind your manners, young fella. You're with a very famous man.

####### SOULE

I ain't ignorant; I'm just drunk. I know who he is…

####### BROWN

Captain Avis, would you mail these letters for me?

Avis takes the letters and leaves.

####### SOULE

If you had your choice Mr. Brown of… Kentucky whiskey or Virginia rye, which would you try?

####### BROWN

Now Silas Soule, you know I don't drink.

####### SOULE

(*totally sober*) Captain Brown, it was worth a try. It may be the last drink you have before they pronounce sentence.

####### BROWN

I think you missed your calling…you would have made a much better actor than that Booth fellow.

####### SOULE

I've come to take you to freedom.

BROWN

Freedom?

SOULE

Yes Sir. You say the word…I've got thirty men ready to fight and free you.

BROWN

Armed men?

SOULE

Yes Captain. I give the signal and we're ready to move tomorrow night.

BROWN

Silas Soule you make my heart soar…but I must refuse your tempting offer. This is my destiny.

SOULE

It don't have to be. I broke Doctor Doy out of that Missouri hell-hole that they had him in. That jail was bigger, better and had a lot smarter guards than you've got here.

BROWN

I remember.

SOULE

There ain't no ifs about this Captain, they mean to hang you. Run away, live to fight another day.

BROWN

Silas…don't you see? I am more valuable to the cause hanging from the end of a rope than living and breathing and fighting those slavers. I must die in this place as a martyr. The abolitionists need a symbol. Someone to inspire the non-believers, the fence sitters. Bring them to their feet. Make them stand up for human justice. If I escape and live, I would just be a fugitive. I have a chance to set in motion the wheels of emancipation…

SOULE

What am I gonna tell my Daddy? I promised him I'd break you out.

BROWN

You tell Amasa, "The Kingdom of God and the affairs of the world are one. My divine mission on earth is to annihilate slavery."

SOULE

Thoreau said, "You are a lightning flash that revealed the corruption of the entire American system."

BROWN

Thoreau said that?

SOULE

Yes Sir.

BROWN

Silas, you know at one time I believed that we might prevail with minimal bloodshed…but I see now that this country must purge its poison…like one might lance a boil. It will be painful, but it is necessary. So, my good friend, it is only fitting that you should be the one to try and save my soul…but I am already blessed. I go to meet my maker and sit at his right hand.

SOULE

Captain…It has been my honor to stand in the presence of your courage and greatness.

BROWN

Now listen, son, when the war comes, for know this Silas Soule, the dark clouds of God's wrath are hovering over these American skies. Prepare yourself.

SOULE

I shall, Captain.

BROWN

When you leave me, recruit those that need you. Leave my soul to heaven.

SOULE

Yes, Captain.

Brown takes out his pocket watch and checks the time.

BROWN

Pray with me.

Silas Soule kneels. Brown kneels next to him.

BROWN

I shall bless the Lord at all times:
His praise shall continually be in my mouth.

The guard, Avis, comes back in with one of the letters. He sees Brown praying with Soule.

BROWN

My soul shall make her boast in the Lord:

The humble shall hear thereof and be glad.

O magnify the Lord with me,

and let us exalt his name together… Amen.

SOULE

Amen.

AVIS

Well, I'll be Goddamned.

Black Out.

SCENE 9

Lights up in a Virginia Court in Charles Town on November 2, 1859. John Brown awaits his verdict. The Judge bangs the gavel to get order.

JUDGE

John Brown, please rise. You have had a fair and just trial. Ten of your men died at the Ferry. We hold six of your men, mostly boys ready to be tried for insurrection…Mr. Brown you tried to rile up our nigras. You were unsuccessful. You have been found guilty of treason to the great commonwealth of Virginia. We found evidence of your treason with the documents you called your Provisional Constitution, maps of the southern states you planned to attack and weapons for two hundred men along with a thousand pikes. Fortunately for us the good citizens of Virginia and her militia were able to pin you down till the U. S. Marines arrived. A testament to the fortitude and resilience of the Southern white man. Is there anything you wish to say to the court before your sentence is pronounced?

BROWN

I have, may it please the court, a few words to say.

In the first place, I deny everything but what I have all along admitted…the design on my part to free slaves. I intended certainly to have made a clean thing of that matter, as I did last winter, when I went into Missouri and took slaves without the snapping of a gun on either side, moved them through the country, and finally left them in Canada. I designed to do the same thing again, on a larger scale.

Had I so interfered in behalf of the rich, the powerful, the intelligent, the so-called great, or in behalf of any of their friends… either father, mother, sister, wife, or children, or any of that class… and suffered and sacrificed what I have in this interference, it would have been all right; and every man in this court would have deemed it an act worthy of reward rather than punishment.

The court acknowledges, as I suppose, the validity of the law of God. I see a book kissed here which I suppose to be the Bible, or at least the New Testament. I believe that to have interfered as I have done…as I have always freely admitted I have done… in behalf of this despised poor, was not wrong, but right. Now if it is deemed necessary that I should forfeit my life for the furtherance of the ends of justice, and mingle my blood with the blood of my children and with the blood of millions in this slave country whose rights are disregarded by wicked, cruel, and unjust enactments…I submit; so let it be done!

Brown sits down.

JUDGE

It is the sentence of this court that you be hanged by the neck till you are dead.

The Judge bangs his gavel. The court room cheers.

Black Out.

Scene 10

Lights up in Frederick Douglass' Dining Room. He has a meal in front of him. It is untouched. He is reviewing pages of a speech. There is a knock at the door. Douglass goes to the door, opens it, and sees a man wearing a wide-brim hat that shades his eyes. He is a conductor. A figure stands behind him in the shadows. It is night.

CONDUCTOR

I've got a passenger.

DOUGLASS

Take him to another station.

CONDUCTOR

This one asked to be delivered here.

DOUGLASS

This is not a good time.

CONDUCTOR

Last station master he talked to was Delilah Copeland; she thought it was a good idea to bring him here. He says he's a friend of Isaac Smith. Says you know Isaac Smith.

DOUGLASS

One of Smith's men?

Anderson steps out of the shadows and into the light.

ANDERSON

Yes sir, Mr. Douglass.

Douglass recognizes his face.

DOUGLASS

Mr. Anderson!! Come in. Come in, Anderson.

The Conductor leaves as Anderson enters.

DOUGLASS

My God man, how did you get out of that impossible situation?

ANDERSON

Luck.

DOUGLASS

Only a few have gotten away. Merriam is in Canada. I didn't know you were a part of that adventure.

ANDERSON

Yes Sir. The tide is turning, sir. Is that cornbread?

DOUGLASS

Yes. Yes! I can feel the tide turning. Northerners want to take action.

ANDERSON

Your man Green and Copeland are in jail. That looks like collard greens.

DOUGLASS

Mustard greens. If Brown were to escape, he could take Shields and Copeland with him...but he is refusing the offer. These white men are not going to take a chance on colored soldiers without their Captain.

ANDERSON

That action seals their fate.

DOUGLASS

How many blacks joined the cause?

ANDERSON

Well, there was five of us. Me, Shields, Dangerfield Newby, Lewis Leary and Copeland. Then when we took some of the slave masters, like Washington and Allstadt, their slaves picked up guns and fought too.

DOUGLASS

I'll be damned.

ANDERSON

Sir, I've got to get to Canada.

DOUGLASS

Don't worry Mr. Anderson, this train won't stop till we're across the border.

ANDERSON

You're goin' too?

DOUGLASS

Some people seem to think I paid for Brown's weapons and arms.

ANDERSON

Did ya?

DOUGLASS

(laughs) Sure did. Ten dollars worth. No, my friend George Stearns and the secret six furnished every rifle, pike and gun… but it looks good if they can lay this endeavor at my black feet.

ANDERSON

You know Mr. Douglass, the last good meal I had was four days ago. Mrs. Copeland fed me rabbit.

DOUGLASS

From Canada, I'll catch a ship to England…start a lecture tour…and you my friend will be the main topic of my speech. You must tell me everything.

ANDERSON

Don't have to tell ya!

DOUGLASS

Of course you do.

ANDERSON

No Sir. Wrote it. Wrote it right here in my journal.

He takes a journal out of his leather pouch and hands it to Douglass.

DOUGLASS

Fantastic! Right now these white folks want to pontificate on abolition, John Brown and what's good for the American slave. Let them. They can only speak from the outside in…but you my friend can speak from the inside out.

ANDERSON

Yes sir. Saw it all…and wrote it down.

Douglass leafs through the journal.

DOUGLASS

Amazing! Only you, Mr. Anderson, can save from oblivion the true facts of what really happened at Harper's Ferry. What is coming out now is propaganda…from North and South. You are an eyewitness and a participant.

ANDERSON

Yes, that's true, I did write about things ain't nobody talkin' about. Is that red beans and rice?

Douglass is reading passages from the journal.

DOUGLASS

Yes. Oh, please forgive me, Mr. Anderson, where are my manners? Here you sit here. This is for you, I haven't touched it.

ANDERSON
Thank you, sir.

He begins to eat.

ANDERSON
Mr. Douglass, guess I ain't gonna be a Congressman after all.

Douglass sits at the table with Anderson; Douglass is distracted by the contents of the journal.

DOUGLASS
I promise you my friend, someday the United States Congress will be filled with black faces. This is damn good.

ANDERSON
This is damn good! You think we can make it to Canada?

Douglass looks up from the journal.

DOUGLASS
Let those hounds that chase us,

View us as the rabbit or the running deer,

But we shall play the fox and silently disappear.

As Douglas reads, Anderson chows down.

Lights Fade to Black Out.

Scene 11

Lights up at the jailhouse. A shadow of a noose shades John Brown as he is taken from his cell by his jailer John Avis.

BROWN

Sir, I have no words to thank you for your kindness. You give me hope for the Southern heart.

AVIS

I don't understand Sir.

BROWN

You are living proof that a Southern man can have compassion, be reasonable and not be swayed by emotion.

AVIS

I just try to be fair.

BROWN

And that is all that God ever asks of any man. I want you to have this.

He hands Avis his silver pocket watch. Avis accepts the watch.

AVIS

I don't know what to say John Brown.

BROWN

Say that as a man you will judge each man on his individual value and say that when you want to know what time it is… John Brown helped you.

AVIS

I will. Mr. Brown I must tell you that…you know a friend of mine…Marty Delany.

BROWN

The black abolitionist?

AVIS

Yes Sir. We grew up together. Played together as kids.

BROWN

Well, that says it all now, doesn't it.

AVIS

Mr. Brown, it's time.

John Brown walks to Copeland's cell. Copeland is praying.

BROWN

(*to Avis*) Do you mind?

Avis nods his assent. Brown stops, Copeland rises to greet him.

BROWN

Mr. Copeland, I have no further use for money. Here is twenty-five cents.

Copeland looks at the coin. He flips it and catches it. Looks at it...

COPELAND

Tails.

Brown shakes his hand.

BROWN

Stand up and do not betray your friends.

COPELAND

I have every intention to meet my destiny with grace.

BROWN

I will see you in heaven.

John Brown walks pass John A. Copeland. Lights to black with a spot on Copeland, as Brown leaves.

COPELAND

My time is at hand. December 16, I would leave this earth not as a criminal, not as a slave, not even as a traitor. These white men would hang me for believing as they had believed, "That all men are created equal." I would leave this earth knowing I shed light in to the dark corners of their souls. If they hated me, they hated themselves. They could no longer hide behind the words of our Lord. For like Jesus was crucified, so was John Brown. And like the thief who stood beside him, the kingdom of heaven waited as our reward. I tried to steal freedom for my brothers and sisters. We shall meet in heaven where we shall not be parted by the demands of this cruel and unjust monster--slavery. If I am dying for freedom, I could not die for a better cause...I had rather die by the rope than lay in my bed an old man knowing that I had not tried. I was ready to die.

Black Out.

The Lights go to a spot on Green.

GREEN

Dey asked me to stand as dey pass sentence on me. Den dey asked me if I had any las' words. Me...a slave. Chattel. I was asked tah speak. Dat is when I saw it. I saw it in dey eyes. Hiding behin' dey shoutin'. I almost laughed, but it could not be denied. Dere it was... Fear. The white man feared me. He was actually 'fraid of me. Dey mouths was full of poison but dey eyes was full of fear. Dere was panic swirlin' around dat fear and in dat moment...I could see destiny stretchin' 'fore me. It was not goin' to end with my death. A war was comin'...a civil war...

A war would save my brothers, it would free my sisters. My grandmothers would see the light dey sang about. My grandfathers would raise dey heads to justice. And de chillun, de chillun would know somethin' I ne'er knew growin' up. Dey laughter would ring like the liberty bell. Freedom was at hand, and dese doomed souls did not know it. I would keep my secret…silent…and let dem wake up one morning to the sound of God's mercy echoing across dis land. I would not utter a word. I would not let dem know what I saw. What dey chillun would have to die for…I stood 'fore white men as a man. An Emperor! Dey emancipated me and didn't know it…and forever locked me in dey history as dey equal. I heard de words say my fate. I was ready to die.

Black Out.

SCENE 12

Lights up in George Stern's Office. Delilah Copeland enters. She has grey hair, is neatly dressed, and carries a small purse. Stearns takes off her overcoat and puts it on the back of a chair. He directs her to sit.

STEARNS
Good afternoon, Mrs. Copeland, please have a seat.

DELILAH
Thank you Mr. Stearns.

STEARNS
Can I get you a refreshment, Mrs. Copeland?

As she talks she takes off her gloves and sets her purse on the desk.

DELILAH
No thank you Sir. Were you successful Mr. Stearns?

STEARNS
It was much more complicated than I anticipated. Would you like some tea?

DELILAH
No, Sir, just my son's body.

STEARNS

As you know Mrs. Copeland, my wife and I asked Reverend Samuel May, to contact J. Miller McKin in Philadelphia to claim the bodies of both Shields Green and your son.

DELILAH

Yes I know.

STEARNS

I thought we might bury the men in Pennsylvania.

DELILAH

I did not know that.

STEARNS

Oh, yes. The idea was to get their bodies out of Virginia as quickly as possible. Then later we would reinter their remains in Mount Auburn.

DELILAH

Why Mount Auburn?

STEARNS

Delilah, I want to erect a monument to the fallen men of Harper's Ferry. I want the nation to know we honor our colored brethren as well as our white soldiers.

DELILAH

Governor Wise gave permission for us to claim the bodies as long as we sent a white person to pick them up.

STEARNS

That is where the mix-up seems to occur.

DELILAH

Mix-up? He is the Governor of Virginia…are not the authorities of Charles Town bound by the laws of Virginia?

STEARNS

Those gentlemen acted hastily and in a barbarous manner.

DELILAH

I would like my son's body, Sir.

STEARNS

Emotions are running high in Virginia right now.

DELILAH

Has lawlessness taken over?

STEARNS

These Virginians have taken reprisals on innocent colored people. They are burning buildings, torturing poor souls and in some cases lynching black people on a whim. Things are in a chaotic state. If they even think someone is an abolitionist or has those leanings, he or she is at the mercy of mob hysteria. Secession is being talked about in Virginia, once again.

DELILAH

Where… is…my…son's…body?

STEARNS

Mrs. Copeland, in Winchester, Virginia, there is a medical college…your son and Shields Green's bodies were…your son and Shield's Green bodies were…dissected.

DELILAH

Dear Jesus.

STEARNS

We don't know…if there is anything left to claim.

DELILAH

Oh, my baby…oh my baby…

She rises from her chair, for a moment she is disoriented.

STEARNS

I have someone investigating the medical school…

DELILAH

Oh dear God, my baby, I have to go Mr. Stearns…I have to go… have to go…

She turns not knowing which way to go.

STEARNS

No, please…stay…Mrs. Copeland…Delilah please.

DELILAH

Noooooooooooooooo! Have to go, have to go, no sir...be by myself...have to be by myself.

She rushes out of the room, leaving her coat, gloves and purse. Stearns goes to the door and watches her leave.

Black Out.

Lights up on Hazlett's Cell, with a Spot on Hazlett. He is barefoot with bandaged feet.

HAZLETT

Bad feet...I can't believe it. My bad feet...Who would think such a thing would be the death of me. At least I have the satisfaction of knowing Osborne got away. He will avenge my injustice...and bring to bear on the white consciousness of this land, the true and honorable thing for Americans to do. The time for talk of what is right and what is unjust must end. We white people must stand for the betterment of our nation, or suffer the consequences of our inaction. I was ready to die.

Black Out.

SCENE 14

Lights up on Harriet Newby. She is sitting at a table. Her thoughts mingle with the ninety-fourth Psalm.

HARRIET

I'se a Christian. I believe Jesus Christ died for my sins. I just don't know what my sin was. I know it ain't for not pickin' tobacco. I'se one of the best tobacco pickers on this here plantation. We got a shed on this here land…It dark, it dirty and it smells of blood. Slave blood. Slaves here call it *de hurtin' room*. Massa, got all kinds of tools in dat shed, but dey ain't tools for the garden. Dey tools for hurtin' a Nigger. Whips? three kinds, pliers, shackles…a post to tie ya up and a bed to tie ya down.

"O Lord God, to whom vengeance belongeth,
O God to whom vengeance belongeth, show thyself."

Massa came and got me from my bed, He threw vinegar in my face to wake me and blind me…I could not see, but I could hear and feel. He had his sons with him…dey dragged me to de hurtin' room. He did not tie me up…he tied me down.

"Lift up thyself, thou judge of earth:
render a reward to the proud.
Lord, how long shall the wicked,
How long shall the wicked triumph?"

I begged for mercy, I ain't knowed why I was in dis room. Massa did not care, dey slid a wooden keg under my belly. I felt him climb on my back, he tore my clothes away from my body, den he shoved his finger inside of me. It was an angry hand. Den I could feel him force his manhood inside me. I thought if I could just look in his eyes, I might understand why. Why?

I screamed for help, I screamed for Missus to help me, I screamed for God to help me and den...den I knew why his anger was so fierce, he say "Why don't you scream for your husband Harriet?" Somehow he knew about my letter to Dangerfield.

"How long shall they utter and speak hard things and all the workers of iniquity boast themselves?"

When he was done I could feel his body go limp on my back. I could smell his sweat, his semen, I tasted the salt of my tears. I cried and I thought that was the end of it; but William his oldest son, thrust his hand inside me. I bit my lip.

"They break in pieces thy people, O Lord and afflict thine heritage."

I heard him crumble the letter in my ears. William took longer, he tore at my breasts, he hit the back of my head with his fists, his daddy cheered him on and I could hear him tell James, he would be next.

"He that...he that...he...he..."

I could not remember it. I tried to take my mind away from *de hurtin' room*…wid words from the Bible…but I could not remember what came next.

I could feel de leather wrapped around my wrists and ankles. I could feel the splinters on my stomach. After de last boy did his deed, Massa used de cat o' nine tails…he gave me new scars on my back.

My seven children …dey all gone now. Sold. Even de youngest, Jedidiah. Sold. Massa make sure Overseer Shaw keep an eye on me.

Matilda told me Massa sleeps wid his gun, now. I don't know what my sin is, dat God saw fit to bring me in dis world a Nigger. I don't know what crime I committed dat I must now carry dis baby and not know which white man is de daddy… but I do know de time will come when Massa will forget his gun…or Overseer Shaw may sleep a bit too late, or I will be in the kitchen and I will season his dinner. I'm just waitin', I'm just gonna wait…and on dat day, I will know why God has cursed my life, because de day I kill my Massa is de day I know my sin.

Black Out.

SCENE 15

Lights up on Anderson. He is writing in his journal.

ANDERSON

In the morning they executed the two Negroes...after they hung my brothers Green and Copeland, they took apart the scaffolding, used new lumber and built a new gallows. Later that same day they execute the two white men Cook and Coppoc. These Virginians would not hang black men on the same gallows as white men. Edward F. Underhill of the *New York Tribune* reported that as John Brown left the jail he stopped at a young slave mother holding her baby. Brown bent over and kissed the child, then was escorted by the soldiers to the gallows. I later found out that incident never happened. They would not let a slave within ten miles of Captain Brown. No, Sir. He didn't kiss any black baby goodbye--too many white guards. Everybody was afraid he might escape...but you can't tell black folks that it didn't happen.

The Fort Sumter, 1861, Union Flag of the United States rises up behind him.

ANDERSON

They know for a fact that it did. Just like they know this war we fighting just ain't about keepin' the Union together. It's also about ending that cruel and unjust monster slavery. Though Captain Brown may not have kissed a black baby on his way to meet his maker...what he did at Harper's Ferry was kiss the future for every black child in America.

Anderson gets up and loads his pistol.

ANDERSON

It's like an omen…and our actions set the wheels in motion …the train has left the station, and that freedom train is picking up passengers as it rides the rails. It cannot be stopped, so you better run and jump on, cause every black person living and breathing believes that when this war ends, so will slavery. We believe it in our bones.

Lights down to half on Anderson, lights up on Brown standing before a noose.

Lights up to half on John Wilkes-Booth; he is standing in front of a Confederate Flag. He is dressed as a confederate soldier and holding a rifle. Osborne is standing in front of the Fort Sumter Union Flag. The figures of Osborne and Wilkes Booth face each other. Both men are armed. Paul Robeson's version of John Brown's Body plays.

BROWN

I, John Brown, am now quite certain that the crimes of this guilty land will never be purged away but with blood. I had as I now think, vainly flattered myself that without very much bloodshed, it might be done.

Lights go to half on John Brown as John Brown's Body, continues to play.

The sound of a cannon explodes.

Black Out.

END OF PLAY

Bibliography

Bordewich, Fergus. *Bound for Canaan; The Underground Railroad.*

Carton, Evan. *Patriotic Treason*, New York: Free Press, 2006.

Cohen, Stan. *John Brown, The Thundering Voice of Jehovah.* Montana: Pictorial Histories Publish, 1999.

DeCaro Jr., Louis. *John Brown The Cost of Freedom,* New York: International Publishers, 2007.

Finkelman, Paul, Editor. *His Soul Goes Marching On*, Virginia: University Press of Virginia, 1995.

Goldberg, Mel. *John Brown's Raid*, Garden City: Nelson Doubleday, Inc. 1961.

Hinton, Richard J. *John Brown and his Men,* New York: Funk & Wagnells Co. 1894.

Horwitz, Tony. *Midnight Rising,* New York: Henry Holt & Co. 2011.

Jefferson County Black History Preservation, *The Capture, Trial & Execution of John A.Copeland and Shields Green*, 2003.

Libby, Jean, Editor. *John Brown Mysteries*, Montana: Pictorial Histories Publishing, Inc, 1999.

Malin, James C. *John Brown and the Legend of Fifty-Six*, New York: Haskell House Publishers, 1942.

Mendoza, Patrick M. *Song of Sorrow, Massacre at Sand Creek*, Willow Wind Publishing Co.1993.

O'Connor, Bob. *The Perfect Steel Trap*, Pennsylvania: Infinity Publishing Co. 2006.

Peterson, Merrill D. *The Legend Revisited John Brown*, Virginia: University Press of Virginia, 2002.

Renehan, J. Edward. *The Secret Six*, Columbia: University of South Carolina Press, 1997.

Reynolds, David S. *John Brown Abolitionist*, New York: Alfred A. Knop, 2005.

Schlesinger Jr., Arthur M. *The Almanac of American History*, Brompton Books, 1993.

Stauffer, John and Joe Trodd. *The Tribunal,* Cambridge: The Belknap Press, 2012.

Taylor, Yuval. *I was Born a Slave Volume 1*, Lawrence Hill Books, 1999.

Lady PATRIOT

Dedicated to

Mel Stuart

and

Dick Anthony Williams

Thanks

To E. Jack Kaplan, who introduced me to the story

and

To Steve Keh, who believed in my storytelling

and

A special thanks to Don Guisinger,

Kay Ley,

and my wife,

Mary Lange

Lady Patriot opened Sept 7, 2012 at the Hudson Theatre in Hollywood California with the following cast:

VARINA DAVIS	Anne JohnstonBrown
ELIZABETH VAN LEW	Connie Ventress
JEFFERSON DAVIS	Gordon Goodman
MARY BOWSER	Chrystee Pharris
OLD ROBERT BROWN	Ted Lange
JUDAH P. BENJAMIN	Paul Messinger
MR. SLYDELL	Robert Pine

Director:	Ted Lange
Set Design:	Adam Hunter
Costume Design:	Mylette Nora
Lighting Design:	Steve Pope
Stage Manager:	Vanoy Burnough
Producers:	Steven Keh, Mary Lange

Lady Patriot opened July 29, 2013 at the HanesBrand Theatre in Winston/Salem, North Carolina, at the Black Theatre Festival with the following cast:

VARINA DAVIS	Anne JohnstonBrown
ELIZABETH VAN LEW	Connie Ventress
JEFFERSON DAVIS	Gordon Goodman
MARY BOWSER	Chrystee Pharris
OLD ROBERT BOWN	Lou Beatty, Jr.
JUDAH P. BENJAMIN	Paul Messinger
MR. SLYDELL	Robert Pine

Director:	Ted Lange
Set Design:	Adam Hunter
Costume Design:	Mylette Nora
Wardrobe Master:	Wendell Carmichael
Lighting Design:	Steve Pope
Producer:	Mary Lange

The Setting

Act I

It is the start of the Civil War and Confederate President Jefferson Davis and his wife, Varina, have moved from Mississippi to the new capital of the Confederacy, Richmond Virginia. They are settling into their own white house and getting accustomed to the idea of war and what must be done to secure their future.

Act II

The War is winding down and things look bleak for a Confederate win. Optimism and options are fading fast and Southerners must consider how to survive a Union victory.

Author's Notes

Lady Patriot is the third play in my historical trilogy about the early history of our country. When I first heard about this story from my friend, Jack Kaplan, I was astounded. My high school history books never mentioned a slave who was a spy for the Union Army. Obviously, this is the kind of story that my history teacher alluded to all those years ago. And so began my research and *Lady Patriot* was born. I conducted internet searches, talked to experts, and read voluminous accounts of this era and gradually pieced together the fabric of this tale. It is the story of three lady patriots who lived during the Civil War: Mary Bowser, Elizabeth Van Lew, and Varina Davis.

Mary Bowser is a college-educated black woman who put her life in jeopardy to fight for the Union and freedom for all black slaves. A patriot! Elizabeth Van Lew is a Southern aristocrat who also believed in freedom for the slaves and did not want to secede from the Union. A patriot! Lastly, Varina Davis is the wife of Jefferson Davis. She was entrenched in the slave mentality of the South, immune to its inhumanity, and believed that her husband was building a new country for the betterment of Southern society. A patriot! Based on their true stories, *Lady Patriot* reveals an intimate look into their prejudices and patriotism as it peels away traditional stereotypes prevalent in our history books.

Other little-known facts emerged for me during the research of this play. Judah P. Benjamin, a Jew, was the right-hand man to President Jefferson Davis. Many Jewish Americans are astonished to learn a man of their heritage was a key influence during the Civil War. Old Roberts' character epitomizes how the house slaves learned to survive and navigate in the master's domain. Jefferson Davis was known to drink and smoke cigars with his house slave at the end of the day.

I have tried to be fair to all views and put the characters in the context of their time. There are words in this play that may be offensive to the reader, actor, or audience. They're a product of that time. A great disservice would ensue if I whitewashed the verbiage of the 1860's and avoided words because they are distasteful to our modern political correctness. The authenticity of the language is vital to the historical context of slavery. It should offend us and educate us in the atrocities that it encompassed so that we can learn from the evils of this degrading aspect of American history and demand a more equal society for all Americans.

For the process of staging the play, I have divided the stage into thirds. Stage right is the Van Lew Pantry/Herb closet. It is later transformed into the Davis White House Kitchen. Center stage is the Davis White House State Room/Dining Room. Stage left is the office of Jefferson Davis. The opening garden scene is played downstage of the Davis Office and State Room. Music is crucial to creating the historical ambiance of the times. The songs for the pre-show audience arrival represent the Southern attitudes of the time. *I'm a Good Ol' Rebel* should be played after the pre-show announcements and right before the show begins.

From the germination of this story, I was compelled to examine this historical time and the little known characters that fought for their beliefs. I was compelled to write this play using drama and comedy to take these events and mold them into a cohesive story line that entertains and educates. *Lady Patriot* is based on a true story--these events happened--check my bibliography. I was compelled to tell this story that lies in the shadows and reveal what was hidden by the victors--only then can we come together as a melting pot and sup in splendor at the same table--free of lies and certain of the truth.

Lady Patriot Music

Pre-Show Music Starts at Half Hour

1. *Dixie* (3:02)
2. *Confederate Song, Wearing of the Grey* (3:02)
3. *Confederate Song, Battle of Pea Ridge* (3:57)
4. *Swanee –Al Jolson Arrangement* (1:54)
5. *Confederate Song, The Battle Cry of Freedom* (2:45)
6. *Southern Soldier Boy* (2:32)
7. *Rose of Alabamy* (2:35)
8. *Mammy – Al Jolson Arrangement* (2:03)
9. Richmond is a Hard Road to Travel (4:35)
10. *Dixie* (3:02)
11. *Battle of Bull Run* (2:40)

Pre-Show Announcements

As theatre goes dark:

12. *I'm a Good Old Rebel* (1:51)

Lady Patriot

Synopsis

The inner sanctum of Confederate President Jefferson Davis has been breached. Information is leaking to the enemy--who is the spy? No one is privy to this information except Jefferson's advisors and they are beyond repute. Based on a true story, *Lady Patriot* reveals an intimate look into the prejudices and patriotism of three ladies who lived during the Civil War: Varina Davis, Elizabeth Van Lew, and Mary Bowser. *Lady Patriot* combines Lange's signature comedy and drama as it peels away traditional stereotypes prevalent in the South during the Confederacy.

Cast of Characters

Varina Davis is the First Lady of the Confederacy. She is the epitome of Southern gentility. She is a woman of strong beliefs, but knows how to support her husband.

Elizabeth Van Lew is a Southern aristocrat. She is a Union sympathizer, but she must mask her true feelings by pretending to be eccentric. Crafty and smart, she uses any situation to her advantage.

Jefferson Davis is the President of the Confederacy. A soldier at heart, he is given the task of running the war and starting a new country. He is a leader, who actually wants to micromanage all details. The war has easily distracted him from domestic duty.

Mary Bowser is a college-educated black woman. She must pretend to be an ignorant slave while she performs her duties in the Jefferson household.

Old Robert Brown is a house slave and an old hand at dealing with white masters. He knows how to work a situation so that he profits. He is past his prime and has given up the fight. He is an old dog that cannot learn a new trick.

Judah P. Benjamin is a Jewish lawyer with a brilliant mind and knows how to deal with gentiles. He comes armed with charm, intelligence, and a way of making others feel comfortable.

Mr. Slydell is a Yankee journalist. He works for Horace Greely and the *New York Tribune*. He is an abolitionist and is soured by the civil war he has to cover.

ACT I

SCENE 1

Richmond, VA. Jefferson Davis's White House Garden, July 1861. Varina Davis, Jefferson's wife, is a Southern white lady who is five months pregnant. She is sitting on a small stool, fanning herself. Elizabeth Van Lew, a southern white lady, is digging up herbs and plants and putting them into a basket.

VARINA

What is that?

ELIZABETH

That's not it.

VARINA

But what is it?

ELIZABETH

I dunno…let me see. You know what that is?

VARINA

No.

ELIZABETH

Me neither...but whatever it is...it's rotten. Come spring, you need to replant this garden, or otherwise you should send your gardener to a place where he will never hear the dogs bark.

VARINA

So much work to be done.

ELIZABETH

Don't worry, Varina, I'll help. You need help, I'll help. That's what friends are for or why would you call yourself a friend. Right? Right.

VARINA

Lizzy, I'm just plain overwhelmed.

ELIZABETH

First priority is the baby. Everything else will work itself out.

VARINA

I hope so. Jeff has got so much on his mind. I just don't want to be a burden.

Everything in the house is my responsibility...it just seems... well...you know...I just think I got pregnant at the wrong time.

ELIZABETH

Children come into this world when they need to come. We don't really have a say. If you don't know that, you're dumb as a bucket of rocks.

VARINA

Child's coming, right smack dab in the middle of a war.

ELIZABETH

Where are your slaves?

VARINA

Most of my niggers are still in Mississippi. It'll be weeks before we get everyone here, moved in and organized. I don't know whether to scratch my watch or wind my butt.

ELIZABETH

Varina, I could lend you one of my girls…if you want. Just for a few days.

VARINA

Oh, Lizzy, that would be wonderful! I'm not moving as quickly as I like. This is my fifth child. It should get easier…but it doesn't.

ELIZABETH

My girl, Mary, can help you around the house. She's good in the kitchen--knows her herbs, cooks like an angel, and she is a hard worker.

VARINA

She doesn't break dishes?

ELIZABETH

Not even when she's mad.

Both women laugh.

VARINA

I'll take her.

ELIZABETH

Just for a few days. I need her back.

VARINA

Two weeks. Lizzy, just let me have her for two weeks, and I promise to give her back. What's that?

ELIZABETH

Used to be ginger. But it's all dried up.

VARINA

Lizzy, this is one pathetic garden.

ELIZABETH

Let's replant it now. You and I could do it.

VARINA

That's crazy Lizzy. We are out of season.

ELIZABETH

Plants don't care. Let's dig this garden up right now, me and you.

VARINA

Lizzy, I'm not digging up this garden. Don't be foolish. That's why we have niggers.

ELIZABETH

Okay, okay, okay, okay, okay. I've got some herbs at home. Okay, okay, okay, okay, I'll share.

Jefferson Davis enters.

JEFFERSON

A beautiful day for picking flowers, ladies.

VARINA

…and herbs.

Jefferson gives her a peck on the lips. He nods at Elizabeth.

JEFFERSON

Miss Elizabeth, how are you today?

ELIZABETH

I'm just a cracker looking for a barrel. How are you doing today, President Davis?

JEFFERSON

Don't you start with me, young lady…no formalities.

ELIZABETH

President Davis, if we are going to build a new nation we must have structure. I'm sure that Lincoln's friends call him

President Lincoln. You deserve no less respect than that Yankee.

JEFFERSON

Aren't you the civic minded one? Okay Miss Elizabeth, I accept your appellation and I will try and live up to all that it engenders.

ELIZABETH

Thank you, President Davis. Well I must be going. I will make sure I get those herbs to you Varina. That is the first thing I must do, then mix the rest of the day with my don'ts till I am somewhere in the middle.

VARINA

Don't forget your nigger Mary and I will send Old Robert round to pick her up.

ELIZABETH

I'll look for his arrival. Good day…good day….good day!

Elizabeth exits.

JEFFERSON

Are you going to give me another son, Varina?

VARINA

If the Lord sees fit, he will bless us with a healthy son or a healthy daughter.

JEFFERSON

You are right. The health of the baby is the most important thing. I just think little Joseph would want a brother to play with.

VARINA

Then let us keep that thought in our prayers.

Jefferson kisses Varina.

JEFFERSON

Your hair looks beautiful in this Virginia sun.

VARINA

You are certainly in a jovial mood.

JEFFERSON

I am married to the most beautiful woman in the South and I just got word that we won the battle at Bull Run. Whipped us some Yankee behind. Our boys were victorious. Who shall we name him after?

VARINA

My daddy of course.

JEFFERSON

That's fair…and if it's a girl?

VARINA

Why Mister Davis, she's gonna carry my name.

He laughs.

JEFFERSON

You delight me Varina. These are dark times and you can actually make me smile.

VARINA

Just doing my wifely duties…which is why I am here in our garden.

JEFFERSON

And what was Crazy Bet doing in our garden?

VARINA

Jefferson Davis, don't you dare call her that!

JEFFERSON

Varina, honey, everyone in Richmond knows that woman is crazy. There is nuttier than a squirrel turd.

VARINA

Well, she did want to replant this garden, but crazy or not she has been very helpful to me. She's gonna loan me one of her niggers till the rest of ours arrive. I think that is a sweet thing for her to do.

JEFFERSON

You get no argument from me. As long as her nigger ain't crazy like her.

Varina suddenly grabs his arm, and starts to drop. Jefferson catches her.

VARINA

Jeff!! Oh, Jeff, help me. Help me.

JEFFERSON

Varina, are you all right?

Varina holds on to his arm trying to catch her breath. She grabs her stomach.

VARINA

Lord have mercy. This isn't going to be an easy birth.

JEFFERSON

Come, let's go inside so you can lay down.

She tries to force herself to smile. Her husband helps her up.

Lights fade to Black.

Scene 2

Van Lew Plantation Pantry. Elizabeth is putting some bottles into a wooden box. She is being helped by a young black slave girl, Mary Bowser. The box is being held by an older black slave, Old Robert. Mary puts an item in the box.

ELIZABETH

(*in a harsh voice*) No, no, no, no Mary! Don't be stupid. I said red raspberry leaf tea.

Elizabeth takes the item out of the wooden box and gets the correct item and places it in the box.

ELIZABETH

See that? That is this one.

MARY

Yes, 'em.

ELIZABETH

Now get me three of those ginger roots over there.

Mary picks out three ginger roots.

ELIZABETH

No, Mary! The biggest ones we've got. Those won't last a week. Find me nice big fat roots.

Mary goes through the roots again and pick out some bigger roots.

MARY

Yes, 'em.

ELIZABETH

Varina's not having an easy pregnancy. These roots will come in handy. Settle her stomach and take the swelling out of her ankles.

MARY

Yes, 'em.

ELIZABETH

You remember how I told you to prepare them?

MARY

Yes, 'em.

ELIZABETH

Sambo…you let me know if Varina complains about Mary. I'll send over another slave.

OLD ROBERT

Yes, Miss Elisabeth.

MARY

His name is Old Robert, Miss Elizabeth.

ELIZABETH

That's what I said.

MARY

No Ma'am…you said Sambo.

ELIZABETH

Old Robert, Young Robert, Black Robert, Brown Robert, what difference does it make? He knows what I mean…don't you Sambo? You know what I mean. He ain't no fool Mary…he just a slave. Sambo, don't you know what I mean?

OLD ROBERT

Yes, Ma'am.

MARY

You said it again.

ELIZABETH

Said what?

MARY

Nothing.

ELIZABETH

Something on your mind Mary B.

MARY

No Ma'am.

ELIZABETH

Damn right. Mess with me. I'll make you feel lower than a toad in a dry well.

Watch her you old coon, she can get feisty. I hear any complaints about your work Mary Bowser...even a whisper... you're coming home. You understand, me?

MARY

I'll be good. I promise.

ELIZABETH

Don't be making no promises you can't keep. Remember you represent me and the Van Lew family. I don't want you bringing shame on the name of Van Lew...even though that ain't your name. You are a Bowser straight up and down. That ain't no lie. Are you a Van Lew?

MARY

No Ma'am.

ELIZABETH

Damn right you ain't. I told Varina you were a hard worker. Varina lost two children. Here, take the olive oil and you be sure to rub it on her stomach every evening.

MARY

Miss Elisabeth, you know I'm the best midwife this side of Richmond.

ELIZABETH

We got to get to the birthin' day, Mary B...for you to be her midwife. Now I don't want Varina lifting anything heavy or staying up too late. It's your job to make sure she is comfortable. You are only going to be there for a little while. You may not even see birthin' day.

MARY

Yes 'em.

ELIZABETH

Tarbaby, you heard what I told Mary?

OLD ROBERT

Yes, Miss Elisabeth.

ELIZABETH

I'm gonna stop by next week to make sure nobody pisst in the punch.

MARY

I promise you Miss Elizabeth, I'll keep Miss Varina comfortable. She ain't gonna want for nothin'. I knows my duty, and I knows, how to do my duty. I done already birth fourteen souls into this world. Mostly white... ready to bring in more.

ELIZABETH

Not worried about you birthin' the baby, Mary Bowser. Witch hazel's in this bottle. It's just that Varina is a fragile woman. Her husband's gonna be busy with the war. I know him...he ain't gonna have time to look after his wife. You're gonna have to do that. Hey, you old darky...you hear what I'm saying?

OLD ROBERT

Yes 'em.

ELIZABETH

Good. Take this box to the wagon.

Old Robert exits with the box.

OLD ROBERT

Yes, Ma'am.

ELIZABETH

(*calls after him*) Don't drop the box or crack the bottles.
(*in a softer tone to Mary, almost a whisper*) Good luck Mary.

She hugs Mary. Mary exits.

Black Out.

Scene 3

Davis White House State Room. Jefferson and Varina are sitting at a table. Jefferson is writing a letter and drinking whiskey. Varina plays solitaire as she sips a glass of absinthe.

JEFFERSON

How's the absinthe?

VARINA

You know I love the green fairy. How's that Kentucky brew?

JEFFERSON

Good. Come here and let me touch your belly.

VARINA

Why?

JEFFERSON

Want to see if this child is gonna be special. Want to know whose bloodline is running strong through his veins… Howell…or Davis?

Varina crosses to Jefferson and he puts his hands on her stomach.

VARINA

I love your touch.

Act I Scene 3 419

JEFFERSON

Oh yes…he got the Davis magic. This boy's gonna be real special.

VARINA

Just like his daddy.

JEFFERSON

This child is gonna raise twenty kinds of hell and leave his footprint where they say it can't be done.

VARINA

Just like his daddy.

Varina glances at the letter on the desk that Jefferson was writing.

JEFFERSON

Varina, I think come September…I'm going to appoint Judah Benjamin as my Secretary of War.

VARINA

The Jew?

JEFFERSON

He's a good man.

VARINA

He's still a Jew.

JEFFERSON

I like the lucidity of his intellect, he's loyal and decisive. Judah has a great capacity for labor.

VARINA

Jeff, you know plenty of Christians who could handle that post. Can't you give someone less…well, you know less…

JEFFERSON

Varina, you handle the house. I'll handle the war.

Jefferson gets up and exits.

VARINA

I'm so mad I could spit.

Black Out.

Scene 4

Davis White House Kitchen. Mary is preparing to bake some bread. She kneads the dough and flours the chopping block as she is preparing the bread. Old Robert enters with a tray of silverware. He starts cleaning the silverware.

MARY

I notice they run y'all ragged in them meetings. You need help?

OLD ROBERT

That's flour from my sack. No, little Mary, I'm fine.

MARY

Don't be afraid to ask. I'm a girl, but I'm young and I'm handy.

OLD ROBERT

I can see dat. I ain't blind; I'm just old.

MARY

Just thought I'd ask, that's all. I am of a mind that we should help one another, whenever we can. Who is the man with all the papers that keeps visiting Master Jeff?

OLD ROBERT

Dat is Mister Judah.

MARY

What he do?

OLD ROBERT

He the Confederate attorney general.

MARY

What's that?

OLD ROBERT

Someone to smoke cigars with. The other cabinet members call him, "The Shylock of the Confederacy."

MARY

What's the Shylock?

OLD ROBERT

Damned if I know, but I don't think it's good.

MARY

Why do you say that?

OLD ROBERT

Just the way they say it…The Shylock. How ya'll skills at brewing coffee?

MARY

Once a white man tells me how he likes it…he don't have to repeat it. And he can count on it being served that way every time.

OLD ROBERT

Little Mary, you full of yo'self.

MARY

Got good reason to be.

OLD ROBERT

Oh.

MARY

Yes suh…I'm the best.

OLD ROBERT

No, you think you're de best.

MARY

I can hold three plates on one arm, and pour honey wine from a gallon pitcher with the other. I can pluck a chicken clean after wringing his neck and never miss a feather, flour him, fry him, and make sure the inside is juicy and the outside is crispy. I can set a table for twelve, put the big forks and the little forks in the right place and make sure the food gets to the table hot.

OLD ROBERT

You can do all dat, can ya?

MARY

Oh yes, I can. I'm valuable. I ain't no ordinary nigger, Old Robert. I'm a special nigger. I know I don't look it…but I am. I know it and someday you gonna know it, too. You just tell me the day you want to educate yourself on the skills of Mary Bowser.

OLD ROBERT

We gone see. Tell you what…I want you to brew me two cups of coffee. One is cream, no sugar. I want dat cup the color of Sarah Mae. De second cup I want black with one-and–a-half spoons of sugar. Dat's for Massa Jeff. Now, he ain't gonna taste it…I is.

MARY

You is…? Well ain't you the one.

OLD ROBERT

If'n it tastes like two spoons of sugar, don't come asking me if I need help. If'n it tastes like one spoon of sugar, don't come bragging to me, 'bout how special you is. If'n it tastes like I asked for…maybe, and dis here is just a maybe…maybe I might let you help me. Cuz, I don't believe in no special niggers.

MARY

You don't.

OLD ROBERT

Waitin' to find one.

MARY

What you believe in?

OLD ROBERT

I believe in special white folks. I know you ain't white so… gwine wait and see if you de other. Dese white folks you dealing with here is somethin' different.

MARY

You think they gonna win this war?

OLD ROBERT

I know dey gwine to win this war.

MARY

Maybe not.

OLD ROBERT

Don't fool yourself little Mary. Yankee talking about dese folks changing their way of life? You think dis white man gwine give up somethin' he love? You think dey gwine take dat kind of talk laying down. No sir. Dey gwine fight cause dey believe dey right. Ain't nothin' worse than fighting with a man knows he's right and think he got Jesus on his side.

MARY

I wouldn't under estimate those Yankees.

OLD ROBERT

Looka here, dese white crackers are some cruel sons of bitches. Seen what dey do when dey mad and seen what dey do when dey just sorta angry. Seen dem pretend to be Christian and seen dem pretend to be genteel. Dey would rather quit the U.S. of A., den give up dey slaves.

MARY

I don't think they gonna win this war. Federal government is too powerful.

OLD ROBERT

Dey already winning de war…and Lord help de child dey find out ain't for dem. Little Mary, heed my words…I can see what you want to happen. Keep dem thoughts to yourself. Dis here war ain't gwine free one nigger. Ain't gwine bring dese white folks back into de fold. Make sure you protect yourself. So dat you can survive which ever way dis wind blows.

MARY

Thanks Old Robert.

OLD ROBERT

Now let me see you brew two cups of coffee.

Black Out.

Scene 5

Davis White House Office. Jefferson Davis and Judah P. Benjamin are looking at some maps.

JEFFERSON

How's Natalie?

JUDAH

She's good. Gonna be harder for me to get those bottles of wine, now that we are at war.

JEFFERSON

Damn if those French don't make a fine tasting wine. She been in Paris how long, now?

JUDAH

Fourteen years.

JEFFERSON

Fourteen years. How can you stand to be away from your wife for such long periods of time?

JUDAH

I see her every summer. She understands my work is here. We're soul mates so I don't think about it much.

JEFFERSON

I believe there is only one soul given to another soul. I lost the soul that was the love of my life. Back in '35. Married her in June, lost her to malaria in September.

JUDAH

Sarah Taylor?

JEFFERSON

Called her, Knox. Oh Judah, what a lady she was. That bastard…her father did everything he could to stop true love. Didn't want his daughter marrying a soldier. Loved that woman so much I stopped soldiering.

JUDAH

What did her daddy say then?

JEFFERSON

Said it didn't matter. I had soldiering in my heart. Truth is I had Knox in my heart.

JUDAH

Varina seems to be the perfect wife.

JEFFERSON

She's a beautiful woman, Judah…but you cannot substitute beauty for passion. Varina's a good woman with strong opinions…but she ain't Knox.

JUDAH

J.D. she loves you.

JEFFERSON

True, fortune has smiled down on me in that regard…but, what is a marriage without the sweet tides of thoughts taking charge of your actions? Sometimes in the oddest moments, Knox will appear in my mind. What would she think of this? How would we share that adventure together?

JUDAH

It is a dilemma…but Knox is gone. Natalie and I never shared work in the same way you and Knox did. I like to keep my private life out of that arena.

JEFFERSON

Not to be dwelt on. Which reminds me…ah, Judah, next time you see Varina, I need you to charm her.

JUDAH

Charm her. Me? I hardly see her…and when I do she is very aloof. I can count the time on my left hand that we have even had a conversation.

JEFFERSON

We are building a new country, Judah. Politics seeps into the domestic as well as the political side of our obstacles. The ancient memories of my lovesick youth must be set aside. We must now solve the problems at hand. Be nice to her.

JUDAH

J.D., whatever I can do...

JEFFERSON

You are a gentleman, sir.

Black Out.

Scene 6

Davis White House State Room. Mary helps Elizabeth with her coat. There is a basket on the table. Varina enters with a mason jar of peach preserves and sipping absinthe.

MARY

Baked you two loaves this time Miss Elizabeth.

ELIZABETH

What are you drinking Varina?

Mary exits with Elizabeth's coat.

VARINA

The green fairy.

ELIZABETH

Absinthe is not good for the baby. You should try bitters. It will settle your stomach.

VARINA

I like the taste.

ELIZABETH

I like the taste of Kentucky bourbon, but I know better than to drink it when I'm pregnant. Send Old Sambo by my place and I will give you my bottle of bitters.

VARINA

Aren't you the sweet one.

ELIZABETH

We want you to have a healthy baby.

VARINA

My nigger Sarah Mae made these peach preserves. Add this to your basket.

Varina hands the jar to Elizabeth.

VARINA

This is my way of thanking you for the use of your nigger. Lizzy, she has been indispensable.

ELIZABETH

I knew you would like her.

Mary returns with two loaves of bread.

VARINA

She keeps my bedroom clean and orderly. She has done wonders for my feet and knows so much about keeping my stomach at ease. When I need her to play with my little Maggie, she knows just how to keep her occupied. Without even asking she keeps Jeff's office immaculate, dusting and washing the floors. I couldn't be more satisfied.

ELIZABETH

Mary makes me proud.

MARY

Thank you Miss Elizabeth.

VARINA

Lizzy, I know we agreed that I would only keep her for a couple of weeks…but may I impose on your generosity for a little while longer?

ELIZABETH

Tell you what Varina…keep Mary till the baby comes.

VARINA

You don't mind?

ELIZABETH

Right now I need Mary less and less. My mother and I have been visiting Libby Prison. We've been administering aid to the prisoners of war…caring for the sick. I know they are Union soldiers, but it's only the Christian thing to do.

VARINA

I don't think I could tend a Yankee.

ELIZABETH

I just hate seeing those young boys treated badly. They are our enemies, but we Southerners are still civilized. You know we got the grandson of Paul Revere locked up in our prison.

VARINA

Guess he chose the wrong side.

Elizabeth puts the loaves of bread in her basket.

ELIZABETH

I would only ask one favor of you Varina…that Mary continues to bake this tasty bread for me. You can do that can't you Mary?

MARY

Yes ma'am. I think y'all will find these two loaves really delicious.

ELIZABETH

It's my weakness. God help me but every Monday morning I feel I have a right to give into my weakness.

VARINA

My weakness isn't bread…but every Monday morning I find myself giving into my own weakness. That is why my belly is in this condition today.

ELIZABETH

Until I find the right man…I'm going to have to settle on my breakfast toast.

I look forward to a good hearty meal. Must be going. Send that old coon around for the bitters.

VARINA

Lizzy, you've got a true Christian heart. May God bless you.

Elizabeth starts to leave as Old Robert shows Judah into the sitting room. Old Robert carries a bottle of olive oil and a towel.

ELIZABETH

Old Sambo speak of the devil and up you pop. You come by my place and retrieve a bottle of bitters for your mistress.

OLD ROBERT

Yes, Ma'am.

JUDAH

I'm early?

ELIZABETH

Yes you are. Just like a Jew.

VARINA

Jeff will be back shortly. Old Robert I want you to go with Lizzy.

OLD ROBERT

Yes sum.

Old Robert gives the olive oil and towel to Mary and leaves with Elizabeth. Judah crosses to Varina and kisses her hand.

JUDAH

How are you feeling today?

VARINA

My ankles swell.

JUDAH

Looks like you are going to have a healthy baby.

VARINA

Mary swears it's gonna be a boy.

MARY

Yes ma'am. That's how you carrying him.

JUDAH

A boy. Good news…another son to carry on the Davis name.

VARINA

He'll be William Howell Davis.

Mary exits.

JUDAH

A fine strong name.

VARINA

William Howell was my daddy's name.

JUDAH

Your son will be able to trace his roots. He will know from where he comes as he helps to build our new country.

VARINA

Our?

JUDAH

Mrs. Davis, you are not fond of me are you?

VARINA

Mr. Benjamin, I don't think about you one way or another. You are a colleague of my husband. He thinks you are valuable to the war effort. I'm a lady. I don't mix into the affairs of state.

JUDAH

You are not just any lady. You are the first lady of the Confederate states. Does my being a Jew bother you?

VARINA

No.

JUDAH

Not at all?

VARINA

Not in the least…however the fact that you killed our Lord and Savior Jesus Christ…does give me pause.

JUDAH

Mrs. Davis, I am fifty years old. He died long before I was born.

VARINA

I mean your people.

JUDAH

I was born in the West Indies, St. Croix.

VARINA

You are a Jew. You know what I mean. You're twisting my words.

JUDAH

No, Mrs. Davis, I am not twisting your words...but I understand how you feel. There are many Southern Christians that feel as you do. Usually those that feel animosity toward me and my heritage know very little of my faith.

VARINA

Did not the Jews kill Jesus Christ?

JUDAH

Actually the Romans did--Herod to be exact. Are you mad at the Catholics who are descendants from those Romans?

VARINA

Ain't too happy with Catholics either...but it was the Jews that betrayed Jesus.

JUDAH

Not all Jews.

VARINA

Most of them.

JUDAH

Mrs. Davis, do you think Jesus was mad at most Jews as he hung on the cross?

VARINA

I don't know.

JUDAH

He asked his father to forgive them. Mrs. Davis, America was founded on religious tolerance. I hope to have that same tolerance in the confederacy. Can you forgive me as Jesus forgave my brethren?

VARINA

(*beat*) I guess so.

JUDAH

Equality for everyone. Let us be free to worship our faith. Jesus was a Jew. You love Jesus don't you?

VARINA

Of course I do.

JUDAH

I'm not asking you to think of me as Jesus, although I sometimes feel unjustly crucified, but he did have twelve disciples. All Jews…think of me as one of the twelve.

Mary returns with more towels and kneels at Varina's feet and rubs olive oil on her ankles.

VARINA

Mr. Benjamin, you certainly have a way with words.

JUDAH

Mrs. Davis, I am a lawyer…and today I am my own client. I am trying to make a compelling argument for your friendship. I think your husband is a great man. We stand on the precipice of a great new experiment. If we win we change the world.

VARINA

And the experiment is working?

JUDAH

I look at your husband as the modern-day George Washington. This is our American Revolution.

VARINA

I think my husband is destined for greatness.

JUDAH

We have been very fortunate…but this is very early on… we have taken the necessary steps of freeing ourselves from a government that didn't have our best interest at heart. The Southern states have united, we have the finest man working for our success…but we have not won the war…yet.

VARINA

I believe you and Jeff can do it.

JUDAH

The Battle of Bull Run was a hard-fought victory. Now the world is watching us. We've been recognized by the Pope. France, Spain, and other European countries are starting to acknowledge our right for sovereignty. I'm here to ask the President to send an envoy to England, so that the Brits might join us in this war and fight with us.

VARINA

You think they will?

JUDAH

It could be very profitable for them. They import a lot of Southern goods. We will make it very appealing for them. It will be an investment in their future business dealings with us.

VARINA

My, my, my…Mr. Benjamin, I like the way your mind works. Remind me never to play chess with you.

JUDAH

Please Mrs. Davis, call me Judah. I love this new country we are building. I love the South. I admire, respect, and marvel at the great qualities your husband possesses.

VARINA

Please Judah, call me Varina.

JUDAH

We are at the dawn of a new age. Anything I can do to insure our place at the table where other nations dine…I will do.

VARINA

Judah, I am so glad we had this little talk. You have set my mind at ease…and reassured my heart. I can see why my husband values your counsel.

Mary replaces the slippers on Varina's feet. Jefferson comes to the doorway.

JEFFERSON

Ah, Judah, there you are. Come let us plot the demise of some Yankee soldiers.

Jefferson exits. Judah kisses Varina's hand.

JUDAH

First Lady Varina Davis, I must leave…but I look forward to our next conversation.

VARINA

Judah, hopefully you will bring me news of a British ally.

JUDAH

Varina, may it come to pass that someday you dine with Queen Victoria.

He kisses her hand, then exits.

VARINA

Mary are you done?

MARY

Yes ma'am.

Varina drinks the rest of the green fairy.

VARINA

I wonder if Queen Victoria likes peach preserves. I'm hungry. Think I'll have Sarah Mae make me a sandwich with some of your famous tasty bread.

Varina exits. Mary gathers the towels.

Black Out.

Scene 7

Davis White House Office. Jefferson is sitting at his desk as Judah enters.

JEFFERSON

Judah, did you bring your notes for the meeting?

JUDAH

Yes, J.D. Before we do that I would like to offer a proposition.

JEFFERSON

Proposition? What kind of proposition?

JUDAH

Strategy...but you must first let me finish with my thought. You must hear me out.

Mary enters and she starts polishing the furniture.

JEFFERSON

Judah, you underestimate your value to me. I want to know how that devious mind of your works. Of course I will hear you out.

JUDAH

I want you to think about this before we present it to the rest of the cabinet.

JEFFERSON

Yes Judah.

Judah pulls out a cigar case from his jacket and he takes a cigar and offers one to Jefferson. Jefferson declines.

JEFFERSON

No thanks.

JUDAH

J.D. We should free our slaves.

JEFFERSON

Have you lost your mind?

JUDAH

We'll put them in the army.

JEFFERSON

No.

JUDAH

I asked you to hear me out.

JEFFERSON

Judah, why do you think we fight this war? Those Yankee devils want us to do just that. They are now using it as a battle cry to enlist more soldiers.

JUDAH

We need help to win this war. England would enter the war on our side if we but free our slaves.

JEFFERSON

Out of the question.

JUDAH

In Britain they have abolished slavery. It is the major sticking point of contention with any nation that might help us.

JEFFERSON

I don't care. I want my niggers.

JUDAH

If Queen Victoria sees that we have freed our slaves, we take away the moral issue Lincoln is counting on to rally his forces. Think of this rationally.

JEFFERSON

It is not a moral issue. It is economics, pure and simple. Slaves are property. I am not being irrational, Judah.

JUDAH

Well, J. D. we could…

JEFFERSON

I can't have young white crackers fighting side-by-side with niggers.

JUDAH

Why not?

JEFFERSON

Because they don't own any slaves. They will see they are not part of our aristocracy.

JUDAH

You can convince them by using Southern patriotism. You are our Washington, we need those black bodies shooting Yankees.

JEFFERSON

Judah, we need their labor in the fields, in the workshops and on the railroads, the canals, the highways. Listen my friend, we need those black bodies in the coal and iron mines. We cannot give up their labor at this most important juncture of the war.

JUDAH

Point taken. I don't agree, but your point is taken.

JEFFERSON

Besides, Judah do you think the rest of the cabinet will agree with that?

JUDAH

That is why I wanted you to lay the ground work now…for what is to come later. We are vastly outnumbered. Right now our enemy is inexperienced and they lack true leadership. Once they find a strong commander our battles will not be so easily won.

JEFFERSON

The Bible says that niggers are the sons of Ham...so it is out of the question. What is our next order of business?

JUDAH

I wanted to free our slaves before the Yanks actually hit upon it themselves.

JEFFERSON

You think those Northern bigots will fight next to a nigger? Let us close this subject.

JUDAH

The Yanks do not want free niggers running around their cities any more than we do...but they will do anything to win this war.

JEFFERSON

Next point of business.

JUDAH

J. D. one last thought... then I am finished.

JEFFERSON

What for God sakes? (*He looks heavenward*) Knox...why do I have to endure this?

JUDAH

If the war keeps taking their men at some point they will enlist niggers to fight side-by-side with white men. Yankee white men.

JEFFERSON

I don't believe it. They are duplicitous. I used to listen to them talk about niggers in the halls of the Senate. They do what is politically expedient, nothing more, nothing less.

JUDAH

And so must we. J. D. free our slaves.

JEFFERSON

No. Yankees fighting with niggers. Not even they would do that. They are uncivilized beasts…but no one would want to fight side-by-side with a nigger. Who would put a gun in the hands of a nigger? For God sakes don't bring this up in our meeting. We will never get anything done. Don't worry about the mule going blind…just load the wagon.

JUDAH

I'd do it myself but I have enemies in that room.

JEFFERSON

As long as I am President your position is secure. Here is what I want to do next with our armies. I want to take Washington. We run that Republican out of the white house…we will have both a moral and physical victory.

Judah looks at some maps on Jefferson's desk.

JUDAH

Let us look at our troops. That is a well-guarded fortress.

JEFFERSON

If we work our way into their territory…start say with Baltimore, we could affect a blow that will devastate their spirit.

JUDAH

Good idea, J. D. General Johnston and General Beauregard had great success at Bull Run.

JEFFERSON

Beauregard is a pain in my ass.

JUDAH

I know that you and Gustave do not get along…but he is a savvy general.

JEFFERSON

We will lay options in front of Johnston. I would rather he led it…if he is of the opinion we are best served by using Beauregard, I will acquiesce.

JUDAH

Spoken like a true commander.

JEFFERSON

Come let us go. I don't want to be late for our meeting. Nothing worse than a roomful of fidgety peckerwoods.

JUDAH

Let me gather my notes.

JEFFERSON

Leave it. You know what you want to say.

Jefferson and Judah exit. Mary dusts the table where they were working. She is alone in Jefferson's office. She goes over his maps and some letters. She fakes dusting, then picks up another letter and reads it. Unknown to her, Old Robert enters the room. He watches her. She dusts some more then picks up another letter and reads it.

OLD ROBERT

I see what you was doin'.

MARY

You see me working?

OLD ROBERT

Naw. I seen what you was doing.

MARY

Old Robert, are you talking in riddles?

OLD ROBERT

No, little Mary…don't know no riddles. Just know what I seen.

MARY

And just what did you think you saw?

OLD ROBERT

Know what I saw… saw you readin'.

MARY

(*laughs*) You know niggers can't read.

OLD ROBERT

Guess you ain't no nigger den, cause I saw you readin'. Is you colored or just a Negro? You play dumb…but you ain't. Been around a long time little Mary…seen a whole lot of things. Good things…bad things, beautiful things and some downright evil things. I used to be young Robert, don't ya know. I knows how to avoid trouble and I knows how to multiply good times. You know how I do that?

MARY

No, Old Robert, how do you do that?

OLD ROBERT

I look a person in dere eyes. A white man's eyes can't hold no secret without him telling you…it's a secret. Oh, I've seen 'em try to hide a secret, but I been around long enough to recognize a lie or see de truth…sitting right dere in dey eye. Know when a white man is scared and know when he's working himself up to beating a nigger's ass. It's all in dey eyes. If'n I take my shirt off, you ain't gonna find no scars on my back. Dat ain't no accident. I know de truth of what I see. I'm gonna ask you a question little Mary…if'n you value Old Robert as a friend, you gonna look me in my eyes and you gonna spread truth all over your words.

MARY

I value you Old Robert.

OLD ROBERT

We gon' see. Little Mary Bowser was you reading Master Jeff private papers?

MARY

(*beat*) Old Robert, I want you to come close and look me dead in my eyes.

Old Robert moves to Mary.

MARY

Old Robert make no mistake…I can read any word put in front of me and write it too if I have a mind to do so.

OLD ROBERT

(*beat*) I knew it. I knew it. Little Mary, little Mary, I got you. Yes, indeedy I got you…got a secret to tell you…I knows my alphabet…all 26 letters. Recognize certain words too. Want to know more…can you help me? It ain't easy around here. Want to be able to read…'fore I die.

MARY

You want a teacher?

OLD ROBERT

Has to be done in secret.

MARY

You want to write too?

OLD ROBERT

Lord ham mercy…ain't you a Go'send. If it ain't a bother?

MARY

One is just as dangerous as the other. If we gonna leap into the river, might as well go with both feet.

OLD ROBERT

Little Mary, you got gumption. Ain't seen that in ah Nigger's eyes since, John Love ran north.

MARY

Old Robert, you ain't exactly what white people think you are. Are you? You have disguised your contempt for this most peculiar institution in a jovial demeanor.

OLD ROBERT

(*laughs*) Love the sound of them words. Promise me you'll show me what dey look like.

MARY

I promise.

OLD ROBERT

Guess you know your secret safe with me.

MARY

It's why I told you the truth. Shylock is the name of a character in a play. He lends folks money.

OLD ROBERT

What's the name of the play?

MARY

Mercantile of Venice.

OLD ROBERT

Who wrote it?

MARY

Willis Shake-the-spear.

OLD ROBERT

I'll say dis for you …you a pretty smart nigger.

MARY

Some might say…I'm special.

OLD ROBERT

Mary answer me this. Why you want to read Massa Jeff's private papers?

MARY

Old Robert, You know how white folks feel about darkies reading. If I open a book, I'm sure to get caught. If I glance at a paper and practice what I see, easier not to get caught.

OLD ROBERT

Yes sir, this is a brand-new day. Gonna use that trick myself when I'm ready.

Old Robert exits humming. Lights slowly fade.

In the darkness the voice of Varina.

VARINA

Old Robert what are you humming about?

OLD ROBERT

Nothin'.

Black Out.

Scene 8

Davis White House State Room. Varina is sitting at a table writing a letter and sipping her green fairy. Jefferson enters.

JEFFERSON

Who are you writing to?

VARINA

Mary Chestnut.

JEFFERSON

Mary Chestnut? That's the woman got an ass like a forty-dollar mule.

VARINA

Stop it, Jeff.

JEFFERSON

A fact is a fact. Your hair looks beautiful.

He touches, the strokes her hair; he then kisses her on the forehead. She pats his hand.

He opens a letter.

JEFFERSON

Why you writing her?

VARINA

The lack of a social circle here...or the lack of my acceptance into a social circle here. Have you been using my stationary?

JEFFERSON

No...why?

VARINA

I'm sure I had more paper than I have.

JEFFERSON

Say hello to her husband. Haven't you been making friends here?

VARINA

Richmond is hard Jeff. I heard a rumor, they like calling me Queen Varina. These women seem to want to criticize you before they get to know you.

JEFFERSON

All of them?

VARINA

Well, Lizzy is a dear. She has been a great help and a blessing to me. I would more of the ladies were as open and kind as she.

JEFFERSON

She may be crazy but at least she has good taste in choosing her friends.

VARINA

And how are things progressing with the war? May a wife be of assistance to her husband? May the lady that is first in your life be the first to hear?

She sips from her glass. He reads the letter in his hand.

JEFFERSON

I'll tell you Varina...General Johnston is really starting to become a pain. First it was Beauregard, now it looks as if he's poisoned the well and I'm getting resistance from Johnston. His animosity leaps off the Goddamn page. He acts as if I was never a soldier or knew anything about fighting on a battlefield.

VARINA

Get rid of him. Demote him.

JEFFERSON

I can't do that--he is too valuable.

VARINA

He knows that. Therefore he is being arrogant...Beauregard too. Promote Lee. You like him and he seems quite capable.

JEFFERSON

Robert E. Lee?

VARINA

Yes. That will give Johnston and Beauregard their comeuppance and it lets them know they can be replaced.

JEFFERSON

That is actually a good idea, Varina.

VARINA

Every once in a while a wife can rise to the occasion.

JEFFERSON

Yes you can.

He leans in and kisses her on the forehead. As he withdraws she grabs him around his neck and kisses him full on the mouth. They break.

JEFFERSON

Tastes like absinth.

VARINA

It comforts me. Oh Jeff. Some days I wish you were a dry goods clerk…then we could dine in peace on a mutton scrag at three and take an airing on Sunday in a little buggy with no back, drawn by a one-eyed horse at fifty cents an hour. Then Yankees or no Yankees we might abide here or there or anywhere.

JEFFERSON

Someday Varina you will have that, except I want a horse with two good eyes.

She laughs. They kiss again.

Black Out.

Scene 9

Davis White House Kitchen. It is night. Mary and Old Robert are sitting at a table. There are writing utensils on the table. Mary is pointing to some letters on a piece of paper.

OLD ROBERT

X. Y. Z.

MARY

You didn't miss a one. You know your alphabet.

OLD ROBERT

Told ya'.

MARY

Look at these five letters. Can you tell me what they are?

OLD ROBERT

A.E.I.O. Uhhh. Is dat a word?

MARY

No… but they are real important letters. They help make a word. Say it again.

OLD ROBERT

A.E.I.O. Uhhh.

MARY

That last letter is pronounced 'U'. Say that…'U'.

Old Robert flirts with Mary as he says...

OLD ROBERT

U.

MARY

Good. Those letters are called vowels. Now, on this piece of paper I want you to write those letters.

OLD ROBERT

Nice paper, where'd you get it?

MARY

You want to learn to write or you want to open up a stationary store?

He clumsily picks up the pencil and tries to write. Mary comes back to the table and helps him hold the pencil. He continues to flirt with Mary.

MARY

We are going to have to destroy that paper you know that?

OLD ROBERT

Damn sho' do.

He continues to write.

OLD ROBERT

Can I ask you a question?

MARY

Don't worry…we'll do the rest of the letters later. First I want you to understand what these letters do.

OLD ROBERT

Dat weren't my question.

MARY

Oh. Sorry.

OLD ROBERT

Miss Elizabeth give you a man?

Robert cannot see her eyes as she answers this question.

MARY

(*laughs*) I ain't married.

OLD ROBERT

Little Mary Bowser, if I was ten years younger…you'd be mine. I'd have Miss Varina buy you for me.

MARY

Ten years?

OLD ROBERT

Okay, twenty years younger.

Mary gives him a look.

OLD ROBERT

Okay, okay, okay, thirty years. Black don't crack.

MARY

Thirty years younger? They should call you "Not so Old Robert."

OLD ROBERT

Damn, can you tell how old I is? All right forty-years younger…and dat is all dat I am admitting too… I would make sho' your master was good to you. I'd make sho' you was fed with dey leftovers.

MARY

You got those kind of privileges?

OLD ROBERT

Little Mary, I knows how to handle white folks. Look at my belly. I come by dat honest.

MARY

Oh, you come by that honestly?

OLD ROBERT

Dat comes from good eating. Dey like me…and dey feed me. How does dis letter look?

She looks at the letter.

MARY

That's good. Don't stop. Keep going.

He writes another letter.

MARY

You was never married.

OLD ROBERT

Oh, I had me a beautiful wife when I were a young man…had her for fourteen years, den they sold her. She some place in Tennessee. We was in love. I sho' did love me some Lorraine Brown.

MARY

Lorraine?

OLD ROBERT

High yellow gal. She loved her some Robert Brown too… had four chillun.

I was young den. Young and hot and full of devilment.

MARY

Where are your children now?

OLD ROBERT

Wished I knew. Sold. Some place in the South…though I think my youngest boy is up North. Boston. He might even be free by now. He was a smart one. Knew how to work dose white folks.

MARY

Like his daddy.

OLD ROBERT

Spittin' image, too. Amos Brown, yeah…he was my heart, don't ya know.

MARY

Amos Brown, of Boston.

OLD ROBERT

Maybe. Wish I could have seen them grow up. Ernestine, Olive, Sylvester and Amos…dose were mine. Lorraine sure knew how to make beautiful babies.

MARY

Those were yours?

OLD ROBERT

Hell, a gal as pretty as Lorraine…you think de master wasn't gonna give her some children? She had twelve. How's dis letter?

MARY

That's good, keep going.

OLD ROBERT

What is dis on top of de line?

MARY

That is a dot. The letter "i". Union win this war maybe someday you see your children. Go, north and find Amos.

OLD ROBERT

Little Girl, think it… don't say it.

MARY

They say union win this war, we all be free.

OLD ROBERT

A little late for me don't you think? It ain't possible. Freedom? Dis dog is too old to learn that new trick.

MARY

Old Robert…look at yourself. Right now you learning how to write, and doing a damn good job.

She lifts up the paper and examines the letter "i" he has written.

MARY

Maybe it's time to rethink your situation.

OLD ROBERT

Oh Lordy, time to go.

MARY

Where you going?

OLD ROBERT
Need to do my favorite chore.

MARY
But you're not finished.

OLD ROBERT
Has to wait…dis is more important.

Lights go to Half.

Scene 10

Lights go up to half on Davis' White House Office: Old Robert stops and leans in the doorway. Lights fade out in kitchen as Mary examines Old Robert's writing. Lights up full in Jefferson's office as Old Robert enters.

OLD ROBERT

Is it time?

Jefferson is sitting at his desk going over some papers.

JEFFERSON

Yes, it's time.

Old Robert comes into the room.

OLD ROBERT

How was your day Massa Jeff?

He gets a decanter of whiskey and pours whiskey into a fine crystal glass.

JEFFERSON

Let us thank God for small rewards.

OLD ROBERT

Yes Sur.

Old Robert hands Jefferson the drink.

JEFFERSON

Deo Vindice.

OLD ROBERT

That's that dead language thing ain't it?

JEFFERSON

That's right Old Robert. Latin.

OLD ROBERT

I knew it was that or French. What it mean?

Old Robert gets a worn mug and pours a shot into that mug. He sits in a chair.

JEFFERSON

"God, Will Vindicate"…think I'll make that our motto. Deo Vindice.

OLD ROBERT

So, we winning, huh?

JEFFERSON

Yes, Old Robert, we've been winning our battles. We won Bull Run. Lincoln has just replaced General McDowell with General George McClellan. McCellan is a joke, that man is a martinet not a strategist. We put those Yankees in a tizzy.

OLD ROBERT

Massa Jeff, I heard Mr. Judah saying something about dat Bull Run…but don't know quite what it's all about?

JEFFERSON

Tell me, what did you hear?

OLD ROBERT

I allowed how some body's bull got out, and us and de Yankees was trying to catch him and get him back in de pasture.

JEFFERSON

(*laughs*) Old Robert, that is quite logical. Very good. That is not the case but I am impressed with your sense of logic.

OLD ROBERT

Is I close?

JEFFERSON

Bull Run is the name of the place where we fought the Yankees. It's in Manassass. We were not chasing a bull. We were shooting at each other.

OLD ROBERT

And we won?

JEFFERSON

Captured almost a thousand Yankee prisoners.

OLD ROBERT

Hot-too-mah-dee-no! Dat's a real whuppin'. What you gwine do wid'em?

JEFFERSON

There is a warehouse here in Richmond. The Libby Building.

OLD ROBERT

Den it's gwine be the Libby Prison?

JEFFERSON

Yes…and my generals gave me a little bonus. Bragging rights to take to Lincoln.

OLD ROBERT

What y'all braggin' about?

JEFFERSON

First…pour me a little more Kentucky Mash. . Deo Vindice, "Putting our hearts in God and in our own firm hearts and strong arms we will vindicate the right as best we may."

Old Robert gets up and pours his master a little more whiskey.

OLD ROBERT

Twelve-year-old Kentuck taste good.

JEFFERSON

Yes it does…and it satisfies my soul.

OLD ROBERT

Massa Jeff, where did my Lorraine go?

JEFFERSON

Lorraine? Lorraine, Lorraine…oh yes, Lorraine. Why do you ask?

OLD ROBERT

You say…satisfied my soul. Dat little gal made my soul satisfied. Just wonder if she safe…in dis war. Wonder where she might be?

JEFFERSON

My Daddy, sold her to Forrest's Memphis slave pen, but that was years ago. She could be anywhere.

OLD ROBERT

You think she safe?

JEFFERSON

No telling Old Robert. This is a war, and things are starting to change.

OLD ROBERT

Why he sell her?

JEFFERSON

It was a business decision, Old Robert. Don't take it personal. She stopped making babies…we needed fertile girls and she passed her usefulness as a breeder. It was time for a new investment.

OLD ROBERT

I shore did love dat gal.

JEFFERSON

She lost her value, Old Robert…had to be done. I'm sure she ended up in someone's house and not in the fields.

OLD ROBERT

You knows for certain?

JEFFERSON

Not sure…she could be anywhere. With this war on…no telling where she's gone. That was so long ago.

OLD ROBERT

Guess I lost dat gal to the mysteries of de unknown.

JEFFERSON

Don't fret, that milk is spilt. Let me tell you about my bonus.

OLD ROBERT

Ready to hear it Massa Jeff.

Old Robert goes to get a box cigars and first offers one to Jefferson who declines then takes one himself and sits down.

JEFFERSON

A Congressman from New York, Alfred Ely came out of Washington to sit in his buggy and gloat. Thought we were going to lose the Bull Run Battle. Sat in his buggy eating fried chicken and corn bread, swilling down hooch. Sat there like he was in a theatre watching a play, ready to cheer on those blue coats.

OLD ROBERT

What's de bonus?

JEFFERSON

He's sitting in my new prison. That'll teach a Yankee to bet against us.

They laugh.

OLD ROBERT

No more fried chicken for dat Yankee. Sound to me like a good omen.

JEFFERSON

I'm not superstitious…but it is a good omen. I'll drink to that.

There is a knock at the door. Old Robert immediately gets up.

JEFFERSON

Who is it?

JUDAH

(*off stage*) Judah.

Judah enters the office and hands a letter to Jefferson.

JUDAH

I was told to give this to you right away.

Jefferson reads the letter and starts to pace as he reads.

JEFFERSON

Old Robert pour Judah a drink.

OLD ROBERT

Yes Sur. Two fingers?

Old Robert gets a glass for Judah and pours him some whiskey. Jefferson is pacing and he is getting angry as he reads the letter in his hand.

JUDAH

Two fingers would be fine.

JEFFERSON

Son of a bitch. Sons of bitches. Those goddamned Yankee, lowlife, conniving bastards.

Mary quietly slips in the room and starts to polish furniture.

JUDAH

What is it? What is the matter?

JEFFERSON

Read this.

He hands a letter to Judah.

JEFFERSON

God damn it Judah, read this. They're stealing my niggers.

JUDAH

(*he reads*) Three slaves, Frank Baker, James Townsend, and Sheppard Mallory had been contracted by their masters to help construct defense batteries at Sewell's Point, for the Confederacy. So...so what?

JEFFERSON

Keep reading.

JUDAH

They escaped at night and rowed a skiff to Old Point Comfort, where they sought asylum at Fort Monroe. The Yankees agreed to asylum?

JEFFERSON

That's outright stealing. Any runaway who gets to the union lines is now classified as contraband. The nerve of those bastards. We have an agreement...the Fugitive Slave Act. They have an obligation to return our slaves.

JUDAH

No J.D., they don't.

JEFFERSON

What do you mean they don't?

JUDAH

The Fugitive Slave Act started eleven years ago. We are now a foreign power. They had an obligation to the United States. We are no longer united. We seceded. This is very clever…very smart. Who did this?

JEFFERSON

You're saying those Yankee bastards can take my niggers? Is that what you're tellin' me? They can legally do that?

JUDAH

We are at war. New rules are made up every day to support each side.

Mary continues to dust around the room.

JEFFERSON

Those three runaways get to Fort Monroe and beg the Yankees to give them asylum… and those bastards do it! Then when we requested their return, sons of bitches started this contraband shit. That's legal?

JUDAH

General Butler…hmm…is a clever son of a bitch. You have to admit this is very smart, J. D. very smart.

JEFFERSON

I don't have to admit a Goddamn thing. Smart or not, I want my niggers back.

JUDAH

The only way we can do that is to take Fort Monroe. They are playing a hard fought game. Score one for the blue. It is time the grey came up with some countermove. Something that will upset Lincoln as much as he's upset you.

JEFFERSON

Damn right.

JUDAH

Let us ruminate on this situation and then come up with a viable counterattack. We must not let emotions dictate our actions.

JEFFERSON

Okay. Okay. What about our navy? Has the Merrimack been converted yet?

Judah checks his notes. Mary continues to dust.

JUDAH

Yes. It is now the CSS Virginia. It should be seaworthy by February.

JEFFERSON

Let's figure out a plan to slap those Yankees silly. Let them look to the land and we shall arrive by sea.

Judah starts writing notes on a piece of paper. Varina enters. She has a glass in her hand and takes a sip.

VARINA

There you are…Old Robert, I need you.

Old Robert crosses to the door.

VARINA

Gentlemen I need two more strong men. Can I impose on you just for one minute of your time.

JEFFERSON

Hell no!

JUDAH

Certainly, Varina…come on Jeff we need a little calming down period.

JEFFERSON

Varina, this isn't gonna take all day is it? What are you drinking?

VARINA

The green fairy.

Jefferson takes the glass from Varina's hand and sets it on a table; then exits, leaving Mary alone in the office. Mary goes and gets a book and opens it and lays it on the table. She gets a pencil and paper from her apron and writes down some notes from the papers on Jefferson's desk. Her back is to the door. Varina returns. She cannot see that Mary is writing but she does see her hunched over the table.

VARINA

Mary what are you doing?

Mary hides the paper and pencil under her dust cloth.

MARY

Nothing.

VARINA

Clearly you were doing something. What was it?

MARY

Just dusting.

VARINA

No, you weren't Mary. I'm not a fool. You dusted this room yesterday. It's clean as a whistle. Now I want you to look me in the eye and tell me what you were doing. You know I can tell when someone is lying. I just look into their eyes and I can see it. Now I am gonna ask you one more time…what were you doing?

MARY

Reading.

VARINA

Reading? You can read?

MARY

Yes Ma'am. Been reading for about two years now.

VARINA

Let me see what you were reading.

Mary hands Varina the open book.

VARINA

Show me what you were reading.

On both of the pages of the open book are pictures.

MARY

I been reading this here.

VARINA

There are no words on this page; it's just a picture.

MARY

That's what I was reading. The picture.

VARINA

You were reading the picture?

MARY

Yes Ma'am.

VARINA

That is not called reading Mary. That is picture-gazing. You were looking at the picture or gazing at the picture.

MARY

I thought that was reading.

VARINA

Oh God No!! No! No!

MARY

That's what this field hand told me, told me I was reading….

VARINA

No! No! Oh, my water, Mary, call my husband, the baby is coming…

Varina grabs her stomach and collapses in a chair. Mary holds onto her. "The Battle Hymn of the Republic" begins to softly play.

MARY

I can't leave you.

VARINA

No Mary…quickly get my husband.

Mary crosses to the door and as she does she stuffs her handwritten note under her dress. Varina doesn't see this.

MARY

Massa Jeff, Massa Jeff….

She runs out of the room. As the lights fade to black Varina clutches her stomach and screams. It is the scream of a mother giving birth. "The Battle Hymn of the Republic" continues to play.

Black Out.

End of ACT I

Left to right: Chrystee Pharris, Connie Ventress, Lou Beatty, Jr.
(Act I, Scene 2)

Left to right: Paul Messinger, Gordon Goodman (Act I, Scene 5)

Left to right: Anne Johnstonbrown, Chrystee Pharris, Connie Ventress (Act I, Scene 6)

Left to right: Anne Johnstonbrown and Gordon Goodman (Act I, Scene 8)

Left to right: Connie Ventress, Robert Pine (Act II, Scene 1)

Left to right: Chrystee Pharris, Paul Messinger, Gordon Goodman (Act II, Scene 3)

Left to right: Chrystee Pharris, Lou Beatty, Jr. (Act II, Scene 5)

ACT II

SCENE 1

Van Lew Pantry. Four years later, Elizabeth and a Yankee journalist, Mr. Slydell are kissing. She breaks the kiss.

ELIZABETH

Kissing you is like brushing my lips against velvet. Tender. You have a way about you…don't you Mr. Slydell? Velvetize me again. (*he kisses her again*). Oh, yes. Soft and tender…yet confident and assured…velvet. Not many men can blend those assets.

SLYDELL

You flatter me Miss Van Lew.

ELIZABETH

Young men are too eager. They rush the moment… overwhelmed by their passion. Satisfy the carnal. Damn the lady…ready or not here I come…but you Mr. Slydell, you understand the virtues of patience. You savor. You use tenderness as a means…to seduce my soul. (*she kisses him*) Spend the night.

SLYDELL

Miss Van Lew I am indeed honored and I thank you for extolling my limited virtues…I sometimes feel that women will play the innocent maiden and pretend they do not want what they really do want…but you…

ELIZABETH

Spend the night.

SLYDELL

Does it show on my face?

ELIZABETH

Does what show?

SLYDELL

I am losing my resolve. Gettysburg has maimed my soul.

ELIZABETH

You are a journalist. You must write what is in your heart…the truth.

SLYDELL

I have something for you.

He reaches into his saddlebag. He has a small sack of flour. He gives it to Elizabeth.

ELIZABETH

Flour.

SLYDELL

So that you might make one of your delicious peach pies.

ELIZABETH

Generous as well as thoughtful…yet, I am incapable of satiating your palate. I thank you but I must return this to you.

SLYDELL

Pray tell what stops you from receiving my gift?

ELIZABETH

There is not enough flour here for half a dozen biscuits, let alone a Van Lew peach pie. This city has been devastated and fresh fruit is not a high priority value time. Plus, I have asked you to spend the night twice to no avail. A woman with half a brain knows that when an invitation is extended and no response is forthcoming--consummation is highly unlikely.

SLYDELL

War has trumped free will. Men like myself must look to the future for the solace of female companionship.

ELIZABETH

Spend the night.

SLYDELL

I have another token.

He opens his saddlebag and produces a mason jar of peach preserves. He gives the jar to Elizabeth. He places the sack of flour on a small table.

ELIZABETH

Peach or apricot?

SLYDELL

Why peach of course. I cannot pass the fruit and not think of you. A fresh ripe peach holds all the mysteries that I share with you. Delicate texture…you cannot squeeze it too hard or its body will bruise…the sweet natural juices that run off its body seduce my every thought.

ELIZABETH

Mr. Slydell you must tend my garden with those strong hands and prune my tree.

SLYDELL

My duty asks of me…obligations. I want to be your gardener… but I must journey to Gettysburg tonight.

ELIZABETH

Pray tell what obligation awaits you in Gettysburg?

LYDELL

I must carry the information you entrust with me to our contact…and President Lincoln is giving a speech. They are marking the day of the great battle on what is now hallowed ground.

Syldell leaves the sack of flour. Elizabeth turns to a shelf of jars and finds a small package among the many jars of herbs. Inside the package are cigars. She hands him the cigar package.

ELIZABETH

The information that our friends seek is hidden among these smokes.

SLYDELL

Will you share with me who is your inside man?

ELIZABETH

Someday.

SYLDELL

There will come a time when we can control our priorities…but death is still at the door…wanting to claim more lives. Good night, my fair lady.

He starts to leave; she stops him.

ELIZABETH

I look to the day of peace. Appease me before you go, Mr. Slydell. Would you at least leave me with the tender feel of velvet?

They kiss again.

Black Out.

Scene 2

Davis White House State Room. The room looks weathered. Things are falling apart. The war has taken its toll on the room. Mary is brushing Varnia's hair and holding Varina's baby. Elizabeth enters. She is carrying a basket.

ELIZABETH

Good morning, good morning, got you something for the new baby.

She takes a box out of her basket.

VARINA

Isn't that sweet. What is it a doll?...Just what she needs. I had her playing with Maggie's toys. What is this?

Varina hold up a pocket watch with a pink ribbon attached.

ELIZABETH

A pocket watch.

VARINA

Trust me Lizzy...she is not old enough to tell time.

ELIZABETH

But someday she will be...and she will be way ahead of children her age.

VARINA

You are one of a kind.

ELIZABETH

Are you ready to have another one?

Varina places the watch on the table.

VARINA

I think my body has been ravaged enough. After that scare three years ago with Billy, I had to be real careful with this pregnancy.

ELIZABETH

No, absinth this time?

VARINA

Not one drop. I learned my lesson. Winnie is one healthy little girl. Mary, where is my mirror?

ELIZABETH

How is Billy doing?

VARINA

That boy is full of piss and vinegar. He is running me ragged. I thank you once again for Mary. Sometimes I need her just to occupy him so I can get work done.

Mary stops brushing Varina's hair and goes to a table and gets an ornate hand mirror. She gives the mirror to Varina. Varina gazes at her face in the mirror.

ELIZABETH

I have another surprise for you.

VARINA

A surprise?

ELIZABETH

Varina, it's very special…and I only want to share it with you. I've got a lovely treat for us.

Elizabeth takes a cloth napkin which has something in it out of her basket. Varina looks in the mirror.

MARY

You look beautiful Miss Varina.

VARINA

Mary take Winnie to Alberta. It's time for her milk.

MARY

Yes, Ma'am.

Mary and the baby leave. Elizabeth takes out a jar of peach jam.

ELIZABETH

You still using Alberta as a wet nurse?

VARINA

Lizzy, no one can suckle a child like that nigger. She must have something special in her milk. (*looking in the mirror*) Do you think the war has ravaged my face?

ELIZABETH

Absolutely not. Other than myself you are the most beautiful woman in Richmond.

VARINA

I see plates, is this treat something to eat?

ELIZABETH

What is the one thing that is getting harder and harder to find?

VARINA

Lizzy, everything is harder to find. Fresh fruit, bread, vegetables, you name it and Richmond doesn't have it. This war is killing us.

ELIZABETH

Well, I brought something to lighten your spirits. Unwrap this.

Varina unwraps the cloth napkin. Inside is a warm biscuit.

VARINA

Oh my God, Lizzy. How did you manage this? Flour is so scarce, everyone is using corn meal.

ELIZABETH

I know. Minerva Meredith got hold of some flour and she baked half a dozen biscuits. She gave me and some other ladies each a biscuit.

VARINA

You want to share half a biscuit?

ELIZABETH

You're my friend.

VARINA

It's half a biscuit Lizzy. You eat the whole thing.

Varina slides the biscuit to Elizabeth.

ELIZABETH

We're friends. We should share. Minerva is a great cook.

Elizabeth slides it back to Varina.

VARINA

That's crazy, I shouldn't really. As much as I want to…I shouldn't.

Varina slides it back to Elizabeth. Elizabeth cuts the biscuit in half and puts jam on her half.

ELIZABETH

Why?

VARINA

Isn't Minerva the one who led the bread riot?

ELIZABETH

No, that was Mary Jackson.

VARINA

And...

ELIZABETH

Want some peach preserves on your half?

VARINA

Minerva was the other woman. If Jefferson ever found out I was eating a biscuit baked by the hands of Minerva, he'd kill me.

ELIZABETH

Varina, I don't have a dog in this fight.

Elizabeth takes a bite.

ELIZABETH

Oh my God, this is delicious.

VARINA

Did you put jam on the other half?

ELIZABETH

No. Want me too?

VARINA

Well, if you did that…I would be forced not to let it go to waste.

ELIZABETH

Well, in that case…

Elizabeth puts some jam on the other half of the biscuit. She extends her hand with the biscuit. Varina starts to take it then hesitates.

VARINA

Oh, you Satan…this has got to be our secret.

ELIZABETH

I won't tell a soul.

Varina starts to take the biscuit, pauses, then decides to take it, she has a bite.

VARINA

Sweet baby Jesus that's good!

ELIZABETH

Told ya'.

VARINA

Secrets, I've got another secret. Can I trust you? Oh hell, I can't tell you. I can't tell anybody.

ELIZABETH

Varina, you don't have to tell me. Just enjoy your biscuit.

VARINA

How is your herb garden?

ELIZABETH

Unattended. I need a gardener.

VARINA

You don't have someone to tend your garden?

ELIZABETH

The war has killed off or maimed any good chance I have of finding a decent gardener.

VARINA

I guess it has.

Varina picks up her mirror.

VARINA

I see more lines.

ELIZABETH

There was a time I didn't have to worry. I knew there would be someone to till my soil, and nurture and coax my garden…so I would bring forth radiant flowers.

VARINA

My face is so consumed by battlefields, I wonder if I'll ever have any more flowers.

ELIZABETH

Now I am not as interested in flowers as I am in having someone with good strong hands to till my soil. Slowly and methodically, someone who can…

Varina takes another bite of her biscuit.

VARINA

Hmmmm. This is a sin and I know it.

ELIZABETH

Why would President Davis be upset with you for enjoying this biscuit?

VARINA

Don't you remember what happened in the riot?

ELIZABETH

I remember how it started. The ladies went to Governor Letcher, asking for help, businesses were raising their prices and they couldn't buy food. They were starving, all they needed was a little help and he turned them down.

VARINA

Right, right…then all the women marched toward the capital and the Washington statue.

ELIZABETH

I wasn't there but I heard maybe five hundred women gathered as they marched.

VARINA

More like a thousand…

Varina takes another bite of her biscuit.

VARINA

As the size of the crowd grew…slap me silly, but this tastes good. I haven't had bread in six months, no nine months, wait…no, no, no, longer than that.

ELIZABETH

Everything is so hard to come by. I need long feet and strong hands.

VARINA

Lizzy! Let me finish my story…

ELIZABETH

Okay, okay, okay, okay.

VARINA

A thousand women were marching down the street. Truth be told, I was kind of proud of them…until they started smashing windows and taking food supplies. That was shameful.

ELIZABETH

I know Varina, but they were starving…and that bastard Letcher wouldn't help.

VARINA

Nothing he could do. So they went to Mayor Mayo.

ELIZABETH

Mayor Mayo, he's as useful as a sixth toe.

VARINA

Oh, he's a horse's ass, alright. Jeff told me Mayo read some gobble de gook to the crowd and then told them to disperse.

ELIZABETH

Who's gonna listen to a man with a squeaky voice. He's a soprano looking for a baritone.

VARINA

That's when Jefferson stood up in the wagon asked for their attention and got it.

ELIZABETH

He's a wonderful speechifier.

Varina stands.

VARINA

"You say you are hungry and have no money; here this is all that I have."

And he reached into his own pocket, took out what he had and flung his dollars and coins into the crowd.

ELIZABETH

And...

As Varina speaks she picks up the pocket watch.

VARINA

No one budged...except for some small children that scrambled for the money. Then he pulled his pocket watch out of his pocket and said; "If you do not disperse within five minutes, the order will be given for the militia to fire on you."

ELIZABETH

And they ran like jack rabbits.

VARINA

Jeff later had them arrested.

ELIZABETH

Who?

VARINA

Minerva and Mary...so you see I don't want him to find out about this.

ELIZABETH

Hell, I can't tell Minerva that I shared this with you...the woman whose husband put her in jail? Uh-uh, that would upset her. It's our secret.

VARINA

I've got another secret. A big one.

ELIZABETH

About Minerva?

VARINA

No Lizzy…about the war.

Varina gets her brush and brushes her hair as she speaks.

ELIZABETH

You gonna tell me?

VARINA

You promise not to tell anyone?

ELIZABETH

My word as a Southern lady and a patriot.

VARINA

There is a leak in Jefferson's cabinet.

ELIZABETH

A leak?

VARINA

Someone is sharing confidential information with the enemy.

ELIZABETH

A spy?

VARINA

Stephen Mallory and Robert Toombs think it's Judah…but I know they don't like him because he's a Jew.

ELIZABETH

What do you think?

VARINA

I don't think its Judah. I trust him with my life. I know he is one hundred percent behind Jeff.

ELIZABETH

Are you sure?

VARINA

Lizzy, some of the ideas he's come up with to help us win this war are brilliant. He's a genius…and I don't mind saying that… Jew or not.

ELIZABETH

Could it be one of the other members of the cabinet?

Elizabeth packs her picnic basket.

VARINA

Personally I think it's John Reagan.

ELIZABETH

What does Jefferson think?

VARINA

He's in a quandary. We've tried on several occasions to catch the culprit to no avail.

ELIZABETH

You've got to use stronger glue. Make a note of that, tell Jefferson…stronger glue. You'll catch him.

VARINA

Glue?

Elizabeth picks up the pocket watch and places it in the middle of the table.

ELIZABETH

It's really very simple. You put the secret on a table, then put puddles of glue near the secret. The poltroon perpetrator steps in the glue and now you know who he is. Just check everybody's shoes. Strong glue lasts a long time.

VARINA

Yes, of course Lizzy…stronger glue. You still visiting the prison?

ELIZABETH

Yes and Chimborazo hospital. Not enough help to go around. Whatever I can do to ease the suffering. Yankee or Reb they're just young boys that need caring for.

Elizabeth rises to leave.

VARINA

Lizzy, you are a good Christian woman. Can I keep the peach jam?

As Elizabeth hands her the jar.

ELIZABETH

Varina, I must confess to you, I know who the spy is.

VARINA

You do?

ELIZABETH

Of course I do…it's the Jew.

There is a knock on the door and as it opens, Judah enters.

JUDAH

The president is meeting with Robert Toombs. Mind if I join you for a few minutes?

ELIZABETH

Speak of the devil and up pops you know who? Mr. Benjamin, I am just on my way out to do my civic duty.

JUDAH

Ahh, Miss Elizabeth Van Lew, please give my regards to your lovely mother.

ELIZABETH

I shall Mr. Benjamin, I certainly shall. I don't think my garden's going to produce any flowers, but that doesn't mean I don't want someone trying. Stronger glue Varina, stronger glue.

Elizabeth exits. Judah sits down near Varina.

JUDAH

Is she all right?

VARINA

Who can say?

JUDAH

And how are you today, Varina?

VARINA

Fair to midlin'.

JUDAH

Anything I can do?

VARINA

Oh, Judah, Judah…oh, I guess I'm fine. How is your wife?

JUDAH

At this point…I don't know. I haven't been able to receive any letters from Natalie…nor send any of mine to her.

VARINA

Miss her?

JUDAH

I miss my daughter Ninette.

VARINA

Will they ever come back to the states?

JUDAH

In her heart of hearts Natalie thinks she is a Parisian. I would like Ninette to see the South…but the way things are going who knows if that will ever be possible?

VARINA

Are you lonely?

JUDAH

I am alone…but not lonely. The war occupies so much of my mind I don't have time to indulge in loneliness.

VARINA

Indulge? Indulge…Judah…sometimes I get so lonely. Jefferson is right here in this house, but he might as well be in Paris with your wife. Everything consumes him. Everything except family.

JUDAH

I understand. When this war is over Varina…you will get your husband back.

VARINA

I had to tie him down just to get him to stop long enough to give me Winnie.

He completely ignores the children. I look at him and see his mind is off somewhere thinking of schemes and tactical strategies. I miss his touch. How do you modify your life without your wife?

JUDAH

Varina, I will be honest. I'm afraid I love my wife more than she loves me. I have had to structure my living in a way that benefits my career, more than my family.

VARINAS

Do you miss her touch?

JUDAH

Deeply.

VARINA

What sustains you Judah?

JUDAH

Before this war it was knowing…every summer would be shared with her and Ninette in Paris.

VARINA

And now?

JUDAH

Why do you ask?

He kneels to her.

VARINA

I need something to sustain me. Win or lose, I need to devise a way of keeping my sanity.

Varina leans in to kiss Judah, but resists.

VARINA

I need to fight for my marriage.

JUDAH

He loves you.

VARINA

That man in the other room is not my husband. He is a President. He is building a nation. He is not the man I married.

JUDAH

Leadership is a tiresome burden.

Judah stands. As Varina speaks, she picks up her mirror.

VARINA

I would like to see the man I married occasionally. I would like to feel the warmth of his touch...the tenderness of his spirit. I want him to gaze upon my face and smile.

Judah takes the mirror from Varina.

JUDAH

Varina...in my mind, I have rooms. In each room I place things I need and things I love. Right now, the room that holds my family...my wife, my daughter, that room is locked. They are shut away. I try not to think on them. Someday I will unlock that door and let the sunlight illuminate that room. So that even the darkest corner gleams like freshly minted gold.

VARINA

You will illuminate that room.

JUDAH

But for now I must work in a room that stimulates my mind and reinforce the work that must be done now.

VARINA

Judah, you are such a comfort to me.

JUDAH

My only wish is for your happiness.

VARINA

Thank you.

She extends her hand. (beat) He takes her hand in his...they look into each other's eyes...Judah leans in to kiss her. She does not resist. Old Robert enters and interrupts the moment.

OLD ROBERT

Sir, Massa Jeff is ready to see you now.

JUDAH

Thank you.

The Judah exits. Old Robert hums as he exits. Varina is alone. She picks up her mirror and looks at her face. Her finger traces a new line she has discovered.

Lights fade to Black Out.

Scene 3

Davis White House Office. Jefferson is sitting at his desk. Judah enters. He hands Jefferson a letter.

JEFFERSON

What's this?

JUDAH

An endorsement, for freeing the slaves.

JEFFERSON

From whom?

Mary enters with a tray with a teapot, cups, and cookies.

JUDAH

Your favorite General. Robert E. Lee. He agrees with me.

JEFFERSON

Damn you Judah.

JUDAH

J.D., we have no choice. It has to be done.

JEFFERSON

If we take them for public service, the government must pay their owners for them. Each regiment of a thousand slaves would cost the government two-hundred-thousand dollars.

JUDAH

Gettysburg devastated us. We're still recovering. If we don't do this you might as well surrender.

JEFFERSON

We would have to sell them at the end of the war or give them their liberty…and that my friend is an odious affair, at the very least.

JUDAH

We have the money.

JEFFERSON

I can't believe Lee approves of this.

JUDAH

He wants men. He's not a fool. You can't fight a war without soldiers. The English refuse to help us. We've run out of options. Who cares if Confederate soldiers are white or black.

JEFFERSON

I care.

Mary hands a cup and saucer to Jefferson.

JUDAH

We are not on the battlefield. As long as a nigger can point a gun at a Yankee and pull the trigger, we live to fight another day. J. D., come down off the cross, we need the wood.

JEFFERSON

But will they pull the trigger?

JUDAH

And that my friend is why we must offer them their freedom. Those Northern niggers have been pulling the trigger against us. We are offering our niggers their legal freedom. No contraband, no counterfeit Emancipation Proclamation. Believe me, offer them freedom and they will take it and shoot a Yankee quicker than a drunken sergeant at a Quaker meeting.

Mary hands a cup and saucer to Judah.

JEFFERSON

That son of a bitch Lincoln, he had no authority to free our slaves…we are a sovereign country.

JUDAH

It's all perception J.D. No one listens to the rules.

JEFFERSON

Those coons ran listened… and they ran to daddy Lincoln… it's illegal.

Mary pours tea into Jefferson's cup.

JUDAH

That's why we must legally free our slaves.

JEFFERSON
I free our slaves…and all hell is gonna break loose.

JUDAH
J. D., we've been living in hell these past four years. This war has devastated our country. What are we really giving up?

JEFFERSON
Everything! Our way of life…the social fabric of Southern society…without cheap labor…our whole economy would fall apart.

JUDAH
You don't do this… we'll lose the war. Even Lee can see that. If we get captured, they will try us for treason.

JEFFERSON
They can't do that. We have legal rights to do what we did.

Mary pours tea into Judah's cup.

JUDAH
J. D. The winner makes the rules. You know that. How much leniency do you think they will extend to you?

JEFFERSON
This just gripes my ass. Niggers in our army.

Mary serves a plate of cookies to Jefferson.

JUDAH

I just want to win and I don't care who is responsible for our victory. If we lose you can always protest this in a Yankee court. History will note your rights to secede have been abused...but you will be swinging at the end of a rope and no one will care what circumstances transpired for you to end that way.

Judah and Jefferson drink tea.

JUDAH

Give them their freedom...but don't give them our rights.

JEFFERSON

What does that mean?

JUDAH

J.D. I'm a lawyer. You let those niggers fight for their freedom okay? Okay, they can become soldiers...after the war, if they live, they've earned their freedom...but we will write laws. New laws...laws that dictate what a nigger can do and what they cannot do.

Mary serves a plate of cookies to Judah.

JEFFERSON

But what keeps them from living in the North?

JUDAH

J. D. we have to be subtle. These laws can't look like they are against a nigger, it has to look as if it is for a nigger. We develop a code. A way of reading the law, so that a sheriff or a judge can use it in a proper way. They will be free, but they will never be our equal.

JEFFERSON

Free but not equal…done. Okay, we enlist colored soldiers.

JUDAH

Do you think you can sell it to the others?

JEFFERSON

I'll explain it…and those peckerwoods will buy it. What have you found out regarding the leak?

JUDAH

J.D. It has to be one of the cabinet members. I just haven't deduced which one. I've narrowed it down to two…but all the pieces don't fit.

JEFFERSON

Which two?

JUDAH

Robert Toombs has plenty of motive…since I took his place as Secretary of State.

JEFFERSON

It's not Toombs. That Georgian's too arrogant. And besides he's been on the battlefield for the last two years. Who else?

JUDAH

John Reagan has had plenty of chances to pass information… but it just doesn't make sense.

JEFFERSON

I think it's Mallory. He keeps talking about resigning.

JUDAH

But he's been very effective with our navy.

JEFFERSON

God damn it, who is this bastard? He's dug in like an Alabama tick.

JUDAH

Whoever it is foiled us once more. Our plan to have Captain T. Henry Hines free our Confederate prisoners from Camp Douglas was defeated. There is treachery about us and for the life of me I am confounded.

JEFFERSON

And what of New York?

JUDAH

Our spies were able to set fire to a dozen hotels and we did some damage to P. T. Barnum's Museum.

JEFFERSON

Keep at it! I want to do to that city what Sherman did to Atlanta. Whoever this traitor is…he'll slip up and I want to catch him and skin him like a cornered badger in a skunk's holler.

Mary drops a book.

JUDAH

We've got to lay a sound trap for him. Something that will smoke him out…even a blind hog finds the acorn.

There is a knock at the door. Old Robert sticks his head in the door.

OLD ROBERT

Is it time?

JEFFERSON

Yes, it's time. Thank you, Judah. I will have something for you tomorrow.

Give this note to Wilkes-Booth.

Hands a letter to Judah. He takes it.

JUDAH

I will set up the meeting with the other cabinet members for tomorrow morning, nine a.m.

Judah exits. Mary gets the crystal glass and pours whiskey into it and gives it to Old Robert. Old Robert hands the glass to Jefferson.

OLD ROBERT

How was your day Massa Jeff?

JEFFERSON

I think God has turned against us Old Robert…but I'll be damned if I will let us be ruled by some corrupt, arrogant Northerners…using slavery as an excuse to glorify control over my country. I've been a good master to you haven't I?

OLD ROBERT

You been my only master. Far as I can remember I been owned by de Davis family.

JEFFERSON

We've been living this way for two hundred years. Yankees want to take away…the best part of living.

Mary hands Old Robert his mug.

OLD ROBERT

Take what away?

Mary pours whiskey into Old Robert's mug.

JEFFERSON

Those Yankees think I'm licked. I ain't licked. This war is over when I say it's over.

OLD ROBERT

Looks like Yankees are getting close to Richmond. What 'cha gwine do, dey take Richmond?

JEFFERSON

Old Robert one must always have an alternative plan. If the Yankees take Richmond, I will travel to Texas, unite the regiments that can get there, and join forces with Kirby Smith.

OLD ROBERT

Start a whole new army.

JEFFERSON

Got enough gold, plenty of silver. I'm a soldier; I'll die fighting. They want my gun? They will have to pry it from my cold dead hand.

OLD ROBERT

Massa Jeff, don't want to see you end up in Arlington.

Mary offers Jefferson a cigar. He declines.

JEFFERSON

Arlington, another example of Northern arrogance.

OLD ROBERT

Not sure I understand what you mean.

Mary offers Old Robert a cigar. He accepts.

JEFFERSON

Old Robert you know that Robert E. Lee's plantation was Arlington?

OLD ROBERT

Yes, Massa Jeff. I know Jim Parke, Massa Robert E. Lee's nigger…know the Union asked him to dig the first two graves for the Yankees that died in Battle.

JEFFERSON

Buried those damn Yankees on Lee's plantation. Turned the grounds of Arlington into a cemetery for Union soldiers. A slap in the face to Lee, just because he chose to fight for me rather than fight for them. Even when we win this war, Lee can never go home.

OLD ROBERT

They say Jim Parke buried some Union colored soldiers at Arlington too.

JEFFERSON

That's outrageous.

OLD ROBERT

Guess they all alike once they in the ground.

JEFFERSON

The true beauty of war is things can change at any moment… Mary pour me a little more Kentucky mash.

Mary pours Jefferson another glass of whiskey.

OLD ROBERT

Twelve-year-old Kentuck taste good.

JEFFERSON

I got plans for Lincoln. He's not getting away with this sacrilege.

Black Out.

Scene 4

Van Lew House, Pantry. Mary meets Elizabeth in the herb closet. Mary drops the slave lingo and speaks as an educated woman.

MARY

Betty, these cigars are from Jeff Davis's private collection. The information is inside. I also found some troop movement. Lee is moving his men to Petersburg.

ELIZABETH

He won't be able to hold that. General Grant will march right into this city. He'll take Richmond, move on to Petersburg and cut Lee off.

MARY

Their only choice will be to retreat to Appomattox.

ELIZABETH

I've got to get this information to General Grant.

MARY

To the point Betty…old man Davis wants to enlist colored soldiers. If they serve they will be emancipated…it's ludicrous.

ELIZABETH

Davis has agreed to use colored soldiers? Never thought I'd live to see this day.

MARY

They enslave an entire race of people and in order to sustain their corrupt, demented view of life… they give the very people they loathe a chance to kill for them.

ELIZABETH

Desperation my dear…but it's too little…too late.

MARY

You think so?

ELIZABETH

Mary, this war is over. It's been over…Jeff Davis just doesn't know it.

MARY

Judah Benjamin thinks they can revive their cause with colored troops.

ELIZABETH

Judah Benjamin better think of an escape route. It's just a matter of weeks, if not days. The Confederacy is ending and there is no way to stop it. We won.

A male figure enters and stands in the shadows observing the two women.

MARY

We did …didn't we?

ELIZABETH

Mary, you are a patriot. You gave up your life of freedom so that others may gain theirs. You returned here for an honorable cause.

MARY

That college you enrolled me in, paid us big dividends in this little escapade. (*slips back into slave talk*) Once you taste freedom, Miss Elizabeth you want everybody to sip from that bowl.

ELIZABETH

I told your husband that you would be returning tonight. I don't want you to stay any longer than necessary. Your work is done.

MARY

No Betty…I'm not finished. I have one more final act to carry out before I escape.

ELIZABETH

Mary, I feel they are getting too close to the truth. I don't want them to discover your involvement. We got lucky when Varina was pregnant with Billy…and we were able to take advantage of the situation. But since the birth of Winnie, you've had too many close calls. Get out now…they are too aware…it doesn't feel good.

MARY

Betty, that is an evil house. You read some of the machinations they plotted in his office. Before I go, I have something to do. Something I must do. I will meet you tomorrow.

ELIZABETH

What do you plan on doing?

MARY

Carpe Noctem.

ELIZABETH

Seize the night? No whatever it is it's too risky.

MARY

Something poetic. The kind of thing Dante would relish had he sat on the third ring of hell and gazed at the impending doom of an enemy.

ELIZABETH

Okay, but I want you meet me tomorrow night at Tom McNiven's house.

MARY

I just need one night.

ELIZABETH

I will arrange transport for you north. Which city do you want to end up in?

MARY

I want to go back to Philadelphia.

ELIZABETH

Where shall I tell your husband to meet you?

MARY

Ask Wilson to meet me in front of the Liberty Bell…at noon on Wednesday. It's been a long time. The man is a saint, Betty. The United States of America owes him. I plan to make his four-year abstinence a memorable reunion.

ELIZABETH

Done. Wednesday, noon. You be careful. I don't want you getting hurt when we are this close to achieving our goals. Mary Bowser, you are real special to me.

MARY

(*slave lingo*) Miss Elizabeth…don't you know, I know that.

Mary exits. Elizabeth crosses upstage to the figure. The man comes out of the shadows and it is Mr. Slydell.

SLYDELL

So that's your inside man. Very clever, Miss Van Lew.

ELIZABETH

Why Mr. Slydell, that woman has done more to keep the Union together than any Yankee gun could ever do.

Slydell kisses her hand and starts to leave. Elizabeth holds onto his hand, smiles and pulls him back into the room. Slydell follows her into her house.

Black Out.

Scene 5

Davis White House Kitchen. Old Robert is sitting on a stool at the kitchen table. Mary enters.

MARY

Look at chu…reading.

OLD ROBERT

Little Mary, I thank you for opening dis door.

MARY

My pleasure Old Robert.

OLD ROBERT

I still got to be careful…don't think it's a good idea for Master Jeff to know my new skills.

Old Robert shows her a piece of paper on which he has written.

MARY

Good penmanship, too. Not bad for an old dog.

OLD ROBERT

Just might write myself a pass and go north, don't cha know.

MARY

North…ain't you the one.

OLD ROBERT

Probably won't have to. Dis war is coming to an end and I am gonna be free and clear. Think I'll visit Boston.

MARY

Boston.

OLD ROBERT

Little Mary, I got a great expectation.

MARY

(*laughs*) You sure do if you thinking of going to Boston.

OLD ROBERT

Reading about dis here young man, in dis book…name of Pip. He had a great expectation.

Mary picks up the book and reads the cover.

MARY

Charles Dickens. He's famous don't cha know.

OLD ROBERT

All I know is…I likes his writing. Now, dat I can read…I think I might be able to find my son, Amos. He's my heart, don't cha know. I'll start in Boston and work my way down.

MARY

If you find him…what will you say?

OLD ROBERT

Nothin'. First two days I'm just gonna look at him. Look at de curve of his face. De shape of his hands, see if he got calluses from work or if he used his brain and was able to make a life without breaking his back. Gonna see if he got fat or if he's strong and lean. Either way, won't matter, cause I get to sit in de room with my boy. Let him know... I'm his daddy. He ain't no white man's son. He's my son...and I will thank God he let me live for dis here moment.

MARY

That's good.

OLD ROBERT

Next two days...it will be just him talking' to me. I want him to squeeze his lifetime into two days. Tell me everything dat happened to him. Who he married? If he got kids? Can he cook? Did he fight in dis here war?

MARY

That's good.

OLD ROBERT

Now the next two days it will be my turn...I'm gonna talk fast so I get everything in. Let him know how I survived dis war. Tell him about some young Nigger gal dat thinks she's special. Tell him how little Mary taught his daddy to read and write.

MARY

That's very good. What happens after that?

OLD ROBERT

Why Mary Bowser…don't you know dat will be the seventh day and dat's the day I'm gonna rest.

MARY

(*laughs*) Why of course Old Robert I should have guessed that.

OLD ROBERT

Maybe eat me a big ol' pot of black eyed peas for luck, with ham hocks dat fall off the bone. What are you gonna do after de war is over?

MARY

Don't know. I have to figure out something special for myself.

OLD ROBERT

Nothing ordinary, huh?

MARY

Why Old Robert…you know I'm a special nigger. Someday you gonna realize that. I got to find something extra special for myself.

OLD ROBERT

If you really are special…won't be too hard to do.

Mary picks up the pencil and starts to hand it to Old Robert as she speaks.

MARY

This war be over soon…and the world is gonna change for a colored person.

Black Out.

Scene 6

Davis White House Office. Jefferson is stuffing important papers into a carpetbag. Judah enters.

JUDAH

J. D., where's your family?

JEFFERSON

Train depot. What are your escape plans?

JUDAH

Florida Coast. It's easier to get to than Canada.

JEFFERSON

Oh, Judah, the South is my heart.

JUDAH

We can't stay in the South. There will be Yankees everywhere. Our cities will be occupied with Union forces. We've got to get to Europe.

JEFFERSON

I'm going to Georgia. There are all kinds of small towns, little villages…Danville is no bigger than a gnat's ass.

JUDAH

No, no, no, you can't stay in Georgia. They'll find you, arrest you and hang you.

JEFFERSON

Judah, the South is my home. I love this land…I'm not leaving.

JUDAH

J. D.…that South you love is gone. Cities have been devastated. The Yankees are on their way to invade this city. Lee has already left for Petersburg. We sit here, unguarded.

JEFFERSON

So, your plan is Florida?

JUDAH

I've got a cousin in Ellenton...then I am leaving America… gonna try and get to Europe.

JEFFERSON

Judah, you would leave this land?

JUDAH

J. D. look at what the land has become.

JEFFERSON

Judah, we convene with the rest of the cabinet in Abbeville, then decide. We could go underground. Lick our wounds. We wait for time to give us a chance to regroup. Reorganize…and we can come back stronger than ever.

JUDAH

Have you forgotten this souvenir?

He picks up a cigar case from Jefferson's desk.

JEFFERSON

Ulric Dahlgren's cigar case. So what?

JUDAH

That was just one year ago and he got very close.

JEFFERSON

We caught him.

JUDAH

We were blessed with a lucky day. He could have assassinated you. If we hadn't found his orders in this cigar case... we have no idea how much damage he could have inflicted. There are spies everywhere. At this moment, who can you really trust?

JEFFERSON

I trust you.

JUDAH

Our cabinet doesn't. I'm not an idiot. I know what's going on.

I see it in their eyes. Ready to blame our failures on The Jew.

JEFFERSON

We've got enough gold to…

JUDAH

It's over Mr. President. We tried and we failed.

Varina brings Mary into Jefferson's office.

VARINA

Jefferson, I can't believe this. Look at her.

MARY

I'm innocent master Jeff.

JEFFERSON

What? Varina, why aren't you at the train depot?

VARINA

No you're not, you hussy.

JEFFERSON

Varina, the train leaves in less than twenty minutes. I want you and the children on that train!

VARINA

I'm staying.

JEFFERSON

I want you to go. I need to know that you are safe in Charlotte. Judah, is Harrison Here?

JUDAH

Think he is waiting out front in the wagon. I'll check.

Judah exits.

VARINA

I am averse to flight. Let me stand by your side.

JEFFERSON

No! The children need you…and I need to know that you are safe.

VARINA

What about this bitch? I caught her…caught her red-handed.

JEFFERSON

Mary, what did you do?

MARY

Nothing.

VARINA

I caught her…caught her downstairs.

JEFFERSON

Downstairs?

VARINA

She had straw and was starting a fire.

MARY

I'm innocent. Master Jeff, I'm innocent.

Varina slaps Mary. She falls to the floor.

VARINA

I'm not a liar. She had a torch…used my silk blouse wrapped around a stick as a torch. She was lighting the house on fire.

JEFFERSON

Is the fire out?

VARINA

I caught it in time. Jesse and Sarah Mae were able to extinguish it.

MARY

It was an accident.

VARINA

She could have hurt our babies.

JEFFERSON

Mary Bowser…what do you have to say for yourself?

MARY

It was an accident.

VARINA

You had a torch!

JEFFERSON

I don't have time for this. Yankees are getting close.

Judah returns and sticks his head in the door.

JUDAH

Harrison's waiting. She's got to get to the depot.

VARINA

I'm giving this gal thirty lashes.

JEFFERSON

Varina, I'll handle this. Judah get me Old Robert.

Judah exits.

JEFFERSON

Remember what I told you. I'm going south to Danville.

VARINA

I want to be with you.

JEFFERSON

I do not expect to survive….you and the children must live to carry on the Davis name. Where's the gun I gave you?

VARINA

I packed it away in my trunk.

He goes to his desk and gets a gun.

JEFFERSON

I want you to be armed at all times. Remember how I taught you to use this?

VARINA

Yes.

JEFFERSON

You can at least, if reduced to the last extremity force your assailants to kill you…but I charge you solemnly to leave when you hear the enemy approaching; and if you cannot remain undisturbed in our country, make for the Florida Coast and take a ship to a foreign country.

VARINA

I love you Jeff.

He kisses her.

JEFFERSON

I love you Knox.

VARINA

Knox?

JEFFERSON

What?

VARINA

Jefferson, you called me Knox.

JEFFERSON

I did not.

VARINA

Yes. Plain and clear.

Judah enters with Old Robert.

JUDAH

Varina, you have to leave, that train won't wait forever.

Varina points her gun at Mary's head and cocks the gun.

VARINA

Let me shoot this nigger.

JEFFERSON

Varina, I said I would handle it. Old Robert…

OLD ROBERT

Yes Sur. Massa. Jeff.

JEFFERSON

Take this child to the kitchen and tie her up.

OLD ROBERT

Yes Suh.

Old Robert exits with Mary.

JEFFERSON

I will be there shortly. Varina, you know I love you.

VARINA
Evade those Yankees, Jefferson.

Jefferson and Varina kiss.

JEFFERSON
I will meet you. Judah, get my family to the train depot.

Judah exits with Varina. Jefferson returns to his desk and continues stuffing the carpetbag with important papers.

Black Out.

Scene 7

The Davis Kitchen. Old Robert is tying Mary up.

OLD ROBERT

Little girl what did you do? You done raised de hackles on Miss Varina something fierce.

MARY

Old Robert, you got to let me go.

OLD ROBERT

Cain't do dat. Massa Jeff gave me an order.

MARY

It's over. Time is up. The Confederacy is dead; they just don't know it. There is not going to be a second country in America. There is only the United States of America. It is a new day for black folks Old Robert. You ain't that old dog no more, you getting educated. You don't have to obey orders anymore; you ain't a slave. You are a man. Yes, you are black…but you are now a man. Let me go. Show these white folks you part of this new world that's coming. Show me you don't have to bow down to a white man. Show yourself what's really in your soul. Let me go, Old Robert, so I can live my life as a free woman. So I can bring babies into this new world…free of their past…and ready to build a new future. Let me go Old Robert and fill your heart with justice.

He looks at her for a beat, then unties her.

OLD ROBERT

Looks like my back gwine get some well-earned scars.

She starts to leave, but stops and goes back and kisses him on the cheek.

MARY

Come with me. You don't need to endure no beating on my account. Come with me Old Robert. Be free with me.

OLD ROBERT

You think dis old dog can handle being free?

MARY

Can you read and write?

OLD ROBERT

Little Mary I believe you done made a point. I think dis endeavor can be fortified wid immediate action.

MARY

Damn right.

OLD ROBERT

You go on. Got to get a few things, I'll catch up.

MARY

Meet me at Tom McNivens' House.

She looks him in his eyes, then runs off. Old Robert goes to get a gunny sack. He goes around the kitchen putting food into the sack. Jefferson enters.

JEFFERSON

Where's the girl?

OLD ROBERT

Gone.

JEFFERSON

I gave you an order.

OLD ROBERT

Yes Suh. I know.

Jefferson looks at Old Robert and crosses to him. Jefferson is defeated. It takes a beat for him to realize that his world has changed.

JEFFERSON

You too?

OLD ROBERT

I ain't no dog. I'm a man. My time has come.

JEFFERSON

I guess it is a new day.

OLD ROBERT

Yes Suh, it is. I'm walking into a new life, Mr. Jeff.

JEFFERSON

A new life.

OLD ROBERT

Mr. Jeff, gwine be free and gwine find my son.

JEFFERSON

What do you think those Yankees are going to do to my wife and children if they catch them? You think they are going to be good to them as I was to you? I need someone to look after them.

JEFFERSON

Old Robert I need you.

OLD ROBERT

You don't want me to be free.

JEFFERSON

What I want is…a favor. I don't have any rights to ask this favor…but I am going ask it, Old Robert. If the Northerners see you with my wife and children they will be less capable of doing harm. If I die, I have no one to see to their needs. If I get captured…I will be hung. I need to know there is someone to look after the Davis family.

OLD ROBERT

Mister Jeff…I gots a chance to live my life in a new way. Gots a chance for dese old eyes to see some joy.

JEFFERSON

I need you Old Robert. Will you consider one last request from me, before you take your freedom?

Old Robert looks at Jefferson. They stare at each other.

Black Out.

Scene 9

1865, Barren Room. Varina is under town arrest. She is living in Savannah, Georgia. Old Robert is with her. She is being interviewed by the Yankee journalist, Mr. Slydell. She sips from a glass. There is a bottle next to the glass.

VARINA

What have I done that I am a prisoner at large? My family in a strange place...I am surrounded by detectives who report every visitor?

SLYDELL

Surely you must find Savannah preferable to the things that are happening in Richmond.

VARINA

Answer this...why am I kept in a garrisoned town? Bereft of home, friends, husband and the means of support?

SLYDELL

You are a traitor to the United States of America.

She takes a sip from her glass.

VARINA

Mr. Slydell, I detect a certain nastiness in your tone. I have answered all of your questions...yet I have noticed that you have gotten progressively hostile as you continue to question me. Is not a journalist supposed to remain objective?

SLYDELL

And who is that man standing behind you?

VARINA

That's my nigger. Surely you will allow me to have one nigger?

SLYDELL

We Yankees look on the Negroes as people.

VARINA

So do I. Tell that to Horace Greely and your *New York Tribune* readers. All my other niggers have fled North…thank God for the loyalty of at least one family nigger.

SLYDELL

What's your name, sir?

VARINA

Robert Brown.

SLYDELL

Robert Brown you know that you are free now?

VARINA

Mr. Slydell, would you take my last nigger?

SLYDELL

I'm not taking him. I'm just informing him he now has a choice. He has rights. What do you say Mr. Robert Brown? Are you going to exercise your rights?

OLD ROBERT

Sir, I have examined my options and I have elected to stand by my mistress in her hour of peril.

Varina is amazed at his use of the English language.

VARINA

Thank you Old Robert. I hope you will print those words for your *Tribune* readers.

SLYDELL

This is an interview to get your side on the record, Mrs. Davis. I am not taking a political position. I would like to remind you that there are those who want to hang Jeff Davis.

VARINA

Hang him? I predict they will never *try* my husband. They hold him in jail at this very moment and they have not brought any charges against him.

SYLDELL

They will bring charges against him and his entire Confederate cabinet. They've already apprehended most of them.

VARINA

Did they capture Judah P. Benjamin?

SLYDELL

He escaped to Europe.

VARINA

Paris?

SLYDELL

No, London. Turns out he has British citizenship.

VARINA

Ah, yes he was born in St. Croix.

SLYDELL

He may be practicing law in London…but they will get him back.

VARINA

No they won't.

SLYDELL

Why do you say that?

VARINA

That Jew is smarter than you.

SLYDELL

Speaking of smarter than you…one of the reasons for your husband's downfall was the Union spy, Mary Bowser.

VARINA

Who?

SLYDELL

You had a slave working for you…Mary Bowser. She was a spy for the Union army.

She takes a sip from her glass.

VARINA

Sir, I think you are mistaken. I do not know a Mary Bowser. Nor was there any nigger I own spying on me, my husband or my family. Ain't that right Old Robert?

OLD ROBERT

Yes 'um.

SLYDELL

You know Elizabeth Van Lew, don't you?

VARINA

Yes I do.

SLYDELL

She has stated that she let you use her slave, Mary Bowser. Both ladies as it turns out were working as spies for the Union.

VARINA

Mr. Slydell, I don't know any slave named Mary and as far as Elizabeth is concern everyone in Richmond can tell you…she is batty as a loon.

SLYDELL

They say your husband wore a dress to disguise himself and evade capture.

VARINA

Why Mr. Slydell, you are not half the man my husband is. Go to Fortress Monroe, go. Look into his eyes and ask yourself, are those the eyes of a man afraid of capture. No Sir. You'll see… those are the eyes of a man unafraid to face his destiny. You will see eyes that shine like freshly minted gold.

SLYDELL

You seem to still love him.

VARINA

Are you married sir?

SLYDELL

Yes I am.

VARINA

Then don't ask stupid questions.

SLYDELL

One final question…in 1845 you married Jefferson. I understand that before you started your honeymoon, he took you to Natchez, Mississippi to the grave of his former wife… Sarah Taylor.

VARINA

Knox.

SLYDELL

Yes, Knox. If he loved you as much as you say he loved you… what was the purpose of visiting his first wife's grave? Are you jealous of the ghost of his first wife?

She looks at Mr. Slydell, then takes her glass and reflects for a moment, she drains the glass.

VARINA

Mr. Slydell, you ever have a brush with greatness? And I don't mean as a journalist. Would you recognize greatness if it stood before you? I know who my husband is and from the moment I met him I knew the aura of greatness sat on his shoulders. I was the lucky one. I was lucky that whatever he saw in me he felt compelled to make it a part of his life. I want to share every waking moment with Jefferson Davis. I will not stop until I have achieved that. I write letters every day to friends, enemies, and powerful people. My husband does not deserve this imprisonment. Every Southern soul that lives and breathes knows the greatness of Jeff Davis. What woman knows what I known or has felt what I have felt? Martha Washington is the only woman that comes to mind. She watched her husband create a nation. A Virginian, I might add. I watched my husband create a nation…but before that baby could barely breathe…Yanks killed it. As nations I think we could have lived together…but now we will never know will we? Am I jealous of a ghost? No sir, she got a few months. I am getting a lifetime and I am securing the name of Davis for future generations.

SLYDELL

Thank you, Mrs. Davis. I think I got a clear picture. Thank you for taking the time to let me interview you.

VARINA

Mr. Slydell…you be sure to print what I said. Every word of it.

SLYDELL

Verbatim, ma'am. Verbatim.

VARINA

Mr. Slydell, I know you think the war is over…

SLYDELL

The union won Mrs. Davis. I know you don't like hearing that but…it's over.

Mr. Slydell starts to leave.

VARINA

My dear boy, you will never capture the Southern heart.

SLYDELL

Mrs. Davis, what you detect in my voice is the anguish that this nation has suffered over the lives that were lost in preserving this Union. What you hear in my voice is the outrage I feel over the assassination of our President. I look at you and I see a woman who has been pampered and catered to her whole life, who ignores the welfare of other human beings, because of the color of their skin. You use the words of God and being a good Christian woman to further the world you want for yourself, not furthering the world for the good of all. You parse out biblical phrases to suit your needs, but I can find no humanity in your heart for your fellow Christians. Deo Vindice, God will vindicate? You started a civil war… an incredibly devastating war. Sons were pitted against fathers, brothers against brothers, mothers against daughters and friends against neighbors…for what purpose? So, that you could maintain a dying lifestyle? The South started a war for the independence of your own private fortunes. You used Southern pride to lure young, innocent, poor Southern souls into a war for your Southern elite. So you could make money on the backs of the less fortunate. So your morally corrupt husbands could continue to do business that tarnished the name of America. Mrs. Davis, I saw more death and carnage in these last four years and I know it will haunt me for the rest of my life… and the enemy was my brothers and sisters. I'm glad you lost this war. Whether you like it or not…America is changing…whether you like it or not…we have become a stronger nation….and whether you like it or not the death of Lincoln is not going to slow down this progress one bit. Mrs. Varina Davis, former first lady of the Confederacy, whether you like it or not…this is now a nation with liberty and justice for all. I want to emphasize…for all. Good night Mr. Brown, good night Mrs. Davis…May God have mercy on your soul.

Mr. Slydell exits.

VARINA

Old Robert would you give me another taste of the green fairy?

He pours more absinthe into her glass, adds water, a bit of sugar and stirs it with a spoon.

Lights go to Half.

Spotlight up on a writing desk Stage Right. Elizabeth is writing a letter to Mary. She lifts up the paper to read what she has written.

ELIZABETH

Dear Mary, I miss you. Things here in Richmond have not progressed as I had hoped…but I am sure time will eventually solve all problems. I am amazed at the cruelty one human being can inflict on another.

Spotlight on a writing desk Stage Left. A light comes up on Mary sitting at a desk; she is reading Elizabeth's letter.

ELIZABETH/MARY

There are Northerners streaming into Richmond taking advantage of the plight of our city and our citizens.

Lights go down on Elizabeth as her voice fades into silence.

MARY

Since Lincoln's assassination, things are not as safe for me as I had hoped. I think I did us both a great disservice by letting people know of our patriotic contributions to the Union. Now that the cat is out of the bag as to our involvement in the war as spies, it is no longer safe for you or I as it once was. My advice to you is to disappear. I'm sure Lincoln would not have allowed all the corruption that our new President Johnson seems to let flourish. He is incompetent. I am ashamed and embarrassed that he is my President. Looking to a brighter future…Sincerely, Elizabeth.

Mary is sitting at the desk begins to write a letter to Elizabeth.

MARY

Dear Betty, wonderful news: I am pregnant.

Lights up on Elizabeth at her writing desk reading Mary's letter.

MARY/ELIZABETH

Finally, time for a family. I am looking forward to a healthy, strong baby.

ELIZABETH

No absinthe for this girl. Wilson and I have been thinking about moving to Boston. A perfect place for us to disappear. It is a big city and there are lots of Negroes there.

Lights fade on Mary as Elizabeth continues to read.

ELIZABETH

To insure that we stay anonymous, we are changing our name. I also want to see if I can find Old Robert's son, Amos. I'd like him to know what kind of a father he has. Wilson thinks he can find work as a leather craftsman. He is a freemason and there is a Prince Hall Lodge located in Boston. There is a school for blacks there called, The Phillips School…maybe I can get a job teaching spelling or Shakespeare? You and I know that dreams do come true. Look what has happened to our country. All my best, Mary.

P.S. Burn this letter.

Lights go to half. Lights come up full on Old Robert and Varina. Old Robert hands a glass to Varina.

VARINA

Thank you Old Robert.

Varina takes a sip, then she gets up from her chair.

VARINA

Where is my mirror?

She crosses the room then stops.

VARINA

Mary Bowser a Union spy. It was not the Jew, it was the nigger.

Varina exits. Music: "America the Beautiful," Ray Charles version plays. Lights do a slow fade on Old Robert standing alone, lights come up to half as the figures of Elizabeth and Mary are standing in the shadows.

Mary rises and picks up a loaf of bread.

RAY CHARLES

(*voice over, sings*) Oh, Beautiful for spacious skies, for amber waves of grain...

MARY

I ain't no ordinary Nigger Old Robert...

Mary crosses the stage to Elizabeth and hands her the bread.

RAY CHARLES

(*sings*) for purple mountains majesty...

Elizabeth takes a note out of the bread.

MARY

I'm a special Nigger...

RAY CHARLES

(*sings*) Above the fruited plans...

Elizabeth and Mary read the note.

MARY

and someday you are gonna realize that.

Lights go to black on Elizabeth and Mary.

RAY CHARLES

(sings) America, America...

Pin spot on Old Robert, he smiles...then laughs.

RAY CHARLES

(*sings*) God done shed his grace on thee...

Black Out.

END OF PLAY

Bibliography

Ballard, Michael B. *A long Shadow.* Athens: The University of Georgia Press, 1997.

Berkin, Carol. *Civil War Wives.* New York: Alfred A. Knopf, 2009.

Boaz, Thomas M. *Libby Preison & Beyond.* Shippensburg: Burd Street Press, 1999.

Carretta, Vincent. *Unchained Voices.* Kentucky: The University Press of Kentucky, 1996.

Davis, Kenneth C. *Don't Know Much About the Civil War.* New York: Prennial, 1996.

Dray, Philip. *Capital Men.* Boston: Mariner Books, 2008.

Evans, Eli N. *The Lonely Days Were Sundays.* Jackson: University Press of Mississippi, 1993.

Foner, Eric. *Forever Free.* New York: Alfred A. Knopf, 2005.

Foote, Shelby. *The Civil War.* New York: Random House, 1958.

Garrison, Webb. *Amazing Women of the Civil War.* Nashville:Thomas Nelson, 1999.

Goodheat, Adam. *1861 The Civil War Awakening.* New York: Alfred A. Knopf, 2011.

Hall, Jasper Newton. *At Death's Door.* Huntington: Blue Acorn Press, 2010.

Holzer, Harold, & Symonds, Craig L. *The New York Times Complete Civil War, 1861-1864.* New York: Black Dog & Leventhal, 2010.

Martin, David G. *Gettysburg July1.* Pennsylvania: Combined Books, 1996.

Mauro, Charles V. *A Southern Spy in Northern Virginia.* Charleston: The History Press, 2009.

Meacham, Jon. *American Lion.* New York: Random House, 2008.

Meade, Robert Douthat. *Judah P. Benjamin, Confederate Stateman.* Baton Rouge: Louisana State University Press, 2001.

O'Brien, Cormac. *Secret Lives of the Civil War.* Philadelphia: Quirk Books, 2007.

Pollard, Edward A. *Life of Jefferson Davis.* Philadelphia: National Publishing Company, 1869.

Rasmussen, Daniel. *American Uprising.* New York: Harper Collins Publisher, 2011.

Swanson, James L. *Bloody Crimes.* New York:. Harper Perennial, 2010.

Stampp, Kenneth M. *The Peculiar Institution.* New York: Vintage Books, 1956.

Tate, Allen. *Jefferson Davis: His Rise and Fall.* New York: Balch & Co., 1929.

Thomas, Emery M. *Confederate Nation 1861-1865.* New York: Harper Perennial, 2011.

Trammell, Jack. *The Richmond Slave Trade.* Charleston: The History Press, 2012.

Varon, Elizabeth R. *Southern Lady, Yankee Spy.* Oxford: Oxford University Press, 2003.

Winkler, Donald H. *Stealing Secrets.* Naperville: Cumberland House, 2010.

CPSIA information can be obtained
at www.ICGtesting.com
Printed in the USA
BVHW042241230419
546377BV00008B/27/P